**stone canoe** | A Journal of Arts, Literature and Social Commentary

2013 • NUMBER 7

EDITOR
Robert Colley

DRAMA EDITOR
Kyle Bass

FICTION EDITOR
E.C. Osondu

MOVING IMAGES EDITOR
Nancy Keefe Rhodes

MUSIC EDITORS
Neva Pilgrim
Steven Stucky

NONFICTION EDITOR
Kenneth McClane

POETRY EDITOR
Cornelius Eady

TECHNOLOGY EDITOR
Megan Davidson

VETERANS WRITING AWARD EDITORS
Karl Marlantes
Anthony Swofford
Brian Turner

VISUAL ARTS EDITOR
Amy Cheng

CONTRIBUTING EDITOR
Doran Larson

ASSISTANT EDITORS
Allison Vincent
Martha Zvonik

ART DIRECTOR
E.L. Cummings Serafini

PRODUCTION MANAGER
Karen Nadolski

SYRACUSE
UNIVERSITY
University College

Stone Canoe, a Journal of Arts, Literature and Social Commentary, is published annually by Syracuse University. Address all correspondence to *Stone Canoe,* 700 University Avenue, Syracuse, New York 13244-2530. E-mail: *stonecanoe@uc.syr.edu.* Phone: 315-443-3225/4165. Fax: 315-443-4174. Web: *stonecanoejournal.org.*

Stone Canoe showcases the work of a diverse mix of emerging and well-established artists and writers with ties to Upstate New York. In so doing, the journal supports Syracuse University's ongoing commitment to creative community partnerships, and seeks to promote greater awareness of the cultural and intellectual richness of the region.

The views expressed in the contents of this journal are solely those of the contributors, and do not necessarily reflect the views of Syracuse University, its trustees, staff, faculty, or students.

Stone Canoe considers for inclusion previously unpublished short fiction, creative nonfiction, short plays, poems, essays, technology writing, and works of visual art in any medium. Unsolicited submissions are welcome from March 1 through July 15 of each year. Submissions must be sent via our web page, and must include a short biographical statement and contact information. Complete submission instructions and forms are available at *stonecanoejournal.org/submission.*

All submissions are automatically considered for one of six *Stone Canoe* prizes in the appropriate category. There is no additional fee required. Details about each prize are provided on our web site.

All rights for individual works revert to contributors upon publication, though *Stone Canoe* may seek permission to feature submitted work on its web site.

Stone Canoe is set in Bembo, a trademark font of the Monotype Corporation, based on a typeface designed by Francesco Griffo in 1495.

Stone Canoe 7 is available for purchase in print or e-book form through our web site, *stonecanoejournal.org.* The print version is $20 and the e-book version is $7.99. The print version may also be ordered by sending a check to *Stone Canoe,* 700 University Avenue, Syracuse, New York, 13244-2530. The educational rate for classroom use is $10, and past individual issues are $14.

Stone Canoe is also available at Syracuse University Bookstores, Barnes & Noble, and *Amazon.com,* as well as at other regional bookstores and at a growing number of other arts venues.

ISSN: 1934-9963   ISBN: 978-0-9836172-6-6

Stone Canoe is a proud member of the Council of Literary Magazines and Presses.

A MIDSUMMER NIGHT'S DREAM

MAR 6 THROUGH MAR 31

BY WILLIAM SHAKESPEARE
DIRECTED BY BILLY FENNELLY
CO-PRODUCED WITH SU DRAMA

"The course of true love
never did run smooth."

—Act I, scene I

HEDI SCHWÖBEL, *Belle-de-Nuit,* Pergamin 30g/m²,
origami folding technique, size of each individual piece: 20cm x 20cm

About the Cover

Hedi Schwöbel, *Belle-de-Nuit,* Pergamin 30g/m²,
origami folding technique, size of each individual piece: 20cm x 20cm

The installation space, the Orangery, the inspiration for *Belle-de-Nuit,* is a beautiful 19th century-style glasshouse, located amidst flowering and fragrant scenery of the baroque garden at Ludwigsburg Castle. In their time, these types of gardens were symmetrically laid out according to mathematical rules, to impose strict ordering on free-growing nature. Even though the Ludwigsburgian garden has undergone some changes over time, the basic concept of the order behind a baroque garden was an initial stimulus for my work. The direct impact of the garden itself and the architecture of the glasshouse finally guided my idea towards the ultimate appearance of *Belle-de-Nuit:* a rectangular field of equal, square transparent paper containers was arranged in strict, serial order.

In order to 'transform' the delicate paper containers, I made use of fire, which is the natural 'antagonist' to paper and can burn it away to nothing. While burning the edges, the different paper layers of the container's sides unfolded and changed completely. The still strict and geometrically shaped container suddenly had assumed the appearance of something organic and seemed to have turned into a wondrous white blossom with fleeting fire markings.

The field of the paper forms was installed on a water area in the Orangery. *Belle-de-Nuit* corresponded beautifully with the changing daylight, and although everybody knows there are no such paradoxons as square blossoms in the natural world, one couldn't help but see a field of water lilies.

Hedi Schwöbel

Hedi Schwöbel is a German artist, living in Ludwigsburg. She travelled to the U.S. for the first time in 2004 when she was invited to a residency at Sculpture Space in Utica, New York. This was her formative introduction to the U.S. and since then she has returned several times.

Acknowledgements

Stone Canoe 7 is dedicated to Shreela Ray (1942–1995), poet and teacher from Rochester, New York, who was an early mentor and inspiration to Cornelius Eady, poetry editor for this issue.

Special thanks to the following people for their contribution to the successful launch of Stone Canoe 7:

Jaime Winne Alveraz, Director of Media Relations and Communications, Institute for Veterans and Military Families (IVMF), Syracuse University

Lorraine Branham, Dean, S.I. Newhouse School of Public Communications, Syracuse University, and creator of the SC S.I. Newhouse School Prize for Creative Nonfiction

Nancy Cantor, Chancellor and President, Syracuse University

Rob Enslin, Communications Manager, The College of Arts and Sciences, Syracuse University

Hedy and Michael Fawcett, creators of the SC Prize for Visual Arts

Allen and Nirelle Galson, creators of the SC Prize for Fiction

Bea González, Dean, University College of Syracuse University and creator of the SC Prize for Poetry

Tom Huff, sculptor and creator of the Stone Canoe carvings

Gregg Lambert, Dean's Professor and Founding Director of the Humanities Center, Syracuse University

Doran Larson, Professor of English and Creative Writing, Hamilton College

Trish Lowney, Assistant Vice President for Strategic Research Development, Syracuse University

Kathleen Masterson, Program Director, Literature, NYSCA

Caroline McMullin, Research Administrator, Office of Sponsored Programs, Syracuse University

Jillian Nakornthap, Curator, Community Folk Art Center, Syracuse University

James Schmeling, Managing Director, Institute for Veterans and Military Families (IVMF), Syracuse University, and creator of the IVMF *SC* prize.

Laura J. Steinberg, Dean, the L.C. Smith College of Engineering and Computer Science, and creator of the *SC* L.C. Smith Prize for Engineering and Technology Writing

Kheli R. Willetts, Executive Director, Community Folk Art Center, Syracuse University

Stone Canoe is pleased to have the following **Constance Saltonstall** Foundation for the Arts alumni represented in the current issue: Craig J. Barber, David Lloyd, Stephanie McMahon, and Jen Pepper.

Thanks, as always, to the ***Stone Canoe* Advisory Board** for their wise counsel and support:

Omanii Abdullah-Grace, Peter Blanck, Carole Brzozowski, Michael Burkard, Carol Charles, William Delavan, Stephen Dunn, Arthur Flowers, Wendy Gonyea, Kenneth Hine, Johanna Keller, Christopher Kennedy, David Lloyd, David MacDonald, Pamela McLaughlin, Philip Memmer, Elizabeth O'Rourke, Minnie Bruce Pratt, Maria Russell, Eileen Strempel, Suzanne Thorin, Silvio Torres-Saillant, John von Bergen, Kheli R. Willetts, and Marion Wilson.

Thanks to a remarkable team of editors, who are listed on the title page.

Thanks to our loyal sponsors, without whom *Stone Canoe Number* 7 would not be possible. See their individual pages in the back of the book, and on our web site.

Finally, many thanks to the University College staff who worked on this issue, for their unending patience in the face of this demanding project.

Stone Canoe is supported, in part, by a grant from **NYSCA**.

Saltonstall Foundation for the Arts
& Saltonstall Arts Colony

Ithaca, New York

Supporting visual and literary artists of New York State since 1995

Juried one-month summer residencies (May - Sept)

- $500 stipend
- five apartments/studios with private baths
- colony chef
- 24-hr. accessible kitchen
- 200 acres with hiking trails

Subsidized retreat space (Oct - April)

- individuals or small groups
- five apartments/studios with private baths
- 7 mi. from downtown Ithaca
- affordable day & overnight rates

Constance Saltonstall
Foundation for the Arts
www.saltonstall.org

435 Ellis Hollow Creek Rd. Ithaca, NY 14850
(607) 539-3146 / artscolony@saltonstall.org
facebook.com/SaltonstallArtsColony
twitter.com/TheSaltonstall

TO CELEBRATE THE 100ᵀᴴ ANNIVERSARY OF STRAVINSKY'S RITE OF SPRING
SYRACUSE UNIVERSITY ARTS ENGAGE WELCOMES
MERYL TANKARD'S THE ORACLE

CONCEIVED AND DIRECTED BY
MERYL TANKARD
FEATURING PERFORMER
PAUL WHITE &
VISUAL ARTIST
RÉGIS LANSAC

THE ORACLE

APRIL 10, 2013 AT 7:30PM
GOLDSTEIN AUDITORIUM, SYRACUSE UNIVERSITY

Inspired by the sometimes disturbing human forms in Scandinavian artist Odd Nerdrum's work, *The Oracle* is set to Stravinsky's seminal composition for the infamous 1913 ballet *The Rite of Spring*.

Please visit www.artsengage.syr.edu for ticket information.

 SYRACUSE UNIVERSITY
arts engage

MERYL TANKARD RESIDENCY FEBRUARY 18-23, 2013
WORKSHOP PERFORMANCE ON FEBRUARY 23

Australian Government

Australia Council
for the Arts

This project has been assisted by the Australian Government through the Australia Council, its arts funding and advisory body.

$OCIETY for $NEW MUSIC

2012-2013 season
(2nd half of 41st season)

RECURRING RESONANCES

11:15am Jan. 25 — MINDY'S MUSIC
Music by guest Pulitzer Prize winner **Melinda Wagner***, Storer Aud., OCC

8pm Jan. 29 — DINOSAUR ANNEX
(Boston's premiere new music ensemble) Music by **Daniel S. Godfrey***
Yu-Hui Chang, Annie Gosfield, Ricardo Zohn-Muldoon*
In conjunction with S.U. Mellon Fund, Setnor Aud., Syracuse University

8pm Feb. 12 — STORIES WITHIN STORIES
Greg Wanamaker* *A Story within a Story* Video by **Carrie Mae Weems**
Also, **Mark Olivieri*, Melinda Wagner*, Diane Jones**
Hobart-Wm. Smith Colleges, Geneva, NY

2:30pm Feb. 24 — 21ST C. PRIZE WINNERS
music by **Ted Goldman** †, **Joseph Rubinstein** †, **David Liptak***,
Libba Cotten, 2011 Pulitzer winner **Zhou Long**, & *The Last
Whirlispring* by **Edward Ruchalski*** with a 'musical' puppet!
Everson Museum of Art, Syracuse, NY

4pm March 30 — VISION OF SOUND
(new music w/ dance) Music by **Sam Pellman*, Mark Olivieri*, Nicolas
Scherzinger*, Zhou Tian, Jesse Benjamin Jones & Nicholas Omiccioli+**
Carrier Theatre, Civic Center, Syracuse

Repeated at Hochstein Aud., Rochester on April 6
& Wellin Hall, Hamilton College April 7

12:30pm April 10 — LATIN SNAPSHOTS
Music by **Roberto Sierra*** & other Caribbean-American & Latin works
In conjunction with **Juan Cruz** exhibit - Utica College Library Concourse

What the critics say:

Great concert . . . magnificent . . . phenomenal . . .
Terrific program . . . absolutely sublime . . . superb . . .

* **SNM commissioned composer**
† **Israel winner**
www.societyfornewmusic.org

41
years of new music

Congratulations on the continued success
of **Stone Canoe**
from the **School of Architecture**

we salute **stone canoe**
and proudly support future generations of
writers and artists in central new york

SYRACUSE UNIVERSITY
SCHOOL OF EDUCATION
soe.syr.edu

A NATIONAL LEADER IN INCLUSIVE URBAN EDUCATION

"The world is but a canvas to the imagination."
-Henry David Thoreau

SYRACUSE UNIVERSITY'S

S.I. NEWHOUSE SCHOOL OF

PUBLIC COMMUNICATIONS

SALUTES

STONE CANOE

FICTION

DRAMA

NONFICTION

INTERVIEWS

REVIEW

VISUAL ART

The YMCA's Downtown Writers Center
is pleased to announce the second annual

CNY BOOK AWARDS

...honoring the best books of poetry,
fiction and non-fiction published by
Central New Yorkers between July 1,
2012 and June 30, 2013.

Nomination Deadline: July 1, 2013

For complete information on prizes,
nomination rules, and nomination
forms, visit us at www.ycny.org/arts,
or call the Downtown Writers Center
at (315) 474-6851 x328.

the **Y**™
YMCA

THE 2013 *STONE CANOE* PRIZES

*S*tone Canoe awards yearly prizes for exemplary work submitted to the journal by emerging writers or artists in various categories. Submission of a single work of creative nonfiction, technology writing, short fiction, three poems, or three works of visual art in any medium will qualify for consideration in the respective genres. No additional fee or application is required.

TOM HUFF
Stone Canoe,
white alabaster,
2006

All prizewinners receive $500 and an original alabaster stone canoe carving by Tom Huff.

The **2013 S.I. Newhouse School Prize for Creative Nonfiction** is awarded to **Amy Monticello** for her essay "Loving Captain Corcoran."

The **2013 Allen and Nirelle Galson Prize for Fiction** is awarded to **Karen Martin** for her story "Re-enactments."

The **2013 Bea González Prize for Poetry** is awarded to **Maud Poole** for her poems "Young Girl with Chutzpah," "Young Girl in Ochre," and "Young Girl with Wasp."

The **2013 Hedy and Michael Fawcett Prize for Visual Arts** is awarded to **Dandelyon Holmes-Nelson** for her oil portraits.

The **2013 L.C. Smith Prizes for Engineering and Technology Writing** are awarded to **Thomas P. Rigoli** (First Prize) for his essay "Experiencing Silicon Valley" and **Betty Lise Anderson** (honorable mention) for her essay "Have You Met Your Engineer?"

The **2013 Syracuse University Institute for Veterans and Families (IVMF) Writing Prizes** are awarded to **Ed Soohoo** (First Prize) for his story "Blue Coast" and **Sam Gifford** (honorable mention) for his story "Mary Alice."

We congratulate the winners and thank the creators of these prizes for their generous support.

WRITERS PRIZE FOR VETERANS

Congratulations to the winners of the
2013 Institute for Veterans and Military Families
Prize for Written Work by a Veteran

First Place—Ed Soohoo, "Blue Coast"
Honorable Mention—Sam Gifford, "Mary Alice"

Thank you to our cohort of veteran judges:

Karl Marlantes
(U.S. Marine)

Anthony Swofford
(U.S. Marine)

Brian Turner
(U.S. Army)

Editor's Notes

Redefining Our Creative Community

Welcome to issue 7 of *Stone Canoe*. For the benefit of new readers, I should explain that our rather unusual name pays homage to an ancient story of our region: the Peacemaker and his sacred canoe of stone. The Peacemaker was a young warrior chosen by the Creator to travel from his home on the shores of Lake Ontario to the Finger Lakes, to make peace among the warring tribes of the region. For his journey, he was instructed to carve a canoe out of white granite, and the miracle of its buoyancy signaled to all he encountered the divine nature of his mission.

The Peacemaker's efforts culminated in the formation of the Iroquois Confederacy, or the Haudenosaunee, on the shores of Onondaga Lake, in the county of the same name here in Upstate New York. This historic partnering of previously hostile nation states resulted in the first recorded participatory democracy in the Western hemisphere, and persists today as a model of the triumph of mutual understanding and cooperation over the forces of ignorance and dissolution.

If our journal can be seen to have a political stance, it is just that—to foster mutual understanding by providing an outlet for an unusually diverse range of viewpoints. In our pages, the voices of Pulitzer Prize winners have mingled with those of high school and college students, neophyte authors, homeless artists, penitentiary inmates, political refugees, and people overcoming major disabilities to produce their art and share their stories with the world.

While *Stone Canoe*'s primary emphasis has always been to showcase the diversity and richness of the creative work emerging from Upstate New York, we have encountered, in the course of our short history, a surprising number of artists and writers from outside the region—expatriates whose work has been shaped by their Upstate roots and others who were affected in important ways by their experiences here. So the contents of each subsequent issue of the journal suggest an evermore complex idea of what might be thought of as the Upstate creative community.

In a nutshell, then, *Stone Canoe* has attempted to present to the world at large both a broader and deeper understanding of the Upstate cultural landscape than is perhaps generally appreciated. Whatever success we have had in this endeavor has been largely thanks to a distinguished group of editors whose expertise and taste have helped shape the contents of our publication. This year, we are especially grateful to the *Stone Canoe* 7 editorial group for their efforts in sorting through the largest number of submissions we have ever encountered and making the hard choices all good editors have to make. (See page 283 for a complete list of editors and their professional accomplishments.)

Amy Cheng, in her curator's statement for the *Stone Canoe* exhibition that accompanies this year's book launch, describes her own criteria for the visual art selections: "craftsmanship, conceptual rigor, and originality, or at least a new take on the familiar." The cover artist, Hedi Schwöbel, is an accomplished German artist whose first American residency at Utica's Sculpture Space had a significant impact on the direction of her subsequent projects. The 27 artists featured this year are a multigenerational group, including a graduate student as well as some artists who have been creating art for more than three decades. Two are Pollock-Krasner Grant Foundation awardees, and one is a Rome Prize Fellow. The paintings and drawings selected represent a wide variety of styles and techniques, and even the photography selections, as Cheng says, "run the gamut" of artistic and technical approaches to the medium. There are artists living, working, and teaching at prestigious art schools and universities throughout the country, from California to Florida to Brooklyn, as well as throughout the Upstate region. The visual arts prize winner this year, Dandelyon Holmes-Nelson, is an arts educator whose teaching experience includes working with chronically ill and at-risk children.

The writing in this issue represents a similar range of experience and perspective. Our poets include a high school sophomore, a financial advisor whose work is being published for the first time, and a poet-in-residence in urban schools who is also editor of a respected journal. There are also several well-established poets with multiple publications and university faculty positions. The poetry prizewinner, Maud Poole (her pen name), is fairly new to the genre, but is an accomplished photographer and author of children's books.

Cornelius Eady gets special kudos for sifting through the mountain of poetry submissions and making his final decisions during the power outages of Hurricane Sandy. Two notable enhancements to the poetry selections are the essay by Cornelius about his friend and mentor in his early Rochester days, the poet Shreela Ray, accompanied by selections of her work, and Jesse Nissim's extended conversation with activist poet and memoirist (and former SC editor) Minnie Bruce Pratt.

Editor Ken McClane's choice for the nonfiction prize this year is a poignant memoir of friendship and lost love by Ithaca teacher Amy Monticello. There is also a beautifully wrought reminiscence by Cornell University professor and novelist Maureen McCoy. The prizewinning fiction submission is by Karen Martin, a Syracuse University graduate student from South Africa. Other selections by editor E.C. Osondu include stories by a Cornell graduate student, a Le Moyne College professor, and a Schenectady-based Iraq veteran.

Stone Canoe could not have been launched or sustained without the encouragement and support of Syracuse University's creative writing program faculty, and we are proud to offer in this issue Rob Enslin's celebration of this legendary program, as seen through the eyes of its teachers and notable graduates.

Our drama editor Kyle Bass has discovered a wonderful play called *Medea, An Illegal Love Story,* by Chiori Miyagawa, a Japan-born playwright and professor at Bard College. Inspired by Euripides' original Medea, it is a beautifully succinct commentary on ethnicity, illegal immigration, and the ironies of the American Dream.

The centerpiece of our music section is Neva Pilgrim and Steve Stucky's interview with two esteemed jazz musicians and pioneers of electronic music: Colgate University's Dexter Morrill and Cornell's David Borden. It may be surprising to many readers that Upstate musicians played such a key role in the evolution of this radical reinterpretation of the limits of musical composition. Samples of their music can be heard on our web site, *stonecanoejournal.org.* Also included in this issue is a provocative analysis of the music of Prince by Osvaldo Oyola, a doctoral student at SUNY Binghamton.

In the area of technology writing, editor Megan Davidson has chosen two pieces by alumni of Syracuse University's L.C. Smith College of Engineering and Computer Science: communication specialist Tom Rigoli's fascinating firsthand account of the origins of Silicon Valley, and Ohio State Professor

Betty Lise Anderson's enlightening articulation of the role of the engineer in our everyday lives. Thanks to guest editor Doran Larson, we are also featuring a new, beautifully written piece on prison life by José Lauriano Di Lenola, an inmate at Attica Correctional Facility.

Finally, this issue marks the successful launch of an initiative that means a great deal to all involved with our publication—the *Stone Canoe* veterans writing prize, sponsored by Syracuse University's Institute for Veterans and Families (IVMF). This is the first of our prizes not tied to a regional connection, and the diversity of submissions has been truly remarkable, ranging from a love story set in post-WWII France to compelling tales of teenage love and revenge to visceral poems by survivors of our most recent wars. The hard choices in this category were made by a team of distinguished editors whose own literary accomplishments are internationally recognized: Vietnam Marine veteran Karl Marlantes, Gulf War Marine veteran Anthony Swofford, and Iraq Army veteran Brian Turner. Despite heavy professional demands that involved international travel, they gave generously of their time and collaborated on the run, as it were, to identify the wonderful pieces we offer here.

It is not easy in a few paragraphs to do justice to the range of offerings in our 2013 issue, but I hope the above remarks will prompt both returning and new readers to give *Stone Canoe* 7 a serious look. Throughout the year, we will also feature additional new writing and art on our web site, *stonecanoejournal.org*. Cinema enthusiasts will enjoy editor Nancy Keefe Rhodes's 2013 edition of our web-based Moving Image section, which will include essays on important new indie films, new appreciations of older films, and a conversation with Kendall Phillips about his new book on the history of horror films. For periodic updates on our web offerings, join our newsletter mailing list by writing to us at *stonecanoe@uc.syr.edu*.

Thanks as always to the wonderful staff at University College, and to all our readers and community partners for helping *Stone Canoe* stay afloat. I suspect we may also have had some occasional help from a more distant source, as did the Peacemaker, but we can never be sure.

Robert Colley
Editor, *Stone Canoe*
Syracuse, New York
December 2012

EPOCH

a magazine of contemporary literature

Study for Transfer, charcoal on paper, 36" x 84", 2008, by Brody Parker Burroughs

EPOCH MAGAZINE
**251 Goldwin Smith Hall
Cornell University
Ithaca, NY 14853-2301**

published three times per year   sample copy: $5   one year subscription: $11

book
DESIGN

Adam Rozum Design is a graphic design studio headed by
Adam Rozum. It offers a full range of design services, from books
and book covers to logos and visual identity programs.

adam@adamdesign.com
315 468 6417

Cornelius Eady

Remembering Shreela Ray (1942-1994)

Born in Orissa, India, in 1942, my friend and mentor Shreela Ray came to the United States as a college student in 1972, first at the Iowa Writers' Workshop, then at the University of Buffalo. Except for four brief trips back, she spent most of her adult life in the States as a writer and teacher. She received scholarships and grants from the *Atlantic Monthly,* the Ingram Merrill Foundation, and the New York State Council on the Arts. Her work appeared in magazines like *Southern Poetry Review* and *Poetry*, and she published her one and only full-length collection, *Night Conversations with None Other* (Dustbooks), in 1977. She died, aged 50, in Rochester, New York, in 1994.

Shreela Ray was my doorway into the literary life, something I wasn't fully aware of when I first met her in the 1970s as a student at Empire State College.

It is difficult to write about Shreela without mentioning the house she and her husband, Hendrick de Leeuw, had on Dartmouth Street in my hometown of Rochester, New York. What a wonder box it was to a bookish kid from a poor neighborhood. They had odd books. They had cool music. The talk was passionate and the food was curried. And the parade of friends (and aesthetic enemies) who walked through what sometimes seemed to be a front door that was never properly locked: people who sang (or wanted to sing), people who danced (or thought they danced), kids, photographers, strivers, burnouts, people with sloppy lives and tidy minds.

Suddenly, at a sprawling dinner table where it seemed there was a seat for everyone, I had to learn not only to talk, but to think fast—or at least consider what I was talking about. This, I think, Shreela was trying to show me, was part of the process of finding one's voice.

In 1994, just before she died, Shreela wrote that poems were to her sort of cumulative maps, a succession of line drawings of who/what/where one has been or become between one poem and the next. They are the art of paying attention. There in the 70s, Shreela gave me a first look at the landscape I was going to walk through. I wasn't fully there yet, she had told me at our first meeting, but she did believe I was a writer. I took that to mean I was now at the door, and it was time to stop gazing in.

This was around the time of the publication of her first book of poems, *Night Conversations with None Other*. After a few meetings, I was invited to move in. Shreela was on her way back to India, back to her family there, as a published poet. I remember the clamor of that moment as I moved into one of the upstairs bedrooms, containing the first opened boxes of her book, rubbing shoulders against the suitcases she was packing for her trip.

How I wish I could tell you what this moment held for her work (and her life), that all of our hopes for her and that first book proved true, how the honest tensions raised in her work—one foot in the English tradition she grew up with, the other jazzed by America and the Iowa Workshop—cleared a way through for a large and long career.

Instead, *Night Conversations* became her one and only book. Reading it now, all these years later, I wonder if she wasn't slightly ahead of the curve, the way she seems to be sifting through her various identities: an Asian woman in 1960-70s America, the tug between the U.S. ("America is so brutal," she wrote sometime in the 1980s), and India ("It is my country of destination because I know I cannot return to it.") The speaking of truth from the point of view of someone from the outside looking in seems to be a familiar subject to readers now. Perhaps the way we live now has finally caught up to her verse.

And if my description of the house on Dartmouth Street sounds faintly to some of you like the Cave Canem Workshop, you might be on to something. Shreela was gone by the time Sarah, Toi and I met that summer on Capri to work out what would become Cave Canem, but we are what we learn, and certainly, one of the reasons Cave Canem is run like a "big table" is a lesson I took from Shreela. I like to think she'd recognize and enjoy the trouble we've made.

The poems I've selected are, with the exception of "Asia," all post-*Night Conversations.* "One Spring" and "The Way We Are" were published as part of a chapbook issue of *The Falcon* in 1979. The remaining poems were collected by her family. They can be found on a web page set up for her work:

http://freepages.misc.rootsweb.ancestry.com/~deleeuw/ShreelaRay/Shreela.html

Shreela Ray

Asia*

Somewhere a boat no bigger than my fist
overturns
and drowns everyone in it.

I do not attempt to save it.
Would you?
Being what I am? Knowing what I know?

Each night, when the red moon and the darkness
marry
I stand on this far shore and mark
with an X the places
where the bodies are washed up.

And I shoulder them one by one
safe conduct
to the vaults in my memory,
where they may lie in state
beyond contempt and further violations.

I build fires on the crosses.
The smoke stretches across these rooms
to make a ring around me.

I shall never know any other
enchantment
but this part mourning.

So I watch my speech and dress,
and do not look long at a man.

*From *Night Conversations with None Other* (Dustbooks, 1977)

Shreela Ray

SONG OF A WOMAN FEIGNING SLEEP

This is nothing more than a painted room
and I, a painted woman in it
by an open window, a brass sun
and a blob of flowers on a cabinet.
Crowds come in every day to look
at the bold brass color of the sun,
the window quite unlike any other;
the cabinet with flowers.

They also look at me feigning sleep.
It's true I elicit no desire
wherever desire is to be felt by them.
It's the artist's skill they admire
for the dark voluptuous flesh.
My parts are disproportionate.

I see too well with these slit eyes.
That man is not so really brave. The fair
young girl in the white cotton dress
sneaks a look at my pubic hair.

I long for the emptiness and shut doors:
to rise and fling the windows wide
to the moonlight streaming in and to dance till sunrise.
Aster, anemone, marigold, bells explode;
and the brave iron knight on his rare
iron horse, the woman reclining in a chair, listen.

Just before sunrise the moon goes brass.
The flowers reassert themselves as a blob.
If there is a change it is perhaps
in a finger covering a little more breast
and the bells returned to the cabinet.

The room is never more than a painted room
and I a woman painted in it.

Shreela Ray

ONE SPRING

1

Don't detain me in love's name
or remind me of the bad endings
of other abandoned children

I ferret the lids of endurance
My breath hurls this self up
against reason and the laws of this land.

A brown speck rising,
losing visibility,
losing different weights
of desire—lungs and heart.

Water and rice transfigured
is kinder to memory
than the saints I knew. They are fizzling
out of sight in a noise of linens
and hired mourners. Now I live
by smoke, not justice.

2

Until sleep removes the dross of sadness
and I sit on your roof to burn the noon flower,
I shall not leave this room.

We hold up our hands to the moon—
in our bones, a spectrum of nations,
coloured strings tremble quietly
and salaam, and salaam for us all
who wouldn't be humble and silent.

THE WAY WE ARE

Somewhere in Arkansas on a Sunday morning
the good people prepare for Church.
I too get ready to pray for my father
who spent a quarter of his salary
on my hopeless education.

I had composed a special text for my mother.
How she cried when she packed
her engagement dress in the black
steel trunk. May her closets fill
with kitchen gadgets from America.
She had such high hope for me.

come back and marry a king;
(if you weren't a socialist)
maybe Gandhi's only grandson!
(If you weren't tired of saints)

But all that is done with.

Baptist USA here I come!
When enter the hostess, Charlene:
"The family would prefer you don't come
to Church. Please understand the way
things are in small towns."

the children of Ham and of Ishmael
have always taken up the burden
of good manners to understand
that sermons are a bore and I'd fall
asleep back home on the coir mat

on my hands and knees between the opening
prayer and letter to the Galatians.
So I spent the morning on a swing.
the sky opened like the throat of God
containing all the truth the world
turns on, and I groped
descending in the universal ichor
with both feet on the ground.

THE PROMISE TO MUNNI

My cook's daughter Munni
has grown up by the river.
Her father minds the temple,
sweeps the floor to pay
the rent on a one room hut.

She is thin and small;
her body slightly bent—an oar
someone leaned against a tree
to season, and forgot
it rains.

She's going to be a tailor;
wants her own shop someday
near the river perhaps, she says
or in Buxi Bazaar. She dreams
of electric sewing machines.

I wandered through Khan Market
in search of the finest
sewing machine; But my wages
were consigned. I bought a sari
made lavish promises instead:

a shop landscaped with mimosa
trees and digitate wood-apples,
a room with a glass case
and superior fluorescent
lights....

if she would not skip school,
if she would write to me
once a month,
if she would be patient.
I spoke of the marvels
of foreign sewing machines:
Bernina, Elna, Necchi, White.
A secondhand Usha will do,
she said, when you come back
from America.

Little girl
by the time I come back from America
the river will have risen
and fallen at least six times
and you'll be married.

By the time I come back
from Amerika, what I'll have saved
And what I earned alone,
wouldn't pay for a fraction of
what I had promised.

DAMNED BEGGAR

Pigeons under dead white sky
feed on sunflower seeds. I
wait in the flare of hard snow
For the postman and know by

now, my chances were always slim.
Still, creedless, I wreathe the grim
wooden form of Shiva, (four
feet offground) yield camphor, thin

stalks of incense…all I brought
from home. If I had been taught
better—how to use my knees…
but the god sees. I will not.

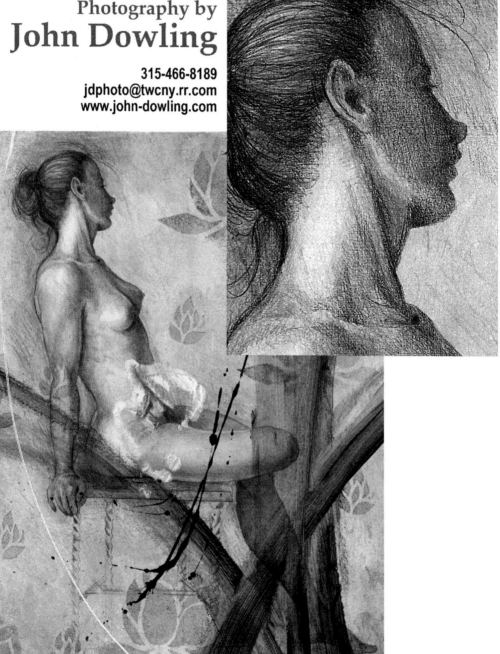

Ed Soohoo

THE BLUE COAST

We were sitting in the semidarkness, downing cognac while watching the couples on the dance floor and eyeing the girls who weren't dancing. I saw one sitting by herself at a corner table. She was small and thin with short, bobbed, coal black hair, dark eyed, with a pale white face set off by a small, crimson-painted mouth and very pretty in the classic French style. She had been sitting with a tall blonde girl who was now slow dancing with a French sailor on the small crowded floor in a room acrid with the smoke of cigarettes. The girl sitting there noticed me looking at her and smiled. I stood up and walked over to her table, and in my very best schoolboy French asked her to dance. She laughed at my halting delivery and said, "I speak English. Yes, why not?"

My shipboard roommate and I were on our first liberty ashore in France, courtesy of the U.S. Navy's Sixth Fleet in the Mediterranean. This was choice duty for the Navy, considering that another fleet was at war in Korea. My roommate and I were brand new ensigns and we were going to make the most of the Old World. We wound up at the Monte Cristo, a nightclub in the old part of Nice.

The girl's name was Jeanne. As we danced, the band was playing "La Vie en Rose," the Edith Piaf song that was sweeping through Europe at the time.

"Where did you learn English?" I asked.

"I was in a convent school during the war and the nuns were Irish," she replied with hardly any accent.

"Then why don't you have an Irish accent?" I asked.

"The war didn't last long enough," she said, smiling and squeezing my hand.

"What are you doing in Nice?" she asked.

"I'm an officer in the U.S. Navy. My ship is anchored down the coast at Villefranche."

"Why don't you have your uniform on then?"

"Too many Americans in uniform make the French government unhappy; so we only wear a uniform when we are on duty."

"Are you here for a while?"

"About a week or so."

"And then?"

"Probably Naples or Athens. We go where the Navy sends us."

"Will you be returning?"

"Sure, I'm on the flagship and the admiral has his family here."

We kept on dancing until the band left and the club started closing. Her blonde friend had left with the French sailor and my roommate had caught a taxi back to the ship because he had to stand an early morning watch. I offered to take her home, but she said that it wasn't far away and that she could walk. Besides, she said that I'd better find a taxi before they disappeared for the night. "Will I see you again?" I asked.

"Tomorrow night if you like. I'll be here" she said.

"Alone?"

"Yes, alone."

I saw her every night that week. She met me at the Monte Cristo or a nearby cafe. Wherever we went, people noticed us right away because Jeanne was striking to look at and because she was with an American. Uniformed or not, we Americans stood out because of our short haircuts and casual dress, which contrasted sharply with the conservative clothing of the French.

When I asked about her family she told me that her father had died in the war and that her mother had remarried and moved to Algeria with her new husband. "No other family?"

She thought for a moment and said, "No, not really."

A few days before my ship was to leave Villefranche, I received a radio message ordering me to transfer to another ship down the coast at Marseilles. I was to replace an officer who had gotten sick and was sent back to the States. I went immediately to the captain and asked whether the orders could be changed so that I could remain on the flagship. He said that since the orders came from the Navy Department in Washington it was out of his hands. I would have to leave on the morning the flagship was to leave. When I saw Jeanne that night I asked her if she could come with me to Marseilles for a few days. She hesitated, then, said, "I would have to tell them something where I work and make some other arrangements. But why do you want me to come?"

"Can't you guess?"

"Because you need a tour guide in Marseilles?" she asked, giving me a smile that made me hold my breath.

"No, because I'm falling for you."

"Falling where?" she teased, her smile getting bigger.

"You know what I mean. Didn't the nuns tell you about that?"

"Very little. Besides, how would they know?"

After she'd had her fun, she said, "Yes, I would like very much to come with you. Let me see if I can do it and I will tell you tomorrow night. OK?"

She told me the next night that she had arranged it.

Early in the morning I stepped from the ship's launch onto the landing at Villefranche. In front of the little hotel on the pier, a taxi stood waiting, its yellow fog lights glowing in the dark. As I turned toward the taxi I saw Jeanne standing beside the driver who was clapping his gloved hands together against the January chill. He wore the postwar uniform of French cab drivers: a long, soft, black leather jacket and Irish tweed cap. She walked over to me quickly, turned her face up to be kissed, and held my waist tightly while my hands held two heavy sea bags. Her breath was warm with the faint odor of French cigarettes. At the same time, I smelled her light perfume. She told the driver to take us to the train station in Nice. We travelled along the Grande Corniche high above the dark Mediterranean.

Jeanne and I got the last two seats in a smoky second-class compartment and sat across from each other with passengers on both sides of us. A frail old lady with very white hair kept looking at us, her hands holding a wicker basket in her lap. I assumed it was my American uniform or that we spoke in English. The French didn't think it rude to stare, I had noticed, and besides, there weren't many foreigners on the early train to Marseilles. A young soldier slept in the corner of the compartment by the window, his cap pushed back on his head. It was not the usual garrison cap but one of those round military hats with the signature white top of the Foreign Legion. I knew that French naval transports were taking soldiers from Marseilles to Indochina every week, trying to save France's last outpost in Asia. Jeanne kept staring at him and I asked her why.

"Because he is a Legionnaire and that means he's going to Indochina," she said with real sadness in her voice.

Jeanne looked at me with sleepy eyes and smiled. She looked especially thin in her black wool dress. She had been a child during the war, and like many others, her slimness was the result of deprivation. I hadn't been sure she would come, since I'd only known her a week. After all, it could be just another shore leave romance and I didn't know if it meant any more to her than that. But now we were together on the train, away from the Navy, family, or friends, just the two of us. I was excited but unsure of where this was going. I was drawn to her not just because of the way she looked, but because of some concealed sadness that I sensed behind her smiles and laughs which I could not fathom but which made her seem mysterious. She was very different from the girls I had known in high school and college who played at being grownups but never quite succeeded. It was part of the excitement I felt about her.

"What do you want to do in Marseilles?" she asked.

"Well, you can show me the sights and we can try the bouillabaisse. We can go somewhere with music and dancing and then...whatever."

I laughed as I said "whatever" and she laughed, too, knowing exactly my meaning.

"And what would you like to do?" I asked.

"I only want to be with you," she said.

It was getting light outside now. We were coming into Toulon; the train slowed, the brakes screeching sharply as it did.

"Are you hungry?" she asked.

"Yes, starving."

"We can buy some sandwiches and some coffee here." She stood up and rolled down the compartment window as the train came to a stop. A bulky lady wearing a large straw hat came up to the window holding a basketful of sandwiches and steaming coffee. Jeanne reached down and picked out our breakfast. I took a small bouquet of violets from the basket and dropped some franc notes in its place. Jeanne looked at me for a few seconds before she took the bouquet and placed it beside her. Most of the other passengers in our compartment had come prepared with little bags of food and were eating already. The Legionnaire awakened and bought his breakfast too. As we ate, the train started again. Jeanne turned to me and asked, "Do you always ask girls to come with you in every place you go?"

"Only if they are very pretty," I replied. "Let's have a good time in Marseilles," I said.

"Yes, let's," and she reached across and took my hand in hers.

As we approached Marseilles, I could see the harbor and the big cargo cranes along the docks. There were old rusty freighters and the sleek gray frigates of the French navy at anchor. The train came into the old prewar station with its soot-encrusted glass dome. The platform was packed with waiting passengers and blue-smocked baggage porters. People crowded the aisles and doorways with their belongings in hand. Jeanne and I were the last to leave, she with her small cloth suitcase and I with my heavy duffel bags.

Jeanne asked about hotels at the station and we took a taxi to one near the harbor. She booked a room there and I went on to the ship and reported in to the executive officer. I asked for some leave time over the next few days. He gave me a long look and then a knowing smile that I was sure had been used many times with other junior officers.

"Got a girl here?" he asked.

"Yes, sir, and my orders only left me 24 hours to get here."

"All right, we need to take on fuel and stores and make some repairs for a few days, so you can have some time until we get underway again. I'll see that you make it up later." He smiled again as I saluted, and I left the ship after I had stowed my gear.

Jeanne and I had dinner that night at a workmen's cafe in the old port, eating the red pulp of raw spiny sea urchins fresh from the Mediterranean, with a *baguette* and glasses of *vin ordinaire*. We had coffee afterwards in a glassed-in cafe facing the main street and watched the passing parade of prostitutes, sailors, Arabs, and dockworkers. There were also soldiers everywhere, waiting to board their ships in the harbor.

In the hotel room that night I told her that I loved her and she laughed softly and said that I had had too much wine. Later, when we made love, she was passionate and eager, almost hungry. Her pale ivory skin and her small body were exquisite. She was not self-conscious at all, but afterwards she was very quiet and seemed lost in thought.

"Is something wrong," I asked.

"No, it was lovely, very lovely. Just the way it should be."

I knew she meant it but she still seemed troubled.

We explored Marseilles. It was not really a tourist town but a gritty working class city where everyone walked fast and purposefully, unlike Nice where no one was ever in a hurry. Over the next few days I felt that I was falling in love with her and thought that she felt the same way, but she never used the word love, and only smiled when I did. I had never met anyone like her or felt as close to someone. Maybe it was the way she smiled or laughed or her lack of artificiality. Maybe I was just young and intoxicated with Europe which was new and exciting to me. Why had she come with me? Was it just an impulse?

At the hotel the night before the ship left I asked her if she would write to me, and I told her that I would probably be back in Nice in a few months. She promised to write. "I do love you, you know," I told her.

"Yes, I think maybe you do."

"Then will you think about you and me, at least?"

"I can't think about anything else."

"Then why not tell me so?"

"I can't."

"Why not?"

"I just can't."

Then I held her for a long time as she pressed her face against my chest, and I felt her warm tears.

A fog had crept in from the Mediterranean the next morning as the ship prepared to leave. Jeanne arrived just as the last lines were let go. As we backed away from the pier, she looked up and waved slowly until she was swallowed up by the fog.

Instead of returning to Nice, we were ordered to Korea where the war was going badly and Navy ships were being used for offshore artillery bombardment against the North Koreans and the Chinese. We spent the next six months on station in Korea. At first I received letters from Jeanne every week, then less often. Even though I continued to tell her I loved her, she never responded. She told me about everyday things in Nice: her job, the weather, the films she had seen, everything but what I wanted to hear. Maybe, I thought, our short time together really hadn't meant that much to her. Perhaps I hadn't been the only one in her life and that this might be just a casual affair for her. Then, I received a letter saying that she did love me but that it was impossible for us to be together and to forget her. But I couldn't.

A year later our ship returned to the Mediterranean for another tour of duty with Sixth Fleet. We dropped anchor in Villefranche in early spring, and I headed into Nice on liberty the first night. I went to the Monte Cristo first to see if she was there, but of course she wasn't. I visited her old address but she had moved and the landlady didn't know where.

On a warm spring Sunday I wandered along the *Promenade des Anglais* fronting the sea, across from the old grand hotels facing the bright, blue green water and the curved coastline that stretched toward nearby Monte Carlo and Italy. Many French tourists and locals were out strolling in the warm sunshine. Then I saw her. I remember that she wore a light blue dress with yellow flowers. She pushed a wheelchair with a young man in it. He wore an olive-drab military shirt with the medals of French soldiers in Indochina. A blanket covered his lower body but did not seem to conceal anything beneath it. She turned toward me as they approached, and recognized me, but shook her head fiercely as I walked toward her. I stopped and looked at them as they passed by. Then, I noticed the gold rings on his hand and on hers. She turned and looked back at me for a few seconds. I watched them until they disappeared into the crowd. ≋

Paul Elisha

U<small>NLEARNED</small>

Just past twenty but ages older,
I turned my back on carnage grown
Familiar as my skin; the battle's din
Beyond me as I stood, shin deep in surf
Yesterday stained red with shreds
Of those who came this far to die.

What I harbored then were thoughts
Of hot meals, shipboard showers,
Hours of forgetfulness and that's
Where they catch you off guard, match
Their canard of clean-sheet, belly-full
Silence against a truth they've hidden and
You've sworn never to forget, yet
Years after, must concede you did.

David S. Pointer

Short Dream of Leveling a Building

Mobile crematory elegy on twin tracks,
a Marine has stolen a tank knowing only

that he needs to make a call, taking out
The Provost Marshal's Office, Okinawa

aboard Camp Butler, I'm sadly too safe,
flying back from Camp Schwab or Hansen

hard on the government gas pedal to save
my good work fellows, but elsewhere the

white hats get the tank stopped, and still
this old war-bound world won't go flat

Mac McGowan

LANDING AT TAN SON NHUT: NOVEMBER 1965

Flying low over the coast,
out of the South China Sea
from the Philippines,
the tendrils of the Mekong
sparkle like sun on steel
through the camouflage
of tangled mangroves—
and even though the cabin
of the plane is cooled by 20th century
air conditioning, I know the jungle bakes
in the primordial soup of muddy slime,
fetid air and forlorn hopes of returned sanity.
Here we will sweat and slog and spend our youth,
our innocence and some of us, our own young lives
in a war of shadows and blurred images,
a conflict of smeared objectives
and diffused intentions.
At this apogee of American wealth and influence,
we descend like wild geese
over the sparkling estuaries
of Southeast Asia.

Rick Christman

No Escape

After the war,
From a safe distance,
I watch teenage Mexican boys on Plaza Garibaldi,
Stripped to bare feet and jeans,
Swallow fire at midnight.
Fire shoots from their mouths
Like bottle rockets
Down the row of boys,
One after another,
Into the dark night sky.

The smell of gasoline
Takes my breath,
Like the boys take fire.
I rush away, escape the burning
Toward the horns and yodels of Mariachis.
I find a booth among the throng
And slide in alone.

But at once men surround me,
Push into my booth from both sides,
Trap me like a rabbit in a wire snare,
Until I know that there will be no escape.
They buy me a cold Carta Blanca
But they feed me fire,
Birria red sauce spilling over my tacos—
I can see the flames.
I switch to green sauce
But I find no relief from fire.

Later that night,
Alone
From the balcony of my hotel,
I watch fire shoot into the Mexican sky and die,
Shoot and die,
Like night fighting, I think,
And I wait to hear the explosions,
But I know it's only fireworks.
A little later still,
I think of Tommy Sorjourner,
Trapped alone,
On fire in his jeep,
And not one of us could save him.

Richard Levine

BEAUTY ON THE WING

The one time I saw a bird alive in Vietnam
it was in a cage. A large, white cockatoo
bobbing up and down and giving off a cry you might
call human, if you'd never heard a human cry.

The cage was suspended from the branch
of a dead tree by a wire that was all
that held the handle of a grenade
to its pregnant body. Anyone

foolish enough to pull on that cage
would become one with the bird
and the trail we walked along, inhaling
what had defoliated a hectare of jungle.

We were trained to ferret out malefic toys
and tactics, but the rhythm of boredom
and sudden death, the trails of a thousand
tense steps when you didn't die made for carelessness.

Even those hiding in wait who saw you
reach for their ruse were surprised
to see how even in hell nothing moves
as easy as beauty on the wing.

Sam Gifford

Mary Alice

Half of the group didn't know what to do or why they were there in the woods with the June sounds of busy insects, scolding crows, and baritone gurgle of Sauquoit Creek. They looked at each other as though one might have an answer. Peter Wallace, his cousin, Billy Wallace, and Harold Newman and his cousin, Mary Alice Newman, stood silently at the edge of a large, uncared-for carrot garden, surrounded by bushes and trees, and downed parts of both.

"What are we supposed to do now?" Peter whispered to the two-year-older Harold, who had engineered this safari with the shrugged assent of his cousin. They had to do something. Harold was more adventurous with forbidden things. He cursed freely and referred to certain acts with girls as a "fug," a word that never crossed the lips of the other two boys. That word, which Peter was certain had a "k" ending, instead of the "g" vocalized by Harold, had magical, evil powers. Of all disallowed words, that one was heard by God, and filed.

"I'm getting out of here," Peter mouthed to Billy, who quickly nodded. It was the best idea he had heard that day. Peter and Billy were reluctant participants in the adventure, though neither knew for certain what it was all about. Billy asked Harold. "Fuggin'," Harold told both, "*that's* what it's all about, *fuggin'*." They listened to the word but did not repeat it, only wincing at the vocalization.

It was cooler in the bushes. They had followed Harold from the backyard of his home near the railroad tracks, along Main Street to short Ellis Avenue, and then onto the dusty tractor path along Sauquoit Creek. The procession had the familiar look of a ritual funeral, the kind held for birds downed by BBs. Peter and Billy shuffled along with bowed heads and now squatted on haunches, waiting for something to happen. Billy and Mary Alice could have a baby, Peter speculated, and they would all have to marry her. Peter waved a deer fly from his face and ran fingers through his shiny black hair. "I won't," he said.

"You have to do *it*, you know, for them to get pregnant," Harold stated. It had replaced the other word for good, hopefully.

"Yeah," Billy's alto voice quavered.

"You know how it is in the morning, you know, when you first wake up? It has to be that way to do it." Harold always had the answers.

Peter and Billy wondered why anybody would ever want to do that. Peter wanted to see what was under her dress, however, but had no mental picture of what might be there, and so he didn't know how to ask. He also didn't want Mary Alice to know he was interested. That didn't seem possible, now.

"Do you like *it*?" an emboldened Peter directed at Mary Alice.

The girl looked at her fingernails. "Like what?" She seemed bored.

"*It*." He felt trapped and feared the other word might have to be used.

"What's *it*?" she pressed.

"Never mind. You know what I mean," Peter mumbled, looking down.

Harold took her hand and commanded, "Come on." She stood up and walked with him into the woods. The other two regarded each other.

"I'm leaving now," Billy said.

Peter stood, then, froze when a voice from the woods ordered: "You stay, or I'll say you did *it* with her." Still a little unsure of what *it* was, Peter determined the threat to be ominous enough. He re-sat, and Billy ran from the woods onto the dry path.

Fear of Harold was not the only reason Peter stayed. He was also held by a curiosity that both excited and sickened him. He didn't want to be part of this, but was captured by a desire to know what Mary Alice looked like down there, and what was supposed to happen, even though he never intended to do *it*. For certain, he never would show himself to anybody, much less a girl. Still, he wanted to see this dark place, but from afar, from a hiding place.

Mary Alice had come to Whitesboro with her parents, who operated a traveling magic and mindreading show. They lived in a house trailer, adjacent to their oblong, circus-like show tent, which was pitched on the large corner lawn of Peter's grandfather's Main Street house, next to an undisciplined herd of rugosas. LeRoy and Margo Newman came to the small town to present the shows and to visit with LeRoy's brothers, Harold and Dennis. Elder Harold was young Harold's uncle, and Dennis was his father. Young Harold was called "Young Harold" by Whitesboro adults. The

Newman brothers were boyhood friends of Peter's father. Billy's father was Peter's uncle, whose family lived in the big Wallace house, which had been divided into apartments by the government department that orders such divisions in times of war. Grandpa Wallace thought it better to move family in than to live with strangers.

Peter lived on Hart's Hill, some two miles from the center of Whitesboro. He seemed, in some ways, alien to Billy and Harold, because his father, a doctor, was naturally thought to be rich. Peter tried to compensate by inserting "ain't" and double negatives into his speech, but it didn't change anything.

At the far end of the tent was a stage. LeRoy tiptoed in and around the cluster of 20 or so locals, holding up an audience member's wristwatch, bracelet, or ring, which the blindfolded Margo would identify from the stage, after some hemming and hawing. Whitesboro people liked the shows, that is, all but Grandpa Wallace, also a doctor, who had paid for his medical education at City University of New York, by teaching Greek at the C.U.N.Y. undergraduate school. The tent and parked cars ruined his lawn, but Sam Wallace could not muster sufficient anger or volume to discourage LeRoy and Margo, or drive the tent show off.

They lived in Florida and spoke in velvety tones and a soft dialect that Whitesboro boys had not heard, except in movies. Mary Alice's southern speech and light red hair gave her a foreign sort of attractiveness among Whitesboro boys, though she was widely freckled and otherwise plain, even by early teen standards of the day. Quiet and reserved, she was at the same time direct and unapologetic in conversation. She wore the same over-laundered dress every day, or so it seemed in that summer of 1946.

She was thirteen, and her nipples were insect bites under the dress. Her new hormones sparked uneducated curiosity, and she gained information through empirical methods. She was innocent and desired to know those secrets of life which her parents had not divulged. She discovered how pleasing it was to be gently touched in those places by certain boys, and how to avoid being touched by other boys. She was unimpeded by rules of correctness and hypocritical morals.

She sat on the grass next to Peter, who, by then, was at odds with himself. "I have to go to the bathroom," she announced, and Harold suggested she do it in the woods. Peter said he wanted to watch. He stared with guilty fascination from his highly visible tree stump seat as she hiked up the little dress and squatted. It was different, and riveting in a way that he couldn't describe to himself. She laughed. Afterward, she wanted Peter to go into the woods with her, but he had seen enough and told her so.

"Don't you want to do *it?*" She looked squarely at his face.

"You said you don't know what *it* is," he responded in a derisive tone.

"We both know very well," she returned with her soft smile, "so what about it?"

"Nah, it sounds boring." He dismissed the subject, sauntering to the path on shaky legs, preparing a story for anyone who might spot him emerging from the woods. Anyway, *it* is a better word than the other one, he concluded.

At eleven years, Peter felt soiled by the adventure, yet thought of it, and walked often the two miles from his Hart's Hill home to Whitesboro just to gaze briefly, and of course, accidently, at Mary Alice. She looked at him differently from the other boys, but didn't say why. She seemed sad when she looked at Peter, as though she saw something past his eyes.

"How old are you?" she asked while they stood outside the tent on a hot afternoon.

"Twelve," he said and turned to walk away. She followed.

"You're eleven," she said with a kind southern downbeat, almost as though she was singing. It made him uneasy. "And you don't have to do *it* to be friends with me." She added with a soft, but digging, intensity. "I'm coming to your house to see you." She wasn't asking.

"Better not," he said, "just better not."

She phoned the next morning, and Peter's father called him to the telephone, grinning. She asked if she could come to the house on Hart's Hill. He said he didn't think so.

"Okay, I'll be right there."

His father admonished him to be nice. Peter thought if he could only tell his father what she wanted him to do, then, there would be no visit. He couldn't, though, and was harnessed to the secret that made him sick to his stomach. If they had to do…*it*, he reasoned, then, they would do it in the playhouse behind the big house, on the edge of the blackberry bogs. At least he wouldn't get caught.

He waited by the old, shingled playhouse, hoping that she would not come, that her father would see the danger if he allowed his girl with little bumps under her dress to play alone with a boy. But, she came. He heard

LeRoy's overused Ford station wagon pop and cough down the long horseshoe driveway. Car doors slammed. Then the exchange: "Hallo, how the hell are ya?" Peter's father and LeRoy had drinking and storytelling in common, which they had shared since boyhood. Despite the youthful ties, Doctor Wallace would no more than nod in passing to LeRoy were it not for the bonding qualities of alcohol.

Peter was beckoned loudly to the house by Norma, the housekeeper who stole silver tableware and hosted a boyfriend in her third floor room, but was never fired, because she was the sister of another boyhood chum. Peter walked to the house with short, stiff steps, as a dog that objects to a command, but obeys. He wondered whether the adults suspected what was about to happen. Mary Alice smiled as their eyes met for a moment before he averted his eyes from her unblinking gaze.

"Let's go outside," she suggested, and they ran on the rolling lawn, past the high deep hedgerow, toward the playhouse, where Peter thought to get *it* over with, once and for good. She stood in the damp little fairy house and said she would live there, given half a chance. The house had two windows in back and a rough stairway that led to a loft that covered half the structure. The only door had a star-shaped window and lock. Mary Alice tiptoed across the room, facing him, and said it was her house and she would live in it and fix it "like I want to." She sat on the ancient deacon's bench with its scaling brown paint for what seemed a long time, crossed her legs, and scanned the house with knitted brow, focused on future décor.

"This is the only house I ever had that didn't have wheels."

"It's not your house."

"It is if we're married." Peter felt sweat in his armpits.

"You're my only friend," her tone was candid and sincere. "I'm in the car or the trailer mostly all the time. I go to school in the winter, but I'm gone all summer, like now. I want my own house with a kitchen and a kids' room, in the same place every day of the week. Of the year. Always. The stove can go right over there," she said as she pointed to the left rear corner of the tiny, dim room. "This could be it, if you marry me. It's bigger than the trailer." Her eyes were clear and blue, and her face told him that she meant it.

She stood up, hugged him tightly, and pressed a thin hand gently to his cheek. He stood stiffly, waiting to be released. She let him go and kicked off her worn, brown leather shoes, then walked about in clean, white ankle socks, twirling as a music box ballerina, offering a curtsey now and then. She smiled tentatively, hummed a sweet tune and searched his face, her eyes wide with innocent passion.

"I like you a lot. More than just that," she said. "Do you know what I mean?"

"I guess I do," he answered. He was resigned.

"I really like you a lot more than the others," she told him, rushing to hold him in her delicate arms and kissing his tightly pursed lips with soft intensity. The move was, to Peter, unfamiliar and pleasant, though he was afraid to take things further.

"Would you live with me—just live with me, nothing else—only just stay here with me?" She presented the question evenly, then paused for a response from the frightened boy. Her fingers squirmed in his dark, straight hair.

"But we're not married," he said.

The conversation veered: "We must have lunch now." She sent him to the house and he returned minutes later with two slices of bread and a pat of butter on a white plate. She buttered a slice with the accompanying table knife and served it to him. She took the other slice and they sat on the deacon's bench, eating. She discussed mundane subjects.

"What are you going to do about the children? They are constantly messing up the house and need discipline. Even punishment."

"I don't want to do…*it*," he burst out. She returned from her dream and focused clear eyes into his, as she always seemed to do.

"Do you think that's why I like you so much?" she said in the tone of a mature woman. "I want to be with you and that's all." Her voice shook now and she whispered: "If you ever decide to do *it*, I will. I'll do anything you want to. But you don't have to if you don't want to. Ever."

She left Whitesboro at the end of August, after most every citizen had seen the show and audiences of 20 thinned to five and six. She wrote a letter to Peter, but he threw the neatly addressed envelope into the garbage can, unopened. He thought of her, however, for the three years that followed.

Peter was 14 when he accompanied his parents from snowy, cold Whitesboro in the family Mercury station wagon, to sunny Tampa, for a two-week vacation. They visited LeRoy and Margo, and Peter saw Mary Alice for the first time since that summer of 1946. She was now a sculptured woman of 16 who no longer wore ill-fitting clothes.

She still looked him straight in his eyes and said again, wordlessly this time, that he could if he wished. She said, too, that he didn't have to do *it* to be her friend. The dream years between 11 and 14 merged as he feasted his eyes on her and smelled the raspberry red hair washed with Ivory dish liquid. "I still like you a lot," she said with a grin that told him she knew he thought of her.

They left the Newman home before Peter had an opportunity to act out the fantasy that had embraced him more tightly with each year. A neatly handwritten letter followed the visit, this one opened and studiously read. He answered, and others followed over the years. In his senior year at Colgate University, his roommate's father, a Disney executive, put both to work at Disney World in Orlando for the Christmas break. Day two of his job as a distributor of restaurant flyers, he heard a familiar voice while walking past an outdoor stage. One of the Thai-dressed dancers on the stage was singing his name in soaring, high-pitched tones with squealing flute accompaniment. He turned toward the stage. The music slowed and ended. The dancer left the stage—she flew, it seemed—and stood before him, breathing hard, laughing. Mary Alice was beautiful in her wispy costume. They ate and talked together every night of his visit. After a time they held each other intimately those nights. More letters followed afterword and they spoke by phone most evenings. At the University of Vermont Medical School, he worked nights at the Mary Fletcher Hospital admissions desk, saving whatever he could for train or air fare.

Peter smiled now at the three-decades-ago recollection. He stood before the large kitchen window of their Hart's Hill house, looking out at blackberry thickets and an old playhouse with a star-shaped window. Peter felt a familiar strength. He hugged the mother of their grown children, and savored the perfume of raspberry hair. ≋

Dewaine Farria

The Raid

"Scared?" you ask.

"Yeah, Simon, I'm fucking scared." Michael hardly ever curses. *Fucking* sounds ugly out of his mouth.

"Me too, Michael," you say gently. Then, with an edge, "Get your mind right." It feels like the team-captain speeches you gave before football games.

You're in your truck, across the street from Novak's house, dressed in the generic tracksuits you bought last week at a Kmart in Oklahoma City. You bought the ski masks you have pushed up on your foreheads at the same place. It's July. The masks were on sale—$3.99 apiece.

It's 2 a.m. and the crickets are chirping the song of the Oklahoma summer. Novak lives in a one-story house about three miles off the road into town. He doesn't have a neighbor within shouting distance. There aren't any streetlights out here. Doesn't matter. You know the place. You know the Ford Escort on cement blocks and two Chevy trucks parked in front. You know where the back door is, where Novak's bedroom is, how many panes are in the window of the front door. You've been watching this house every evening for a week.

The day before your Kmart shopping trip you asked Michael if he has a baseball bat.

"Why would I have a baseball bat?"

So you brought two of yours. Turns out you had three baseball bats in your basement. You never liked baseball much, but you played. What teenage boy in small-town Oklahoma doesn't at least attempt to play baseball? Michael, that's who.

Yesterday morning you and Michael drove down to Dallas and checked into a Holiday Inn near the West Side bar district. You sold the idea to your parents as a final bash before you and Michael go your separate ways—the best friends' last summer together. In a few weeks Michael will leave for Columbia University and you will report to Ft. Benning, or as Michael puts it, "indulge your fascist side." You made a big deal about the trip: booking the hotel, plotting the route, choosing the CDs you would take. You arrived in Dallas around 11:30, took a nap, and then drove the four hours straight back up to Harrah, Oklahoma. It's a good alibi.

You pull the mask over your face. The wool feels unnatural against your skin in the summer heat.

Michael looks down at the bat between his knees, nods, and pulls his mask over his face. You sewed the mouth holes closed while watching Novak's house a couple nights ago. You've thought of everything. You can do this.

"Let's go," you say through the wool.

You step out of the car with purpose, cross the street, and crunch across the gravel driveway. You smash the tip of the bat through the small, square glass windowpane above the door handle. The sound is louder than you expected.

Novak is good and passed out by now. You think this thought forcefully, hoping that will make it true.

You reach through the square windowpane, suddenly very aware of the warmth and moistness of your hands inside your leather gloves. In the week that you watched Novak's house, you never saw him fiddle with any keypads upon entry. He's not the type to have an alarm. Shotgun, yes. Alarm, no. You find the lock above the doorknob, turn it, and open the door until the chain pulls taut. You watched Novak return home, piss drunk, an hour ago. You're surprised he had the presence of mind to set the chain lock. You yank the doorknob hard with both hands. The chain snaps. You and Michael enter the house and walk straight to the bedroom.

• • •

Your teenage social scene revolved around the convenience store down the street from your high school. The name of the place has changed three times that you're aware of. First it was *McCloud 66,* then *Kwik Stop,* now it's *the Kickapoo Convenience Store.* You'd park at the *Kickapoo* on a Friday night, shoot the shit, yell at girls driving by, and try to find out what parties were going on.

It's the quintessential Midwestern teen hangout: slushies, windows plastered with advertisements for *Milwaukee's Best,* hot dogs on greasy rotisseries, and employees who had been your classmates a couple years ago. What does failure look like? Like working at the convenience store a stone's throw from where you graduated three years ago, that's what.

During your sophomore year you fought Zack Stanton in the *Kickapoo* parking lot. Stanton was a solid defensive lineman on the football team.

You fucked Stanton's girlfriend, Sally (dirty blonde, small tits, not much of an ass) at a party. Your most vivid memory of the drunken sex was her theatrical, "Oh, Si! Oh, Si!" alternating stress between syllables. "*Oh,* Si!" As if she was surprised by the act itself. Then, "Oh, *Si!*" as if she was surprised that you were the one doing it to her. The fight at *Kickapoo* was a week after the Sally incident. In your high school, fights are scheduled like school dances. You and Stanton moved in the same social circle—the jocks. It was a tense and awkward week at school.

It was a relief to finally be in the parking lot of the *Kickapoo* that Friday night, listening to Stanton describe to your classmates how he was going to kick your ass. You smile and wait—lips, fists, and asshole clenched. As an athlete, people assumed you could scrap. Not counting wrestling matches, you hadn't actually been in a fight since grade school. You're a prototypical wide receiver—tall, lean, fast, strong. But there's strong and then there's *strong.* You're gymnast strong. You could do 20 pull-ups when you were in the eighth grade. Stanton was corn-fed, Oklahoma football strong. He outweighed you by a good 75 lbs. and you'd seen him push 300 lbs. on the bench for reps. You were guessing that Stanton could punch his weight.

You never find out for sure. Someone from Stanton's crowd tires of the wolf tickets, runs from behind him and smacks you in the head with a beer bottle. Everything goes hazy. It was like falling asleep on the couch while watching a TV show about a teenage brawl. You're vaguely aware of blood, beer, and gravel on your face. Your friend Craig, a big, white offensive lineman, comes into focus slamming some poor bastard to the ground like a rag doll. You almost laugh when you spot Michael summoning up all of his courage to plant a boot in some supine fucker's side. Then it's all indistinct yells, scampering feet, and sirens.

In the back of the ambulance, a paramedic presses a bandage against your forehead. The other medic intermittently shoves a plastic tube in your mouth to suction the salty, metallic tang of blood out of your airway.

"Just relax, kid," they keep saying. That, and, "Okay, spit," sounding annoyed. You feel like you're in a moving dentist's office.

"Zack Stanton, the black kid?" your mom asks Michael in the emergency room.

"Yeah, Mom, Zack Stanton, the black kid," you say.

She shakes her head, then grabs your chin and surveys the bandage, acknowledging your wound but not your presence.

The play at racial solidarity annoys you. You've heard your mother, more than once, complain about these "country-ass-Harrah-Niggas." Her southern drawl melding the insult into one word. Most of the blacks in Harrah were associated with the nearby state prison. Your mom and Michael's parents work there. The Stantons were homegrown black hicks.

On Monday the whole school is talking about your stoic stance and heroic wounding at the hands of Stanton's evil henchmen. That was your sophomore year. Now, two years later, the scar has almost faded, but the story just keeps getting better. Last you heard, Sally picked you up from the emergency room after the fight and you nailed her again. (A few weeks later you do nail her again.) Being rushed to the hospital with an "acute bottle noggin injury" (as your mother called it) bequeathed you tough guy status for the rest of your high school career. Whoever smacked you with that bottle has no idea what a favor he did for you.

Normally, Michael avoided the *Kickapoo*. He referred to the place as, "a microcosm of everything we hate about Oklahoma," and you would smile at the implied complicity. Now you understand the real reason Michael avoided the place: Novak works there. But Michael was there that night—scrawny, useless, and shivering in his *Smiths* t-shirt—daring you to tell him to leave. He was the only one who didn't scatter at the sound of sirens. The only one with you in the back of the ambulance. Your mother spoke to you in clipped, aggressive sentences for a week after the fight. She spit out only two words during the drive from the hospital: "Thanks, Michael."

• • •

You expect the inside of Novak's house to be a dump. You're not disappointed. You step over empty Sonic and *Little Caesars'* cartons on your way to his bedroom. You glance in the kitchen to see a large trash can overflowing with beer and soda cans. The place smells of piss, sweat and chewing tobacco.

Subhuman motherfucker.

Michael wanted to take Novak as he drunk-stumbled from his truck to his house. The breaking and entering scared him more than the real work. You convinced Michael that it was better to let Novak pass out and then make your move.

The bedroom door is open. The cracked curtains let in enough moonlight to see Novak passed out shirtless on the bed, looking like a blond, beached manatee. He's still wearing his jeans, shit-kicker boots, and baseball cap.

He took his shirt off then put his hat back on?

You lean your bat against a dresser, take the electrical tape out of your sweatpants pocket and hand it to Michael. He nods. You dart onto the bed and flip Novak onto his stomach and pull his wrists over his ass. You hear the *rrrrrrip* of Michael pulling the tape before Novak starts to resist. The deftness with which Michael tapes Novak's hands surprises you. He then roughly tapes Novak's legs, mouth, and eyes. You stick your fingers in Novak's nostrils to make sure the bastard can breathe. You rise from the bed and wipe your fingers on Novak's jeans. Everyone's breathing hard. You lift Novak off the bed by his taped wrists and drop him on the floor. You push your mask up over your mouth. Michael hands you your bat.

• • •

You moved to Harrah, Oklahoma, from Baton Rouge, Louisiana, when your mom was promoted to the managerial ranks in the prison system. She had been working as a corrections officer in Baton Rouge for about five years at that point. Frank Mathias, the deputy warden of Harrah's Antoine Prison, was her new boss. Your mom bought a house within walking distance of where Frank lived with his wife Clairetta and two sons, Michael and Gabriel.

"What type of people name their kids after angels?" your mother asked. Only people raised by single parents get asked these types of questions when they're 11.

Michael was your age. Gabe was four years younger. Michael didn't play sports or video games. He didn't like being called Mike. He rode a skateboard. He listened to *Radiohead* and *Dinosaur Jr.* The walls of his room were plastered with his drawings, everything from elves to ballerinas. *Ballerinas?*

You immediately liked Frank, though. He was a Vietnam vet who ran every morning and did pull-ups in his backyard. Frank speaks to you as if you are grown and never mentions anything about your dad not being around. You and Frank lift weights together during the summers. Deadlifts, Clean & Press, Snatch—all old school Olympic lifts.

"Everyone who works in a prison should be ready to do a forced cell movement," Frank would say.

Michael skateboarded and Gabe danced, but otherwise the two expressed no interest in athletics.

You tell Frank about your decision to join the army between sets in the gym in his garage. He never talked about his service in Vietnam before, but once he starts, it is like he can't stop. Frank tells you about drugged up black sergeants and honorable white lieutenants, about some white soldiers calling him a high-yellow nigger, while others asked him to look up their sisters when he rotated back to the States.

"Combat, drugs, and race defined my service." Frank pauses, then adds, "mostly race."

You're not sure if he's trying to talk you into the military or out of it. It seems that Frank's not sure either. In the end he drives you to the recruiter's office.

• • •

When you showed up in Harrah Junior High, Michael was in desperate need of allies. There were fewer black kids in Harrah than in Baton Rouge. This resulted in race mattering a lot more. At your old school in Baton Rouge, Michael would have been a goofy anomaly. In Harrah, he was a liability. Could this kid, with his *The Cure* t-shirt and ballerina drawings, be depended on? The black kids would trip Michael in the hallway just for the fuck of it.

"What the hell you going to do about it, faggot?" You don't yell this question at someone unless you already know the answer.

More than different, Michael was wrong. He had no respect for the *blackrequisites:*

- Sports: basketball, football—OK; skateboarding, hockey—no (you wrestle, and even that was a bit suspect)
- Speech: broken (best to drop all forms of "to be," and the word "niggah" (not nigger) was an acceptable and encouraged alternative for "dude"—*Where you at, Niggah?*)
- Reading habits: monitored (one risked being accused of "acting white" if seen with books too often). When your cousins came up from Louisiana, the Badger comics and *Forgotten Realms* novels were replaced with *Sports Illustrated* and *Vibe*. (It was also best to move the *Stranglers* and *Siouxie and the Banshees* CDs to the bottom of the pile.)

Mr. Charles Roan was Michael's and your homeroom teacher your freshman year. You and the other football players in the class call him "Chuck-Dog," once or twice to his face. Roan was a youngish white guy, enthusiastic in that way that freshly certified teachers are.

During "Black History Month," Roan assigned the class an essay comparing slavery and indentured servitude. In the hope of sparking debate on the topic, Roan had the students read their essays aloud. There were 24 students in the class. The seven or eight black kids favored indentured servitude. Most of the white kids favored slavery. Before this discussion, the divides in homeroom were along conventional lines: jocks, overachievers, wasters, and Michael. Now you listened in dumbfounded silence as a lot of your football buddies described the advantages of being provided for and the difficulty in finding employment at the end of indenture.

What about middle passage? Forcefully separated families? The whippings? The rape?

"Get over it," their shrugs said.

Michael read his essay last:

"Race runs along a spectrum in the United States that only Americans understand. Everything from the casual light-blue *(Look at that brotha's shiny new ride.)* to the more subtle lime green *(What's he want to meet my parents for? I'm just fucking him, we're not getting married.)* to full blown, flaming red *(Thank you, you fucking trained orangutan.)*. American blacks pretend to hate the spectrum, but can't handle it when someone evaluates them without it. We need the glare of the colors."

You're lime green. You happily play the Mandingo tribesman to the white girls who flock around you at pep rallies. You even get off on it. Frank preferred his racism bright red—no pretense. And scrawny, bespectacled Michael, with his comic books and ballerina drawings, is the only black person you know who utterly doesn't give a shit.

When Michael finished, you notice Roan and a couple of your teammates snickering.

"Hey," you say in a loud clear voice, "shut up."

"That's enough, Simon," Roan tells you, pretending that he thinks you're only talking to your classmates.

You wink at him, "My bad, Chuck-Dog."

• • •

You're with Michael when he meets his first girlfriend later that year at a Pizza Hut in Oklahoma City. High school football players are local celebrities in Oklahoma. You're surprised when a cute brunette walked into the place with a group of her friends and makes eye contact with Michael and not you. They hold each other's gaze. Finally, Michael looks down at his slice of meat lover's pizza. The girls sit in a booth facing Michael.

"Soul meets soul when eyes meet eyes. Does your true love stand recognized?" A line from *Elfquest,* one of our favorite comics. Michael doesn't answer.

"You know her?" you ask.

"No," Michael whispers. "Do you?"

"No, but we oughta get to know them." You look over your shoulder and give the girls your coolest nod. "And stop whispering, retard."

"Will you please stop looking," Michael begs.

There was no way on God's green earth you were going to let Michael leave that Pizza Hut without at least a phone number.

Exasperated, Michael asks, "Should we just go talk to them?"

"Nah. You should ask her to dance."

"Ask her to dance," he repeats, in an exaggerated mongoloid tone. "We are in a Pizza Hut, Simon."

You are thoroughly enjoying yourself.

"Yeah, motherfucker, ask her to dance. No matter what else happens in her life you will always be that dude who asked her to dance in a Pizza Hut. That *ballsy* dude that asked her to dance in a Pizza Hut."

Michael stews on this for a moment. Then, his face set in a heartbreakingly sincere look of determination, he nods and stands up. You lean back in the booth and watch him walk to the girls' table. *Water Runs Dry* is playing on the Pizza Hut's stereo. Now, whenever you hear that sappy song, you remember Michael's moment.

"Would you like to dance?" he asks.

"Dance?" the cute brunette asks, all smiles. Her friends laugh. "Here?" She sweeps her arm to indicate the families eating, the salad bar, the *Street Fighter II* video game in the corner.

Michael holds out his hand.

"C'mon."

Michael's little brother Gabriel is the dancer in the Mathias family. But that evening the wait staff, the moms and dads, and the kids on the video game watch Michael and his new girlfriend, Jennifer, dance.

And when the song's over the place bursts into applause.

• • •

You and Michael don't say a word to each other. Michael doesn't even look at you before he starts swinging. The bat falls with cruel thuds. You swing twice. Halfheartedly. You agreed earlier—only body shots. Michael swings with all his might. Workmanlike. He doesn't look up. Michael pounds every insult, every slight. He pounds out the disrespect. Novak's muffled cries only make him swing harder. You place your hand on Michael's shoulder. He turns to you—eyes crazed, satisfied—nods and steps back.

• • •

Novak stuffed his dick in Michael's mouth when he was 11 years old. It happened in the coach's office in the male locker room at your junior high. Novak was volunteering as a P.E. teacher's assistant at the time. He must have been in his mid-twenties. That was seven years ago. Nowadays, Novak is a part-time assistant baseball coach and full-time manager at *Kickapoo*.

While ringing up your slurpies in *Kickapoo*, Novak would talk your ear off about his glory days as a standout on the Harrah High School football team. What does failure sound like? Like a dude still talking about his high school football career when he's in his thirties, that's what. He has a military style "high & tight" haircut. His gut hangs over his nut-hugging coach's shorts. A couple weeks ago graffiti reading "Novak is a fag" appeared on the side of the high school gym.

Driving home from a comic book store in Oklahoma City, you ask Michael if he'd seen the graffiti.

"That's some funny shit," you say.

"He's a rapist, yeah. But he's not a homosexual." Michael doesn't take his eyes off the windshield.

Novak got Michael in the office on the pretext that Michael refused to shower after class. Then he forced his erect penis into the scared, frail black kid's mouth. He used one hand to grasp Michael's hair, the other he clasped around his throat. Michael gagged and vomited when Novak came.

"Jesus Christ. Clean it up." Michael mocks Novak's voice when he retells this part. He's silent for a moment then continues. "He's not gay. He did it with anger. Real malice. Like he was taking revenge."

"For what?" you ask.

It was one of those movie moments, Michael's chance for a great line. Instead, he drops his eyes and shrugs.

"Why didn't you tell someone?"

"Would you have, Simon?"

No. You wouldn't have.

You and Michael sit in your truck in the Mathias's driveway staring at the windshield. The raid is your idea.

• • •

You look at Novak's broken form, writhing on the carpet in muffled agony.

This isn't a person.

You whip out your dick and piss on him. You aim for the back of his head. The piss splashes off his stupid "high & tight" haircut onto the carpet. He shakes his head violently.

Sorry, pal, you can't deflect piss like that.

You walk to the kitchen. There's a phone on the wall. You pick it up, dial 911, and place the receiver on the counter top. Then you and Michael walk out the front door, across the gravel driveway to your truck. You get in and drive. You're almost to the highway before you think to take off the mask. You pull onto I-270, heading south. It's four hours to Dallas. Neither of you have spoken yet. You're thinking of consequences. Things that could give you away. Things that could go wrong.

Nothing. You think forcefully.

"I saw you in your basement masturbating once," Michael says, so abruptly that it frightens you. You regain your composure, laugh.

"Oh, yeah?"

"Yeah. It was when you guys first moved out here. You were eleven. I'm pretty sure I didn't even have a sex drive yet, but there you were, stroking like your life depended on it."

You make the sound of laughter again, but feel like crying. Michael's voice sounds like he probably is. You fix your eyes on the road.

"How'd you see me doing that, Michael?" you ask, trying hard to make the question not sound accusatory.

"We weren't friends yet. But I wanted to be, so I came to your house to get to know you." He turns his head to the passenger side window. "Your mom wasn't home and no one answered your door. I went into your backyard and could just see you through the basement window. You were watching porn. Where'd you get porn from back then anyway?"

"I traded Lee Hines five comic books for that tape. Five good comic books."

"I never told anyone."

"You know I wouldn't have cared if you had, Michael."

"No. Now you don't care, back then you would have." He's quiet for so long you think—hope—that he has fallen asleep.

"I so wanted us to be friends."

You don't answer. You have a long drive ahead of you. ▧

Edward Cuello

St. Francis

I saw St. Francis just over the top of your skull, where the needlework of
your scalp met the flushed peak of your forehead, where arches repeated
upwards from the top of your lip, through the lids of your eyes past the
living prayer of your eyebrows. He wore his familiar monk's robe of brown,
tied chastely at the waist with two white chords hanging down from
above his hips, a safe distance from his cock. The arms were crossed, right
over left, and a white dove was descending near his elbow. His skull was
inclined back like yours (only he was standing up) and there was a similar
repetition of the arches of desire from his top lip to the top of his tonsure.
His expression was more placid, even bored, as if he were enduring
something; maybe it had something to do with the stigmata on his right
hand. In any case, he was still, a bookmark saint and you were moving. You
were receiving the inertia of my body and it rolled from the base of your
spine to the top of your head, again, again, and again. I watched your face
as you came (St. Francis was still looking up), your mouth opened, the tip
of your tongue extended and searched for the secret word. Watching you,
watching St. Francis, I gave myself up to the feeling that was rising, a wave
that pushed the dreary cargo ship of my identity off course, capsized and
sank it.

J.p. Lawrence

Dry Heat

Small, green trolls infest the shooting range at West Point. They pop up from the tall grass. They grimace at me, so I shoot them. My nose kisses the rear of my rifle's charging handle. I see the green target in the middle of my iron sights. I fire. And it's gone.

My weapon is the M4A4, a gas-operated, rotating bolt carbine with an effective range of 500 to 600 feet. I carried one for 12 months while deployed. Two months in Fort Lewis, Washington. Ten months in southern Iraq, in Basra. Fort Lewis is where I met Maj. John Harvey. Harvey was an intelligence officer. His job was to talk to the CIA. He loved fly-fishing and life on the river. Before deploying, he met Spc. Marianne Summers, a cook with the unit. Summers was a blonde with a nose like Meryl Streep and an air that suggested she knew the minds of desperate, hungry boys.

My buddies would whisper to me that Harvey and Summers would skip training and sneak off into the woods like young lovers. But Summers was 23 years old and Harvey was 48. Sexual relationships are prohibited during deployments. And everyone sniffed trouble.

In Iraq, I always carried my rifle, but my real weapon was my D200 digital camera. I was a military photojournalist. I would fly from base to base, writing stories about the people there. The heat was relentless, but dry. The story was that there was no story: the war was over.

Young boys with dreams of blowing up villains and winning medals sniped each other in video games played on big screens. The staff officers and one of the generals spent their Thursday nights playing Risk in air-conditioned conference rooms.

One morning my bosses told me to take my camera to a special mission. A suicide. I stood outside the doorway of a plyboard hooch, half-completed. The military policemen and the criminal investigators were already there. Harvey was inside. The investigator ushered me in.

There is a halo of blood around the body. The inner ring is dark red. It has coagulated and formed a raised plateau. The outer ring is brown and thin: the blood had dried up and left nothing but a stain. His eyes are open and his jaw is agape, giving him a slack-jawed and ghoulish overbite.

Harvey holds a M9 pistol in his right hand. There is a hole in his right temple where there is nothing but blackness. There is a hole in his other temple and a hole in the wall. There is a bullet in the next room. "Good thing it wasn't a hollow point round," the military policeman says. "That would've made a mess."

The military policeman tells a story about a man who tried to kill himself with a shotgun and missed. A few centimeters would have been death. But he missed and had to live the rest of his years with no face. Brain damage. Pain every day.

Spc. Tom Hannah is the military policeman's name. He wants to know if this is my first dead body, if I'll crack. But I am just doing a job. I ask the investigator to close the door so I have even lighting. I feel nothing. I feel nothing in the presence of the dead. I aim. I press a button. The shutter clicks. And there's a flash.

A target pops up on a fire range. I swing my weapon toward the target. I fire. A crack of lightning. A flash. The target goes down, as if in a dream. Another target. I look. I fire.

Gone.

I think of playing football in the backyard, or learning how to throw a spiral for the first time; there's that moment when you realize you're good at this, when you understand just how much you control. You see someone open, running down the field, and then the next thing you know, the ball is in their hands.

It's as if the self subsides. The self becomes a spectator. The self becomes an instrument. Another target. Gone. Another. And another. And another. Gone. ▰

CLAIRE SEIDL, *Swimmer (Night),* selenium-toned gelatin silver photograph,
14"x18", 2011

I am very interested in how we see (or don't see) what is right in front
of us. The camera gathers and records more visual information than we
can, especially over time or in the dark. While our eyes can see only
incremental instances of time and can focus only at specific distances, the
camera takes in a record of movement across the entire observed space.
The resulting image documents a continuum of space and time not visible
to the human eye.

In *Swimmer (Night),* a flashlight was used to illuminate the subject and the
film was exposed for about a minute. The time it takes to gather light on
the film is an important part of my process. Time becomes enmeshed with
the representational subject matter and then becomes the subject itself.
The resulting images feel like a memory, a moment held.

My photographs are intimate studies with an elusive topic: the ephemeral
nature of things.

Claire Seidl

Barry Perlus, *Nightscape,* digital photograph, size variable, 2011

Panoramic Vision

The works shown here are equirectangular projections from 360° x 360° (spherical) panoramic photographs. An image of this type differs radically from a conventional photograph, with its frame and single point of view. The spherical photograph has no intrinsic frame, and combines multiple views into one—in front, behind, left, right, above, and below. In the equirectangular projection, the spherical image is converted to a rectangle, and, in the process, the visual information is distorted in unusual ways— some parts remain relatively literal, while others are expanded or stretched beyond recognition. The forced inclusion of multiple views in one scene can be disorienting and difficult to comprehend at first.

In producing these images, I consider the subject the way a cinema-tographer might consider the scenic possibilities of a location. I think about how the different views will function when rendered, and work with imaging software to suggest the emotional sense of this different way of seeing.

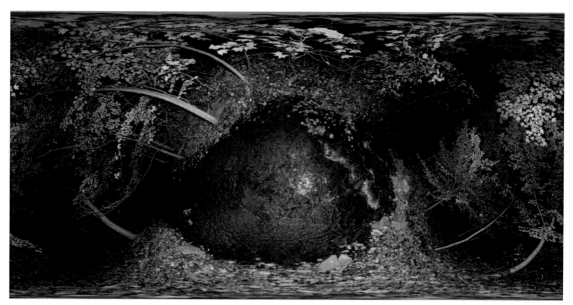

BARRY PERLUS, *Jantar Mantar—The Jaya Prakasa at the Jaipur Observatory,* digital photograph, size variable, 2004-2008

In the *Nightscapes* series, light at the camera's position illuminates an area close by, but diminishes with distance. We find ourselves in a solitary place within the forest, surrounded by darkness, yet illuminated by a source that seems to come from everywhere and nowhere at the same time. The series draws on this effect to explore ideas of presence and relativity. The image reproduced here centers on a view downward, above a small seasonal creek, its water emerging from, and disappearing into, the darkness of the forest at night.

The *Jantar Mantar* series is based on the astronomy observatories built in India in the early 1700s. These observatories comprise numerous buildings of unique design, each with a specialized function for astronomical measurement. In my panoramic renderings, these structures, with their striking combinations of geometric forms at large scale, become curved, folded, and re-oriented, producing images that are strongly abstract, yet rich with architectural and scientific detail.

Barry Perlus

JANET ZWEIG, *Lipstick Enigma, 2010,* aluminum, electronics, resin, glass, language generating program written by Janet Zweig, using software developed by Jon Meyer, 10.5'x18"x12.5", 2010 Client: Florida Arts Council, Harris Engineering Center, UCF, Orlando, Florida

Credits:
Engineering and fabrication: Franklyn Berry, Jon Meyer, Benjamin Cohen, Todd Holoubek, Stuart Heys
Photography: Stephen Allen

This computer-driven sentence-generator—using rules and lexicon written by the artist—invents and writes a new line of text, and displays it on the sign when triggered by a motion detector. The sentences mix the language of engineering with the language and syntax of beauty advertising.

The sculpture is made of 1,200 resin lipsticks powered by 1,200 stepper motors, controlled by 60 circuit boards.

Janet Zweig

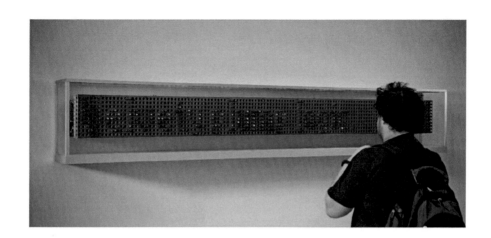

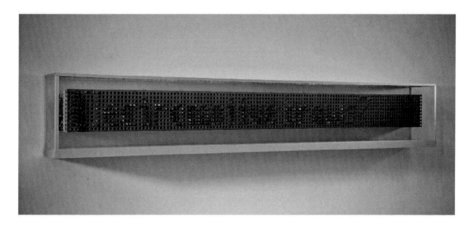

SHARI MENDELSON, *Five Vessels,* plastic from discarded bottles, hot glue, acrylic polymer, paint, sizes various, 2009-2011

I mine art history for intriguing objects that become a source of inspiration for my current work: ancient Greek and Roman ceramics, Islamic glass vessels, Egyptian Faience Sculpture, and the paintings of Georgio Morandi. I love these pieces for their formal beauty, and the insight into past cultures that they reveal.

I construct reinterpretations of these historical pieces using found plastic bottles, cut them into pieces, and use the parts to create new sculptures. Some of my pieces are coated with mixed materials and/or glaze-like layers of polymers and paint, which vary the levels of transparency and opacity, emphasize or obscure the original material, and alter the visual and actual weight.

Using today's trash as material for sculptures enables me to comment on our current throwaway culture while playfully exploring issues of authenticity, originality, materiality, history, culture, and the relative value of objects.

Shari Mendelson

Amze Emmons, *The Reorganization,* graphite and gouache on paper, 22"x30", 2011

For the past several years, my artwork has begun as an investigation of images found in documentary sources, such as the Sunday Edition of *The New York Times,* online news sources, and web sites for international aid agencies. I start with clippings depicting the smoking shells of bombed buildings, wreckage left after receding flood waters, tsunami-mangled villages, car bombings, refugee migrations….Through erasure, drawing and collage, the world of the source begins to change. By editing and combining imagery to make visual connections between seemingly disparate events, constellations form, and something new emerges. My media-isolation experiment is intended not to glorify or monumentalize the dystopian events unfolding around us. My interest is in distilling and cataloging the patterns and forms of our daily world through an intuitive editing process. We normally see these kinds of documentary images as topical, disposable, something to process and consume quickly. By sifting through the pictorial evidence of displacement and strife I discover what is hidden in plain view: essential visual elements that let the eye linger and keep the viewer from turning the page.

Amze Emmons

PORTIA MUNSON, *Cosmos Sun,* pigmented ink on rag paper, 43"x 42", 2011

I create large-scale photographic prints using fresh flowers grown in my garden as the medium. The flowers are arranged directly on a scanner, capturing detailed configurations in high resolution. Every constellation is unique to a moment in time, preserving what is in bloom on that day. I experiment with the color and structure of flowers, slicing into buds, pulling blossoms apart and layering them onto one another. My optically intense arrangements of flowers conjure the ephemeral nature of the botanical along with its innate utopian beauty. The images are printed on rag paper with archival inks.

Portia Munson

Maureen McCoy

STILL LIFE WITH DIEGO RIVERA

Whenever I see a reproduction of *The Flower Carrier* I smell paint. I taste it. I go straight down the rabbit hole to childhood wonder and fear. The simplicity of line in the painting, the hunched bulky body and the presence of flowers belie the dark mystery of action. How could someone be so weighted by, of all things, flowers? As an eight-year-old child I did not know that the painting was famous art, only that it was essential to our home.

On our dining table, which served as a sewing station, typing stand, and game board, a pocket-sized book of paintings lay open to *The Flower Carrier* for who knows how long. This was my mother's doing. The presence of a great painting amid our family hubbub stands out in relief only years later, as urgent conjury of my mother's dreamer's spirit. She would dream dreams beautifully beyond our small house; she would hex out what should not be.

Mine was a mother who went about observing in an Old English song of a voice, "Sumer is a coomin' in, lood sing cuckoo." She sang to babies and dogs alike, "Sweetest little fella, everybody knows; don't know what to call him but he's mighty like a rose," and urged us on with "Wonderful, wonderful Copenhagen," and "June Is Bustin' Out All Over." Periodically, out came the stamp collections, hers and mine, and together we marveled at the official names and spellings of certain nations and noted the countries vanished and modified since her day. We admired the size and intricacy of certain countries' stamps: Ceylon, Togo, and Tobago. At nap time, my mother would read me to sleep from another world beyond us: Charles Addams's first cartoon book, the ghoulishly witty (and not entirely comprehensible to me) *Homebodies*. By redeeming supermarket S&H Green Stamps, Gold Bond and others for sports equipment, my mother introduced the neighborhood kids to croquet. She spread cement and made a base for a tetherball pole, and she built a little brick grill for the purpose of roasting hot dogs and marshmallows. Children and mother, we walked to the bookmobile every Tuesday, and we each brought home the maximum six books to read. What a richly textured existence, anyone might say, and I would proudly agree.

Diego Rivera, circa 1959, shone in our outwardly placid and wholly humble quarters in Des Moines, Iowa. But at my grandmother's house, the mother-in-law's, we were ushered to stand politely before a very different print, Gainsborough's *The Blue Boy,* and hear the story, once again, of how our father, when just a boy, took all his money and presented this work of art to his mother. *The Blue Boy* constituted the only official artwork in this grandmother's house, *The Flower Carrier,* in ours. Beside the open book lay a piece of thick paper on which my mother, using a set of tiny tubes of oils, was copying out the painting. She had sketched it in pencil first, a magical accomplishment to me. After school, or in the mornings, I would hurry to the table to see what new work she had done, what colors had appeared. I sniffed the paint, so different from my runny pots and little squares of watercolor blocks set in snap-to lozenges of metal. My mother's paints lay neatly side-by-side in a wooden box that opened with a swivel latch. The paints appeared alongside the Diego Rivera and, as far as I know, disappeared from our home when Diego Rivera did.

My grandmother clung to her "Blue Boy" tale. She would not acknowledge directly the fall from grace, the fact that her son had us living rather meagerly on "the wrong side of town," the fact that he had married a Catholic—still a woe to her, the fact that the Catholic sewed her daughters' (gorgeous, suspect) clothes herself. The repetition of this story—my father's gift, his caring—was the worry of a mother who knew her son's fragility and void; reveling back on the past was her love's anchor and, perhaps, a plea for our faith, or at least our patience. The past was insurance, goodness pawned and waiting to be claimed. By insisting often on an idealized past—boys in breeches—surely a more decent present would materialize. Still, this was the mother-in-law who, time and again, was called on to bail out the son who once more had not brought home the money, who once more had quit, or perhaps was fired from, a simple job beneath his education and abilities.

Psychologically, he had never gotten past World War II, but no one had the words for that. My mother, too young to have sniffed out doom when they courted at Drake University, married him as a hero and lived in a small box home surrounded by many other small box homes from which art and music and croquet sets did not emanate.

My mother was neither a gossip nor a joiner, yet neighbor women found their way to her, sensing her good spirit and common sense. What they could not pinpoint, and what must have helped her through everything, was the same dreamer's spirit developed in her own childhood. She was the ignored second girl, born after a blazingly perfect son and a prima donna daughter, tumbled forth awkwardly before the birth of a darling blond baby boy who got to ride around on a pony even before he could walk. She became bookish, a solitary experimenter, a hungry mind. Perhaps, too, descended from hard-working miners of northern Minnesota, from a time and place less fractious than the present, she was able to kindle the life of the mind as pernicious luxury *and* necessity, and so, just maybe, deflect the rough terrain of the present.

At some point *The Flower Carrier* book and the painting-in-progress disappeared. Had my mother run out of paint and lacked the money to continue? Did something else overcome her? I wondered, but only later. To my child's eye, the painting effort seemed extraordinary and beautiful, but there it was, half-finished and gone.

Painting *The Flower Carrier* proved to be an anomaly, perhaps a quirky indulgence not visceral enough for my mother. Her artistic urges flourished fully in practical necessity: sewing dresses, knitting sweaters, reupholstering chairs and couch, running up curtains, embroidering, hooking rugs, caning chairs—all performed with energetic curiosity. Before undertaking her first upholstering job she indicated the couch and told my sister, "Somebody made that, so I can too." She casually imparted a rich vocabulary of sewing and fabric terms that pleases me still: piping, pin tucks, batting, tatting, ticking. Tattersall plaid, windowpane check, houndstooth, Swiss dot, yokes, whipstitching, cummerbunds, ruching, flat-fell seams—I had them all. I went off to school knowing exactly what I was wearing and assured, always, that my plaids matched perfectly at the seams.

By age five my sister was sewing on her own little machine, and soon after, we were given chemistry sets. Nothing was said (and surely not thought) about earnest efforts at gender egalitarianism. Sense was sense, chemistry figured and, by the way, having only a boy pictured on the metal cover, we were made to understand, was sheer nonsense. Always ignore nonsense.

The year that Diego Rivera had come and gone, a woman at the top of Monona moved away and rented out her small house to some young relatives. The girl—"Karen is only eighteen," my mother stressed—started coming down the hill, wanting to sit and talk with my mother. Baby cocked on her hip, Karen had endless time to sit, and sit some more. In the way that children do, I blocked out the talk. I said hello and hurried by the cigarette smoke, catching Karen's glance that as much as said, *Childhood, how strange. Childhood!* My mother stayed in the kitchen working while Karen sat in the dining room, at what was called the dinette table, which my father's parents had purchased for us, and which my mother declared atrocious. "Dinette" signaled a kind of post-war liberation from tradition: table and chairs were distinguished from their heavy forbears by a total absence of wood. The set was a terrible tan color, with shiny surface, and pointy legs tipped in gold tone. Its chair coverings looked as if bits of leaf lay under the surface, reminding me of the plates I yearned to eat from, what many people around us had: Melmac. Melmac dishes were made from a kind of plastic that came in light blue and green, yellow, and even pink, with gray flecks throughout, beautiful to me. "For Pete's sake!" was how my mother acknowledged my wish. Melmac was, of course, nonsense.

In summer the plastic-covered seats crackled and stuck to the backs of bare legs. Here Karen would sit, the baby sticky and dull, my mother commenting from the kitchen as she continued to work. Karen became a fixture for a while, and the whole business worried my mother. Why would she tell me, as she did, that Karen's husband was a no-account who not so long ago had been banished to a juvenile home, locked up for stealing cigarettes from a pharmacy, and something she called pep pills. It was a *break-in*, she told me and the stupidity was vivid. I imagined Jim crawling through a jagged window, on his knees amid glass, scooping up cartons of cigarettes. This man had hood hair, blond and simperingly curly, combed straight back at the sides and slightly duck-tailed at the neck. His face was the blistered red of anger, or indulgence. I gathered from the tone of Karen's voice, rather than any actual news I heard, that they were on different sides of something. There sat Karen, eighteen, with a baby. Who knows what she was trying to do to get along with this Jim, who flaunted himself in tight black pants, never the soft hues of his neighbors' work clothes, and useless, hard, black shoes. Plus, he had friends over. No one in this neighborhood had friends over. The occasional relative showed up and, in turn, people went off to visit a family farm. If someone lived too far away to walk over, they did not visit.

One day that summer, Karen showed up as usual. From the enclosed front porch, hidden from living room and kitchen, but within easy earshot,

I heard sounds of gasping and consternation. No milk for the baby, was the problem. Karen had nothing for the baby. Extras were unheard of in our refrigerator and we always rationed milk, but now I closed my book and came in to see my mother hand over our only quart of milk. I watched as Karen walked up the steep hill with her baby cradled on her left hip and the quart of milk grasped in her right hand. I was so astonished by this sight I may as well have been viewing Cecil B. DeMille's parting of the Red Sea. Karen held the milk carton before her, slightly elevated, as a torch of victory or hope must be held. That night, sitting down to dinner, my mother explained to us kids, "Karen needed the milk. The baby had to have milk." Seeing a glass of water at my place put me into a library book of romantic orphanage deprivation. Drinking water, suffering almost, so that a baby would have milk, was noble. Sacrificially, I sipped at my water. I was helping someone simply by drinking water.

Another morning that summer I went to the back door to let Karen in. She stood as always, baby on her hip, but looked away to the backyard oaks, in profile. When she turned her face full on me, it leaped forward, creature-like. The formerly hidden side shone black-purple. The white of her eye bled red. Her mouth hung down and the cheek swelled out.

Did anyone say hello? Did I even open the door? I turned and fled, saying, "Karen's here," and ran to the farthest point in the house—that front porch—where I would not have to look at anyone, just listen and learn what was to be done. My mother would know what to do.

My mother cried out. Many times she cried, "Karen. Oh, Karen. Oh, no."

I clenched the chenille spread in order to stay put, stay in one place—the little davenport seemed to be rising up under me—and not scream with feeling. I had never seen such a face. I had never seen an injured adult, an adult's face hurt. I had never considered that an adult could get ugly, ugly hurt.

Karen told the story. I strained to hear and disbelieved it at the same time. Friends had been over the night before, Jim's friends. Everyone had gathered in the basement for a party. Suddenly Jim went crazy. He threw Karen down. He began bashing her head against the basement floor. The friends stood there and looked on. No one helped Karen. No one stopped Jim as he bashed away at his wife, the tiny girl upstairs howling a scalding cry. "I thought I would die," Karen said. She didn't cry as she spoke to my mother, slowly, as if navigating through cereal.

Surely my mother urged her to get help, but what help or advice would she have offered? This was the 50s, now glamorized by television series and extolled by some public figures as a time of serene order and bliss. My mother may have insisted to herself, with her characteristic hopeful determination, that nothing was beyond repair, and that she'd keep an eye out, that she would certainly be Karen's friend. We saw doctors only for the rare shot, and everyone knew that private matters were not police business. Calling the police was, I am sure, not remotely considered. Shelters did not exist and even now the act of showing up at a doctor's office in such a condition, to sit and await one's turn among other people with invisible ills, quails the traumatized hearts of many. Karen went home, and gradually she healed, looked better, and then like her old self. My mother had not approached me on the porch to repeat Karen's words or to say, "I know you saw something terrible," though she irrevocably despised Jim by then. Whenever his name came up, rarely, she would say, "Egads" or "ugh."

Just as we did not talk about the disappeared Diego Rivera artwork, we did not talk in detail about Karen and Jim. We did not talk about sex or money or the philosophy of the religion we followed, or why in the night my father sat alone in lamplight and talked to himself, reliving the war. Perhaps there was no mental space for my mother to consider and interpret. Perhaps to do so would have broken into, and so broken apart, her native bravery, good sense, and good cheer. Perhaps—to use the words she often said in jest—she would have gone "stark raving mad." Instead, we sang and read. We talked about violets and watched ants work the peonies; we regularly looked at *Homebodies* cartoons, and laughed. We collected our stamps, and we wore our beautiful clothes. Beauty, wonder, and creation staked a claim to a blossoming world.

College-aged, when trips home were occasions to subject family life to dumbfounded scrutiny, I asked my mother, "What happened to the Diego Rivera painting you copied? You do know it was Diego Rivera?" She snorted. "Of course I know." One day our grandmother had come visiting, and though the entire dinette table was clear except for the partially completed and very wet painting, and though my mother cautioned her, my grandmother plopped her great pocketbook right on the painting. "Oh," she said, once my mother went into a scramble, "I thought it was a magazine." A rise of revulsion or fury caused my mother to give up the project on the spot.

After the summer day that shook me so, I avoided Karen whenever she drifted back down to our house. Then one day she came to say good-bye. She and the baby were leaving Jim, going away. My mother murmured her sympathy and approval. Later, Karen returned just once to see my mother, and they sat together in the backyard with the baby. I fidgeted around them, feeling older and shy when Karen noticed me. The awful Jim stayed on in the house up the hill, those friends coming over in cars all the more frequently.

One winter evening the awful Jim entered our home. I watched him come in and treat my mother like an aunt, a friend. I stood back and watched as our house shrank around him. Just that once I had to see him standing in our house, big and bristly, talking loudly, laughing in huffs, offering us a dog. How could he come here? Laugh, even? Hold a dog? Disguised as a new man, Jim wore a full-length coat, fuzzy and belted—"camel hair," my mother would note after he left. "Oh," she said about the small black dog Jim set panting and skittering at her feet, "I don't know. Really, no."

Some time later, Jim moved away. Eating Sunday dinner on a cold February afternoon, we realized that the little dog he had toted down that night was outside, racing around the neighbor's house. The creep Jim had left the dog behind. When my mother realized this, she went right out and scooped the dog to her. Inside, the little dog ran to the heat register and ate ravenously. For two weeks he buried bits of food under carpets, disbelieving his good luck. Bloody paws and a scraped nose were evidence that he had not just been turned out, rather, he had escaped captivity.

When my mother gathered the dog in her arms she was calculating how many days—possibly a week—he had been trapped in that house. She could not know that he, our Muffin, would live eighteen years with us, eating the same daily breakfast as she: Rice Krispies and whole milk. When she put down that first bowl of milk, I wonder if she saw the connection that I see now. My mother had not been able to so roundly rescue Karen, but she gave milk to the baby and she would give milk to this dog, supporting, again, as she could, life menaced and disregarded by Jim in that house.

The house stayed empty. Eventually it was demolished. In the meantime, a friend and I, now eleven, used the front step to meet and discuss the possible existence of sex in the case of our parents. Once, two brothers and I went inside the vacant house. The younger had run to us swearing there had been a murder in the house: it was filled with blood and bandages! Peeking through the window, he had seen the evidence. Of course we followed. The door was not even locked.

The house smelled like soggy clothes. Its ugly dirtiness disappointed us right off. In a kitchen corner we found an open trash bag topped by used menstrual pads. They were rotted, raggedy, the blood rusted by time but definitely recognizable as blood. The older boy and I looked away, embarrassed. He punched his brother in the shoulder and we clomped down to the basement. As the boys snooped around, I stood still and it came back to me, the story from before, about Karen and Jim, three years ago by then, an eternity in a child's life. I felt, eerily, the way a place retains memory, and that its memory, not mine, could razor my arms like crazy, and thump my heart out my eyes. I touched the hard cold floor that Karen's head had been slammed against. A skin of greasy dirt coated my finger. I thought of people watching, of how Jim's red face and oily blond hair would have looked as he did such a thing, and I knew that even as I stood right there where it had happened and the same picture burned in my heart as when Karen described the scene to my mother, the blankness of the basement emphasized that I was missing something. I hadn't asked or perhaps even known to ask my mother the crucial unanswerable question: *Why?*

In the basement with the boys I looked at my feet, at the concrete floor all around, and pictured a crushing weight on Karen, her cheek hitting cement. I had a small urge, if not for the boys' presence, to lie down in that cold grime and feel what I had never felt, my cheek laid on cement. I heard my mother's voice say, "Karen, oh, no, Karen." I pictured myself, jumpy and hollowed by shock, listening to Karen's story from the front porch. Friends, even other girls, I remembered Karen saying, had watched Jim beat her. Gathered for a party, these girls would have worn slim shifts and bubble hairdos with bangs that hid emotion. They would leave later with their boyfriends and have sex which, I believed, was required of them. Our dog Muffin would have been present in the house while it happened. He would have been panting in distress and, finally, barking in high staccato, the only bark he had. When Jim locked Muffin in that basement, I wonder if he made a nasty connection between the events. I wonder—it makes me sick to say so—if he went so far as to think deep in his thick protected skull that letting a dog die in that house would be just deserts for Karen's leaving him. He drove down Monona—we may have seen him from our kitchen and porch windows, not knowing he was going for good. He may have smirked at our house or driven with his blazing red face fixed forward. Jim would never know that through a little open window too high for any but a circus dog or a dying dog to scale, our Muffin escaped that basement. In their different ways, Karen and Muffin escaped the monstrous Jim.

Done scuffing around in the basement of what had been Jim and Karen's house, the older brother poked at the naïve one again and said, "There's nothing here. Come on." I followed them upstairs and out. I did not mention our trespass to my mother. It was as if, by then, I knew better than to speak of pain in terms of cause and effect, or in any terms at all. The mystery of adult pain rode bright and still as flowers on my mind, an increasing pressure of brightness that seeing the Diego Rivera painting always provokes as a leap in my heart and a shiver across my unbowed back. I never said to my mother, "Remember when Jim beat up Karen? I saw where it happened. I imagined everything, except why." Perhaps I sensed that to concoct answers to certain questions was beyond, way beyond, my mother's dream of life as it should be and her desire to hold onto and fulfill her dreams and, so, secure ours. ⧉

Tricia Asklar

BECOMING A WOMAN FILM

They handed us pamphlets as we entered, diagrams
of the whirlpools of ourselves, bleeding and bandaged.

After, the women teachers marched us out, our charts
marked with an X of completion, back to our exams,
chemistry tables, lab partners, Bunsen burners on high—
the kinds of experiments with predictable results. Unlike

Grace, who ran her Corolla into a tree because
she was pregnant, or Elaine and her shooting up.
Few admitted the future in the darkened room
as the film rolled itself from its wheel and clicked
like the rapid fire hits of playing cards clipped

to our bikes. The white screen offered a fleeting
place for our silhouettes until someone thought
to shut off the machine and turn on the lights.

Amy Monticello

LOVING CAPTAIN CORCORAN

I didn't care that John Lacy wore sweatpants—I loved him anyway. John didn't love me back, not the way I loved him, but he loved the Miami Dolphins. His sweatpants were orange and Kelly green, like his baseball hat that I stole at every opportunity.

"You want me to chase you, is that it?" he'd say. The blacktop basketball court at Ann G. McGuinness Elementary stretched behind him like an oily lake.

"*Nooo*," I'd say, meaning yes. Then I'd run off in my hot pink stirrup pants, and when I was lucky, John would humor me and follow.

My friends would say it's no surprise I loved the sweatpants kid, just like they weren't surprised when they met my husband, his heavy amber beard and wire-rimmed glasses, his calm intelligence. John Lacy could have come to school draped in George Castanza's velvet sweatsuit and I would have picked him. I don't mean to sound self-righteous. I really did love the smart ones, and especially the smart, weird ones, and even more, the smart, weird, *quiet* ones. Call it opposites attracting. Call it wanting men who are nothing like my father. I loved John for his sharp and peculiar mind, and it's one thing about myself I'm secretly proud of. When I say looks don't matter, I mean it.

My mother said John was a good influence on me. Of all the ways kids compete, John and I competed for grades, and not just grades actually, but any form of accolade or recognition the school could bestow upon our kiss-ass, praise-junky heads. John sat behind me in the fifth and sixth grades, and when Ms. Eckert handed back tests, I turned around for our weekly confrontation.

"So?"

I beat him in spelling, he beat me in math. I was an ungracious winner, lording over him every victory, while he demurred, giving me his test so I could see where I'd gone wrong. When we had an afternoon exam, it wasn't unlike John to quiz me during recess, and sometimes, when he could tell I was struggling through a problem, he threw his eraser at my back and used the basic sign language we had learned: *FOIL,* he signed during our algebra test. *F*irst, *O*utside, *I*nside, *L*ast.

But it was under the spotlight where John and I were closest. In the sixth grade, we starred in the school production of Gilbert and Sullivan's *H.M.S. Pinafore*. I played Little Buttercup and John played Captain Corcoran.

I remember everything about that musical, from tryouts to closing night. I remember the chaos of rehearsals with Mrs. Neiburg, the chorus director, when two of the sailors got into a fight that destroyed *Pinafore* bow #1, and when John fell off bow #2 during dress rehearsal, spraining his shoulder. I remember the peasant dress my grandmother sewed, and practicing my solos morning and night, much to my mother's annoyance.

But what I remember most about the play are the actual romances that budded from it. My best friend Jaime Sabol, who played Josephine, couldn't resist the idea of authenticity. After school one day, she suggested we turn the pretend into real life. The next day, she started going out with Mike Poling, who played Ralph Rackstraw, and they convinced (coerced?) John to go out with me. For a few precious weeks, we all sat together at the long cafeteria tables during lunch, where Jaime and I pushed our mushy French fries to the edge of our trays in front of the boys.

John and I had one duet in *Pinafore,* a number called "Things Are Seldom What They Seem," which references Buttercup's secret about Captain Corcoran's true identity. The lyrics are allusions—"Things are seldom what they seem. Skim milk masquerades as cream. High low pass as patent leathers. Jackdaws strut in peacock feathers"—and Mrs. Neiburg choreographed a dance for us, circling, bowing, and exchanging stage positions, symbolizing Corcoran's eventual "exchange" with Ralph Rackstraw. During practice, John and I acted embarrassed to have to hold hands and curtsy to each other, but on opening night, the touch of John's slick palm was like our song—we could hardly contain our smiles in that serious moment of the play. The real bond between us was like a secret we kept even from the audience, and though we were supposed to look forlorn, and my peasant shawl kept slipping off my shoulders, and we screwed up more than a few dance moves, we nailed that number.

Jaime Sabol and Mike Poling's relationship lasted through closing night, promptly ending in a public defacement on the playground when Jaime stomped on Mike's hand at recess and he yelped like a kicked dog. John broke up with me in a note a few days later, probably in retaliation for Mike. But while Jaime and Mike parted for good, John and I remained friends, entwined in other quests for stardom—all-county orchestra, all-county chorus, piano guild, and of course, our tests in school. Going out or not, we were together, in band practice, on the stage, and in pictures along the corkboard bulletin of the school foyer.

John had his vivid sweatpants and puffy trumpet cheeks. I had braces and frizzy hair. We were both just a little bit chubby. By the end of sixth grade, I was predicting the future in the margins of my math notebook. *Little Buttercup + Captain Corcoran 4 ever.*

. . .

John told me he was moving at the first school dance of seventh grade. We were sitting on the top bleacher in the gym, watching couples cop a feel below. Girls wore baby doll dresses circa 1994, and boys wore the ageless school dance uniform of khaki pants and polo shirts. The universal middle school experiences apply. Five elementary schools in Endicott, New York, converged at Jennie F. Snapp, a squat, gray building down an alley off South Loder. My old class of sixty kids rocketed to over three hundred. Somehow, the pretty girls were suddenly *so much* prettier, and with every attempt to improve myself—ratcheting my hair with curling irons and gel, wearing baggy clothes to hide my dumpy figure—I made things worse.

At Jennie F., as we called it, students were divided into "teams." I was on Team A, and John was on Team B. We didn't have any classes together, and without him there to goad me into learning, I became mute, dismissive of my schoolwork. The material got harder, especially in math, and I had a hard time keeping up. Instead of studying, I wrote John long notes that I'd slip through the slats of his locker, and drew crosshatching in the margins of my notebooks like Robert Crumb, and watched rain pelt the plexiglass windows in the dreary Upstate New York fall. I became the opposite of a standout—I became invisible.

But I waited each day, counting the seconds of ninth period until I could catch John at his locker before boarding the bus home. Our conversations were mixed. Some days, we still compared grades, at least until mine started slipping, and some days, I acted sarcastic and moody until we were both uncomfortable and slunk away to our respective buses. John started wearing jeans to school, and a new Marvin the Martian hat that he wore ironically, and though he tried to be sympathetic to the plight of middle school girls, I felt a rift slowly opening between us.

We had our dance in *Pinafore,* but we were not one of those couples swaying on the gym floor that September night. I asked John to dance for real two months earlier at the summer social before middle school began. My polyester dress had static cling, and we were both sweating in the mid-July stuffiness, our limbs moving like planks. I doubt anyone else was faring much better, but that kind of embarrassment at twelve years of age is so private, held hostage inside where it breaks down confidence like cafeteria spaghetti. On the outside, John and I seemed to be the only ones who couldn't navigate this new terrain. Hands? Where to put them? Feet? How to move them? Boys and girls paired off more seriously in the popular crowd, which got more exclusive and mythic, while adolescence trickled down to the rest of us slowly, more imitation than reality. Desperate to keep up, I wanted John to enter this world with me, to mimic what we saw at recess until it felt real. But John wasn't interested in faking it, and unlike me, he was brave enough to abstain.

Below us, the colored lights of the DJ booth spun Skittles-colored circles across the lacquered floor. John covered his face with his hands. "I have to tell you something," he said. "I'm moving."

A slow song, probably Mariah Carey or Celine Dion, bolstered this news, and I might have laughed at that if I didn't immediately feel like a rubber dodgeball had whacked me in the face. A vacuum seemed to form. It felt airless up there in the bleachers, the two of us separated from our classmates, and now, inexplicably, from each other.

"When?" I said.

All the doughiness was suddenly gone from John's cheeks. He looked almost gaunt, as though he hadn't eaten or slept in days. "IBM told my dad he could either transfer or be laid off. We leave in January," he said.

I waited for him to say something else, to tell me this was all a joke so I could punch him in the arm. But when that didn't happen, when he looked away and went silent, I stood and hobbled my way down the bleachers, then ran to the back of the gym and pushed through the double-doors that read, *No Re-entry.*

My mother was waiting up in the kitchen when I got home, smoking and drinking boxed zinfandel in her flannel nightgown. She asked how the dance went, and I started sobbing, one of those really big cries that's about a lot more than you think. Like middle schoolers the world over, I was crying for my frizzy hair, the ten extra pounds I carried in my hips and thighs. I was crying for the loss of school as a validating place. I was crying for the only boy who wasn't embarrassed to talk to me in the hallways. The sadness pushed down on me until I was hugging myself on the linoleum.

My mother stubbed out her cigarette and rubbed my back in small circles. She instantly recognized this sadness as the kind rife in the adult world—bad things happen no matter how good you try to be. Things my mother knew well, and from which parents wish to shield their children as long as they can.

My mother gently pulled me to my feet and took me to bed. As she yanked the blue comforter up to my chin, she said, "All you can do is make the best of the time you have left. Make it count." Then she flicked her lighter on a fresh cigarette and inhaled.

• • •

International Business Machines opened its Endicott plant in 1924. For nearly seven decades, it operated alongside the Endicott-Johnson Shoe Company, the largest employer in town until the 1970s, when E-J began to ship its business overseas. But unlike other manufacturing towns like Buffalo, Cleveland, and Detroit, the loss of E-J was cushioned by the rise of IBM, which flourished in U.S. defense throughout the Korean and Vietnam wars, extensions of the lucrative Cold War. Whereas teenagers once planned their futures around the tanneries, they now planned them around IBM's sprawling engineering and computing interests. Well into the 1990s, when John and others would begin disappearing from our school, my classmates would describe their futures at IBM. They planned to follow their parents, who largely took their high school diplomas straight to North Street, where IBM still sits in a maze of gray concrete and steel.

In college, I had to write a paper for an economics class, and in a fit of nostalgia brought on by the poetry classes I was also taking, I wrote about IBM. I learned that the plant developed the very punch card system used by the Nazis to catalogue European Jews in concentration camps during World War II. I also learned that John's family was considerably luckier than others when the plant began its twenty-year descent into computing irrelevance. Many employees received no such offers of transfer with their pink slips. During my middle and high school years, the layoffs spiraled out into town: first the IBM employees themselves, then the small businesses they frequented, then the banks that financed the businesses, until the empty, gutted buildings of IBM Endicott began to look like ground zero.

My mother understood before I did that some fundamental part of our town was disintegrating. Around the time John told me he was moving, she began securing her job in the school district where she worked as a secretary, taking on so much extra responsibility that she required a nightly crying spell to relieve the stress of her work day. She started saving money, refusing me anything outside necessity, including the clothes from The Limited and the Gap, for which I threw memorable tantrums. She started taking Prozac. She visibly aged.

I'm sure what Mom meant by "make it count" was for John and me to be good to one another while we still could. But I didn't get the subtlety of my mother's words, her gentle nudge towards worrying only about what I could control, a lesson I would fight learning the rest of my life. I was still operating on the lessons of grade school that taught me if I went for something—really, really wanted it—my drive would deliver me, and if you showed someone you cared enough, they wouldn't—they couldn't—let you down.

So, Little Buttercup got to work, launching her campaign to save Captain Corcoran. I started with letters to the IBM headquarters in Armonk, and to IBM Endicott's management, asking them to spare Mr. Lacy's job.

To Whom It May Concern:

My friend John Lacy and I are in seventh grade at Jennie F. Snapp middle school. Recently, your company decided to transfer John's father, Mr. Lacy, to Connecticut. I do not want John to move because he is my best friend. John is also an excellent student. He plays trumpet in the Christmas parade every year, and won second place in the science fair. If you save Mr. Lacy's job, then I will volunteer at IBM after school. I can clean, do filing, and anything else you need. As you can tell, I have very good communication skills.

Sincerely,

Amy Monticello

I felt bereft when headquarters didn't reply. A month later, IBM Endicott wrote on anguished letterhead that the company was "very sorry to cause disruption in [their] employees' lives." When another round of layoffs was announced in the newspaper the following week, I went to Plan B—the classifieds. I knew John's father worked with computers, so I circled in pink highlighter anything with the words "computer," "typing," and "office." I brought the ads to school and slid them into John's locker.

My mother became worried about how much time I spent looking through newspapers instead of doing my homework at night. It must have disturbed her to watch me, paper spread across my bed, push back futilely against change, trying to preserve not only a friendship but a dying sense of security in Endicott. She started leaving my math book conspicuously out on the kitchen table. "Your grades come first, young lady," she reminded me at dinner. I answered her with silence.

The day before Christmas break, John told me he would not be back at school after the New Year. "I have to pack," he said. I noticed he was unloading the contents of his locker into his book bag. Some of the ads I'd clipped for his father were crumpled inside, the pink highlighter marks giving them away.

"You never took those home?" I said. John looked away. What was the point of all this if he wasn't even going to try, if he was just going to give up? In a fit, I kicked his locker door shut, the wind of it knocking his Marvin the Martian hat off his head, and started down the hall. Like he had hundreds of times, John followed.

"I'm the one that's leaving, you know!" he shouted. "Did you forget that? Don't you think this is worse for me than it is for you?" The hallway was nearly empty, but the kids who lingered watched us in shock.

I stopped walking and turned around. "Then, why?"

John leaned against the tiger mural painted on the wall, our school mascot's fanned claws reaching up over his head. His face reddened and he started crying the way boys do, shoulders lifting and falling, but no sound coming out. His hair was matted from wearing his hat all day, but little sprigs popped up in back, and I fought the urge to walk over, smooth them down.

"Because we already sold our house," he said. "It was done before I even told you we were moving."

I walked over and leaned against the wall beside him, and we both slid to the hallway floor. We were kids. We couldn't do anything about our parents' jobs. We sat for a while and didn't speak or touch, and then we walked out of school and onto our buses.

• • •

I've got a flair for the dramatic—school plays, surprise birthday parties, weepy reunions, drunken fights with boyfriends in the middle of the street. But my reaction to John moving away is a bit strange even to me. Friends move away, especially in childhood, and it's sad for a while, but most twelve-year-olds would get distracted soon enough by what's still there—the blossoming opposite sex, the hunt for popularity, the easiest way to make a B in history. In my adult life of nontenured college teaching, my husband, Jason, and I move every few years, leaving the precious people we come to love in each place for another unfamiliar one. This transient life exposes us to parts of the country we'd never otherwise see—the Northeast, Midwest, and Deep South so far—and our careers mean we never have to give up learning, nor the university environment that sustains us the way grade school once sustained John and me. Still, Jason is much better at change than I am.

I hate change. The morning we left Columbus, Ohio, where Jason and I met in graduate school, I watched him in the driver's seat of our rented U-Haul, working our way down High Street for the last time. Behind us was the apartment where we'd completed our thesis projects, the university with our professors' reassuring offices, our friends who sent us off after a weeklong spree of parties and tears. In the rearview mirror, the city shrunk.

"You and me now, darlin'," Jason said, smiling behind his sunglasses. Maverick, I called him. He sounded excited at the prospect of our aloneness, our new life in the South. It was time for work, time for health benefits and car payments and commuting, and time stretched endlessly ahead of that overloaded truck containing only us.

I sobbed most of the way to Alabama. Even now, when I feel parts of Ohio slipping away, when I notice myself not thinking about it, I force myself to recall that moment when we passed the city limits, and I experience those losses, regain them. I make sure the part of me Columbus filled stays unfilled by any other place.

Unlike most Millennials, I have a baby boomer's penchant for nostalgia. For much of my childhood, I spent Thursdays with my father and watched him get drunk at the En-joie Golf Club lounge. After four or five Labatt Blues, he would pontificate about my mother: how she was the only woman that meant anything to him, how he was so sorry for all he'd done to cause the divorce. Though it pained me to witness his loneliness, I found an unexpected solace in my father's longing. His devotion to my mother, however latent, affirmed my existence somehow—loving my mother became the same as loving me.

My father, an avid reader, used to take me to Barnes & Noble on our afternoons together, and he once bought me a massive copy of Shakespeare's collected works. I read it cover to cover over the course of a few years, and though I didn't understand much of what I read, I could follow the love stories because my father had taught me to recognize a certain template for tragic love. My parents were *Romeo and Juliet, Antony and Cleopatra, Troilus and Cressida.* Love had to end in order to be epic.

I was convinced of the value of suffering for love by the time John Lacy told me he was moving away. So, if Little Buttercup couldn't marry Captain Corcoran, she would simply stay stuck in time, losing and losing him so that he would never be gone.

• • •

The night before John moved, my mother knocked on my bedroom door. "Would it help if we went over tomorrow morning so you could see him off?"

Not every mother would allow her daughter to miss a day of school to say goodbye to a childhood crush, especially my mother, whose usual policy was deathbed absences only. She didn't think twice about sticking a thermometer in my mouth, or under my arm, or worse. This was a rare bout of compassion.

"Really?" I said.

She blew out her cigarette smoke. Looking around our duplex on West Franklin Street, it was easy to see life hadn't exactly gone my mother's way. Two leaky roofs in five years. Wood siding in desperate need of a paint job. Clothes from two seasons ago that no longer fit. We couldn't afford the lives she had planned on, but this she had control over. This she could make happen. "I'll call Mrs. Lacy," she said.

It was the first time I had ever been to John's house. For all the time we spent together in school, our relationship never made it past the goalposts of the football field, and until then, this had never seemed weird to me. School wasn't just part of our lives. It *was* our lives.

John's old house was on Boswell Hill, part of a grid neighborhood IBM built around a large, splendid park my friends and I would use in high school to smoke weed. The houses were all split-level, brick-and-vinyl sided homes with bay windows and tight, manicured shrubbery. It was Rockwellian, only with a Budget moving truck parked in the driveway.

Shyly, John led me to what used to be his bedroom. We sat on a small rug in the middle, and I looked around, trying to get a sense of what things looked like before. Worn spots and pinholes on the wall suggested pennants and posters recently taken down. A circle around the light bulb on the ceiling betrayed a fixture unscrewed and packed in newspaper. There were a few dust bunnies clumped in the corners, long hidden by beds, dressers, and desks.

I didn't know where to begin, so I started with the obvious. "What's the name of your new school?"

"Fairfield," John said, making a face. "It's even bigger than Jennie F."

Fairfield. John Lacy was going to live in Fairfield, Connecticut. I had an image of him hurling a football down a leaf-covered field, and then one of him playing his trumpet in a band of gleaming instruments, not the old ones our school provided. It even sounded right—Fairfield, Lacy—and the idea that John was not only leaving me in Endicott, but leaving me for someplace that sounded synonymous with happy made me feel embarrassed and deeply sad. Tears spilled down my cheeks.

Tender and uncertain, John slid closer to me on the rug and rested his forehead against mine, the way my mother used to when I was a toddler, trying to make my eyes cross. "You know I'm going to miss you, right?" he said.

I stared down at the colors in the rug and nodded. It was the first time we'd ever touched this way, the first touch not instructed by the chorus director, the first of John's volition. He opened my palm and placed in it a slip of paper with his new phone number. "It won't be hooked up until Wednesday," he said.

We heard a soft knock, and Cheryl Lacy poked her head in. Cheryl was a church organist who had also played the accompaniment for *Pinafore*, and, like John, she had a reserved disposition that contained a surprising amount of warmth. At the sight of us on the floor together, she smiled, but quickly recovered the motions of her face so as not to embarrass anyone. "John, Amy's mom has to get to work. I'm sorry, but I think we're going to have to wrap things up," she said gently.

She left the door open a crack for good measure, the suburban mother's way of saying she knows what's going on in there. John turned back to me. "I'll still visit," he said.

"I know."

We stood, and he stepped towards me, circling his arms around my waist. As I hugged him back, I felt his soft, unwashed hair lightly brush my face in a sensation so intimate I almost pulled away. But I didn't, and instead I tilted my face towards him just as his lips found the corner of my mouth. It lasted a second, a small lifetime.

We stepped back from each other with reddened faces. Then, John led me back to the living room, where my mother was knocking the snow from her boots out the front door, an unlit cigarette at the ready between her lips.

"Oh, Amy, it's been fun, hasn't it?" Cheryl said, hugging me. "We're going to miss it here so much."

"You'll be great in Connecticut," my mother told John, patting his dirty hair. John followed us out the door and watched as we climbed into our old Chevette, its tail pipe spewing exhaust in the morning cold, and then he watched us pull out of the driveway and turn down the hill. I left my seat belt unbuckled so I could turn around and wave. John waved back. We waved until we couldn't see each other anymore.

• • •

"You wouldn't do it. Come on."

"Probably not. But that doesn't mean I don't think about it. I got yelled at the other day for sleeping in class, but actually I was just daydreaming about how pretty the mountains would be if I waited till fall."

"Well, how long would it take? I mean, really?"

There was a pause on the other end while John calculated. "On my bike, I think about a week. But maybe longer because I couldn't take main roads."

"Why not?"

"The police would find me."

"You think your parents would call the police?"

"Wouldn't yours?"

It was past nine o'clock when the long-distance rates went down. My mother had bought me a hand-me-down waterbed for Christmas, a queen size model that took up my entire room. Sometimes I talked to John while walking the plush, cushioned edge of it, pretending I was a gymnast on the balance beam. Alone, I was poised and confident, recognizable to myself in the privacy of my room, which I turned into a stage. I walked and walked the waterbed's perimeter, pretending I was in the Olympics, until my mother shouted that it was time to get off the phone. She could always tell when I was talking to John. Unless I had a calling card, which I'd buy whenever I had money, I was only supposed to talk to him once a month for fifteen minutes. It was all we could afford. But we talked once or twice a week, sometimes more if I couldn't stand it, and dialed his new area code compulsively. It didn't matter that the phone bill would inevitably arrive at the end of every month. Without a social life to give up, I took my groundings in stride and kept dialing.

For our clandestine phone calls, like this one, I waited until my mother went to sleep, then crawled under the covers at the far end of the waterbed, the farthest point in the house from my mother's room. I pulled the covers over my head to muffle the sound of my voice, and there, surrounded by damp heat, John and I made plans we'd never follow through on and became archeologists of our own memories.

"You know what I was thinking about today? When they took down the *Pinafore* set. Remember how sad we all were?"

"I remember you and Jaime crying through lunch while they did it. The bow broke apart when they took the supports out, and you two burst into tears at that pile of plywood."

"Shut up. You were sad, too. Don't lie."

"I was, a little."

We went on like this for three years, carrying on a relationship via telephone. By ninth grade, my looks had settled out some—I dropped some weight, had my braces removed. My interest in English was rekindled with *Great Expectations,* which I read three more times for fun, loving the way Pip never gets Estella, but has her somehow anyway, forever. I also discovered a love of watercolor painting in my studio art class, even began flirting with Dave Arnold, who shared a drawing desk with me, though I didn't tell John about it.

Sometimes I asked John to describe things in his new life—his school, his neighborhood, his bedroom, where I increasingly pictured him talking to me in nothing but boxer shorts—but mostly those things were taboo, as though acknowledging them would negate his old life, the one I had claim to. The glimpses I did get of Fairfield were of its wealth and insularity, and though I vocally lamented each of John's failed attempts at fitting in—his second-string spot on the football team, the cliques at school—I was secretly grateful when the place rejected him.

My mother's worry about the situation was only partly because of my melancholy. Staying locked in my room after school was a small infraction compared to the phone bills I kept racking up. After John moved, she signed me up for horseback riding lessons, something I'd wanted for years, but which my mother only agreed to in an effort to yank me out of my self-imposed funk. A distraction, that's what I needed. We spent hours in the car riding to the barn and back each week, and she took these opportunities—me, trapped with her in the Chevette—to lecture me about my long-distance addiction.

"Amy Lynne," she said, using my middle name, "You can't keep this up anymore. I can't keep this up. Do you know what's going to happen if you don't get a handle on this?"

Snow began to fall outside. Mom sat all the way up in the driver's seat, squinting through the opening sequence to *Star Wars,* those snowflakes whizzing at us, then spreading out across the windshield as we plowed through darkness everywhere.

I felt exhausted, like every feeling was getting squeezed out from some unrelieved pressure inside. I had no name for what was wrong.

"What on earth do you two talk about all those hours anyway?"

I slipped into a wintry trance as the rhythm of the car ground through the slush. Each of those snowflakes became a tiny light flaring up, then going out. "Nothing," I said. "Everything."

• • •

The nature of pining is that you love the possibility, the ache of how it all might turn out. In *Pinafore,* Little Buttercup waits a lifetime for Captain Corcoran to grow up, learn who he really is, and realize that the old friend whose counsel he consistently sought was more than a friend. All the while, she waits aboard Corcoran's ship, quietly watching, quietly pining.

I'm convinced a smidge of contentment lies in every longing, for there is no disappointment in longing. You can have as many imaginary conversations with your particular ache as you wish, as Buttercup does at the start of Act II. You catch glimpses of your ache everywhere—passing you on the highway, checking out at the grocery store, walking across a crowded parking lot—just a little too far out of reach, just a little too unclear to be certain. But it's there. You know something that could be real is out there.

John returned to Endicott only twice. The first time was for his cousin's baptism, or confirmation. We went to the Ann G. McGuinness playground, and he told me about the hymns, how they were so outdated. I asked him what he meant, and he said the whole sermon was too somber, and it was weird how he didn't remember church being that serious before. Then he told me about his new church's sound system, and how they just hooked up a screen so the congregation didn't have to juggle hymnals anymore.

"Yeah, well, let's just hope they don't come up with a replacement for your mom's organ," I said.

John kissed me for the second time, another closed-mouthed peck on the lips, and gave me his Marvin the Martian hat. "It should stay here with you," he said, pulling the brim down over my eyes.

John visited again the summer after ninth grade, and this time, we had a whole afternoon together at my house. We cracked the door of my bedroom half an inch—my mother's rule—and listened to the Jars of Clay CD he brought. I didn't know Jars of Clay was Christian rock. They had a hit single on American Top 40, which I listened to every Sunday at Northminster Presbyterian while my mother directed the children's choir practice. All the teenagers piled into a spare Sunday school classroom and listened to Casey Kasem's voice drip sex into our ears from an old stereo the size of a small car, while the adults set a good example for an hour each week. Church wasn't much more than an extension of school, and that's the only reason I didn't protest going.

On that second visit, John and I had our first real make-out session. We were lying together on my bed staring up at the Christmas lights I'd hung when I turned my bedroom into what my mother called an opium den, complete with lava lamp. John's skin smelled like Irish Spring, and his tongue in my mouth was not as tentative as I had thought it would be. I felt it behind my teeth and against the roof of my mouth, and I was surprised by its boldness and reluctant retreat. We didn't go any further—I didn't slide my hand underneath his t-shirt, as I'd wanted—but that visit left me hungry and confused.

For spring break of tenth grade—three years since John moved—my mother surprised me with a trip to Connecticut to visit him. We would have five whole days together, including Easter Sunday.

Dave Arnold and I began seeing each other five months before the Connecticut trip. I told him I was checking out colleges. Like John, Dave was quiet and intellectual, but more cynical and funnier, a talented artist, and we had already gone to second base in the backseat of his parents' Acura. I liked Dave very much, but being with him was full of guilt, not really knowing how far I should go with him, and where John fit into the life I had somehow fallen into with Dave. There I was, going to parties at the floodwall off June Street, drinking Miller High Life and stealing cigarettes from my mother's pack, and there I was again, dialing Connecticut and talking about English class as though it was the altar at which I worshipped. John and I weren't exactly in a relationship, but we weren't not in a relationship, and I was afraid that he would break off whatever we were in completely if he knew about Dave.

My mother watched me closely. "You can't have them all, Amy," she said. She had noticed my swollen lips when I came home on Friday nights and had begun mentioning condoms during dinner conversation.

We arrived in Connecticut on a Wednesday night, and I should have known the visit wasn't going to go as planned when Cheryl Lacy announced we were going to church.

"Wednesdays are kind of a social thing," she explained to my mother, whose distaste for non-Sunday worship must have shown in the way she immediately lit a cigarette. "The kids usually hang out in the gym, and the adults do Bible study in the café. There's coffee and cake," she added for incentive.

"You got a café in there?" my mother said.

Our first night in Fairfield—the town as quaint and colonial as I'd imagined, the dogwood-lined streets covered in spongy white flowers—I watched John play basketball with his friends. The church was as big as Jennie F., and once again, I sat in the bleachers while the action happened below, the boys horsing around and shooting air balls, as wholesome as can be in their bowl-cuts. After the game, as they toweled off and talked on the court, I noticed John's friends looking at me strangely. Then they said things to John with serious expressions.

"They didn't like me or something?" I said on the ride home. John and I sat in the back while our mothers chatted about baking up front.

"No, they did. I mean, they don't know you, so how can they not like you?" John stared out the window and wouldn't look at me.

We ate dinner back at the Lacys' house, and with actual candles burning on the dining room table, they told us more about Fairfield. Tom Lacy, who had spent some time in the local library, said it was a renegade settlement of Puritans from the Massachusetts Bay Colony, who were fighting Anglican reform and its condoning of divorce. In other words, Fairfield was God's town, and it probably didn't approve much of people like my mother and me. But Cheryl also complained that people were more private than in Endicott, and how she missed good pizza and the Grand Union grocery store.

"Can you believe I used to sample the green beans right from the bins, and no one said a word?" she said. "Isn't that a hoot?"

"Folded," my mother said through a mouthful of lettuce, apparently having left her table manners in New York. Cheryl looked confused, and my mother held up a finger while she finished chewing and swallowing. "Went out of business."

After the weird vibe I got at John's church, I wasn't much into my roast beef. I picked at my salad and snuck pieces of meat to the Lacys' cocker spaniel, Sissy, who lay at my feet under the table. My mother leaned over and squeezed my knee, code to knock it off. I squeezed hers back, and we stifled our giggles, acting like two misbehaving cousins during Christmas dinner. I almost wished my mother and I were alone to talk about how bizarre this trip was turning out. But more than that, I wanted to be alone with John.

After the adults went to bed, John and I moved to the den to watch a movie. I combed through the VHS tapes on the shelf and pulled down *Spaceballs*, thinking of Princess Vespa's saucy relationship with Lone Starr. I thought it might set the proper mood.

John unfolded the futon and produced a fleece blanket to wrap around our shoulders. I used this as an excuse to snuggle right up against him, breathing in his musky post-basketball scent. We watched the movie with its crude, vaguely sexual humor, but I could tell neither of us was really watching. Eventually, we stretched out on the futon, John's front curled against my back, and John's breath on my neck made my whole left side tingle, like when Dave Arnold put his mouth around my earlobe. We started kissing. It felt like his visits to Endicott when we didn't really know how long to kiss, except that now I did, and I also knew what to do next.

"Here," I said, rolling over. Through the mesh fabric of his gym shorts, I felt his erection push against my thigh. I put my lips to his neck, just under his jaw, and ran my hands down his chest, his stomach, my fingers grazing the skin at the waist of his shorts.

"No, don't," he said. He flung the blanket off and sat up.

"I'm sorry," I said. "I didn't mean to." But I didn't really know what I hadn't meant to do. A current of shame rushed down my spine as I tried to figure out what just happened, and if John was mad at me.

"Listen, I'm just tired," John said. "You go ahead and finish the movie if you want, but I'm gonna go to bed. See you in the morning." He turned and went upstairs.

• • •

Our visit to Fairfield included two more church services on Good Friday and Easter Sunday. The Good Friday service was held at the church, and John did not sit next to me while I pretended to sing the hymns that scrolled along the bottom of the eight-foot screen. Since the incident in the den two nights ago, he'd only spoken to me when our parents were present, and he made sure one of them was in the room with us at all times.

I was mortified by this constant chaperoning. I kept searching John's face for recognition, for my old friend, even for signs of a horny teenage boy, someone I could understand. I began wishing I could just go home.

The Easter service was held at the beach at sunrise. I suppose it symbolized the resurrection, the world experiencing the dawn of God's infinite compassion. The church's impressively large congregation squatted in the rocky sand and listened to the Pat Boone-ish pastor deliver his televangelistic-style sermon.

"Father, we thank you for the miracle you performed nearly two millenniums ago, Father, for the sacrifice of your only son, who died on the cross for our sins. Father, we accept this gift with great humility, Father, and our hearts are full of Jesus Christ's mercy, of which we are none of us worthy…"

My mother made an *oof* sound as she pulled her sleeping leg out from under her. "Don't they know old ladies can't sit like this?" People's hands were randomly shooting into the crisp air like resilient daffodils. "Goddammit, if he says 'Father' one more time," she said. She glanced over at Cheryl to make sure Cheryl hadn't heard, and then leaned closer. "Did you know John's family were such holy rollers?"

The sun began to rise out of the ocean, and a weak light spread across the upturned faces of the congregation. Puny, gray waves lapped against the craggy shore. I thought about John's tongue in my mouth, the melting feeling of kissing him, and then the way he left me with the movie still playing, Rick Moranis sputtering and lisping until I had finally fallen asleep. I had waited on that futon for hours thinking he'd come back and explain, and when he didn't—when I accepted he wouldn't—I sat there longer, feeling like the dirtiest, most unworthy soul even Jesus couldn't save. "No, I didn't," I said.

The next morning, we said a quick good-bye to the Lacys, turning down their offer of breakfast. "I got a hankering for an Egg McMuffin," my mother said. John waved to me from the couch, not even getting up as we pulled on our coats. We blared Bob Dylan and Led Zeppelin all the way to Endicott because, as my mother said, we needed the devil to get all that God out of our hair.

A few days later, I received a letter from John. He said he wished he'd told me about the purity pledge he'd taken shortly after his last visit to Endicott.

Even wanting you is a sin, he wrote. *Instead, I want to thank you for being there when I needed someone to help me through such a hard time in my life. You are my best friend, and I realized that seeing you this week.*

He wrote about the church pulling him out of the despair of leaving his hometown three years ago. Like it does for many, but never would for me, church gave John the community he needed in Fairfield, and now he felt he owed it something—his chastity. That's what his friends were whispering to him on the basketball court. They told John I would tempt him to compromise his pledge. And when I didn't shy away at his arousal during the movie, he knew they were right.

You will always be special to me, and I hope I'll always be special to you too. But doing God's work is my first priority. I won't be able to call you so often. But I care, and I'm praying for you. Love, John.

I balled up the letter and threw it away. But that wasn't good enough, so I emptied my wastebasket and took the trash out to the curb. Then, after a week went by and I still felt haunted by John's words—no, his prayers— I asked Dave Arnold to come over when my mother wasn't home, and we took each other's virginity.

· · ·

My father is just about the best ex-husband in the world. When I was five, he sent me home from our Thursday visitation with an inflated child support check so my mother could put a new roof on our duplex. When I was ten, another five grand to help her pay off her credit cards. He took care of my braces, and bought my school clothes, and sent me to summer camp so my mother could have a week of annual peace. She started dating again when I was in high school, and when her boyfriend left her for another woman, my father brought over Consol's pizza and listened to my mother cry. If you ask him why he does these things, he'll say, "Because I love her. That's what matters."

· · ·

John and I didn't talk as often during college, but we called each other for the big stuff—scholarships, missionary trips, relationships. He called me when he met Sarah on a mission to Belize. "I want her to know I like her before we go home for the semester, but I don't know if I should kiss her yet," he said. "What will she think?"

I had chopped my brown hair into a curly pixie and was wearing a lot of black in Ithaca, New York. I read slam poetry at the Wownet café, ate things like hummus and kale, and routinely smoked Camel Lights in my dorm room. "Are you insane?" I said, exhaling blatantly into the receiver. "She'll think you like her. Yes, dummy, kiss her."

He did. And two years later, he asked her to marry him.

I was grateful to be dating someone when the invitation arrived in my campus mail. Spencer was Jewish, and intrigued by my stories of John and his church. "Let's go," he said. "It'll be anthropological."

Secretly, though, I wouldn't have missed John's wedding for the world. Not only did I want a good look at his fiancée, who was also Italian and who John described as being "a lot like you, only Methodist," but I also wanted him to see that I had turned out fine without Jesus, that I was happy with my life. I wanted John to pray for somebody else.

I chose the exact wrong dress. I bought it at a thrift store in Ithaca— short and yellow, with little purple flowers all over. Buttercup, I thought, pulling it off the rack. But it was short. Way too short. The stretchy material clung everywhere to my too-skinny body after years of vegetarianism. It rode up when I walked. The spaghetti straps showed off the tattoo I'd gotten on my shoulder when I was seventeen, using the ID my mother borrowed from the day-care girl at Northminster Presbyterian. With my hair short enough to leave my neck unencumbered, I was practically all skin, and what wasn't skin was a sickly, unflattering color, the color of flu.

The first embarrassment of the wedding trip was running into Cheryl Lacy. I had foolishly arrived early, thinking I might get to see John before the ceremony. Spencer and I wandered around the sanctuary, sitting in the hard, straight-backed pews, getting up, sitting somewhere else. Cheryl came breezing through with a large vase of flowers for the altar, and when I said hello, she looked at me funny.

"It's Amy," I said.

Her face disentangled itself. "Oh!" she said, "Oh, Amy! My gosh, I didn't even recognize you!" She gave me a hug, but there was something surprised about it. "I'm sorry, but I have to deliver these. You'll be at the reception, right?"

I said, yes, but now I was dreading it. What was I thinking, coming here? I realized then that John had meant for the invitation to be a courtesy, a gesture to an old friend to spare hurt feelings. He didn't expect I would actually show up.

Cold sweat erupted on the back of my neck. I turned to Spencer. "Do you wanna bail?" I said. "We can get takeout and bring it back to the room." I suddenly had the desire for Kung Pao chicken and loud sex.

Spencer looked around the sanctuary, at the lavender and white flowers, and the white tulle, and the tall, white candles. "No, let's stay," he said. "I've never been to a Christian wedding. It's interesting."

John and Sarah got married at Sarah's hometown church, the sanctuary bright with August sun. I wish I could remember the vows, the color of the bridesmaids' dresses, Sarah's gown, but I don't remember anything except John. His chestnut hair swept back like a bible-thumping David Hasselhoff, his olive complexion, his tuxedo, everything about him was gleaming and certain. He looked more certain about what he was doing than I had ever been about anything.

The ceremony was traditional but short, and I gave a little nod of appreciation to the cross for that. Did I look away while John kissed his wife? I don't remember. But I did follow the caravan of cars to the reception, figuring that I might as well see the experience through to the end, the experience of watching someone you once loved, will always, in some way, love, choose someone else. It would, as Spencer put it, be something to study, to write about, to read passionately at the Wownet café to others who found such self-imposed pain beautiful.

Spencer and I found our place cards at a table in the very back of the reception hall. There were only two other people at our table. A tall, muscular girl named Kim sat down next to me along with her date, a lanky guy who kept looking around nervously at the glasses and plates, picking up his fork and setting it down again.

Kim introduced herself as John's ex-girlfriend, though I knew exactly who she was. "We dated in college," she said, shaking my hand and laughing what sounded to me a bitter laugh. I smelled liquor on her. "I think I was his first kiss. That boy was so inexperienced."

Heat climbed my face. Had John really never mentioned me, his actual first kiss? And did he think me so immature that I should be seated at this, the official Ex-girlfriend Table, as far away from him as we could be? I wished I had just sent a gift. A nice wine decanter, maybe.

Because, to top it off, it was a dry reception. No alcohol, not even a champagne toast. I hadn't thought to bring a flask, but Kim did. Every so often, she snuck away for a nip, and each time she returned, her opinions and her breath were a little stronger.

"Jack Daniels and I have decided this is too goody two-shoes even for John," she said. "Are they, like, Mormons?" She leaned towards me conspiratorially as she spoke. I'm sure my prostitute-like dress gave my usual vodka-chugging lifestyle away.

"I don't think John drinks," I said, sipping my water and trying to sound as measured as possible.

"Well, most *normal* people do," she said. "Weddings aren't just about the bride and groom. They're about the guests too."

John and Sarah had their first dance. The best man gave his speech. The chicken or fish were served. I told my boyfriend we'd leave after the cake was cut. We each ate a piece with too much frosting, and as the music swelled up again for dancing, I began planning our exit, the route quickest and stealthiest through the crowd. That's when John appeared at our table, standing over me with his hand extended. It was the first time in five years we stood face-to-face.

"Me?" I said.

"Of course, you."

Along with most of the details of the wedding, the song we danced to has been jettisoned from my memory. I remember only the feel of his hand at the small of my back and my nervous movements in his arms.

"How's Kim doing?" he said, the hint of a smile on his lips.

"Are you kidding me?"

The smiled opened fully and he laughed. "I thought she might have a hard time today. I figured you would help her through it. You're good about stuff like that," he said.

"I think Jack Daniels is doing a better job of that than I am."

I stepped on his polished black shoes twice, and couldn't relax or look him in the eye. "I think we're going to leave after this," I said over his shoulder. "You understand."

I felt his arm tighten around me. "Hey," he said. "That's why I wanted to do this now. I didn't want to miss our chance."

I did look at him then, and that's when I knew what he was really saying, why he had invited me here, and why it was okay that I came. As the song faded and we let go of each other, I realized that John knew exactly who I was—a girl who needs an ending, a girl who might not wholly let herself move on until a chapter of her life closes appropriately, with meaning, however cheesy or artificial, like the kickline at the end of *H.M.S. Pinafore*. And maybe, if I haven't been wrong about all of this, if I haven't misread the kernel of romance at the center of our friendship, John, too, needed an ending.

He squeezed my hand and smiled, and then let go to make his way back to his wife across the room. As Spencer and I pushed through the doors of the hall and walked to our car, the bride and groom were sharing a second piece of cake. It was the last time I saw Captain Corcoran.

· · ·

When my father had a heart attack on New Year's Eve 2009, I was living in Alabama with Jason, who I would marry the following year. My mother went to the hospital and sat in the waiting room while a surgeon performed the first round of angioplasty on my father's heart.

"He's scared, but he's going to be all right," my mother said when she called with news of the surgery. Her voice was full of relief.

When I could speak again, I thanked her for being there. "It means everything to him," I said. "You have no idea."

"That's not true," she told me. "Just because we aren't married anymore doesn't mean we don't love each other. I will always love your father in my own way."

• • •

John and Sarah had adopted twin girls by the time my Jason and I sent our wedding invitations. I expected they wouldn't make it, but didn't expect their R.S.V.P. to arrive so close to the deadline. They had tried everything, John said, and had even visited the web site of our wedding venue, a greenhouse conservatory in Columbus where a former professor, not a minister, would marry us. But in the end, he and Sarah couldn't find a viable solution for their family needs: *I'm quite bummed about that, actually,* he wrote. *I know we will find a way to catch up with you one summer so we can meet your husband and you can meet our girls.*

It touches me to think so. At twenty-eight, John and I have been friends across distance longer than we were friends in the same town, sharing an elementary school's slim spotlight, and it has been a long time since I've wondered how things could have turned out differently. But sometimes, as I grade my students' papers, I recognize some similar eagerness for approval, a certain performative quality, a fundamental sincerity that reminds me of John, or maybe of me—a younger me, perhaps a better me. Six adjectives when one will do. A word plucked from a thesaurus. Dialogue that smacks of the stage.

It is rare. But it is enough. ≋

Lily Chiu

In the Bath

We are naked   in the bath

when you tell me about   the first time

how you left   the shower on

so your mother wouldn't   find you

for a long, long while.   One minute

I'm Pretty Woman   your body wrapped

between my legs, and then I hold you   like an anchor

so you know there is another   kind of weight.

suzanne rae deshchidn

FRAGILE

i await their pilgrimage   the arduous
journey of the delicate monarchs migrating
south through my one acre of texas
cornfield   battalions of them   streaming
by   orange flares set off by some
internal clock   some ingrained need
to mate in deep forests   drink from
salt pools   i remember counting them
as they waft by   carried by will and
beauty   she sits across from me and
weeps telling me how she's locked
into her marriage   *trapped*   she says
and doesn't know how   to get out
i don't know what to say   how to
tell her it is a lie   that being trapped
is all   an illusion   *you just can't see*
your exit yet   but it's coming   i leave
it at that   and we find another soul
locked in her home   *we've been*
fighting   she says   waking the dead
she means   we sit   understanding
as women   with children   what can
be done   how to get away from
the men who control our lives
i told you   it takes courage to leave
she said   and i begin to understand how
 can something   so fragile   so
beautiful   possibly make   the journey
alone   there is too much danger   to go
too much danger   to stay

SANGRE DE DIOS

i pass the line of migrant workers whose
dark oval faces   black hair
almond eyes   are the faces of all
those i have ever loved   those faces
not so much hopeful   as determined
mama back at home flips the tortilla
dough between her hands   singing
ese lunar no puede cielito lindo
junto a la boca   the flat tortilla pan
and white linen towel used for pressing
the dough on the fire   the slender
figure of the worker   trained not to
eat too much   until he gets home
to mama's comida   paid too little
for grueling work   standing in the sun
all day   waiting   endlessly waiting
the children dressed in cotton summer
dresses   worn thin from too much washing
if laughter were wages   we'd be kings
mama is the world   and when papa
comes home   having drunk his wages
at the bar with his buddies   she paints
his toenails pink   as he's passed out
in the living room   a rookie cop beats
him for a fag when he sees the nails
papa never mentions it   but we know
the story   i remember it   every
time   i drive past the workers

Chiori Miyagawa

Medea, An Illegal Love Story

Actors

Medea .... a woman of color in her late 20s to early 40s
Friend .... a woman of any ethnicity or age
Creon................................... an older Caucasian man
Jason................................... a man of color in his late 20s to early 40s

Place
New York City

Time
Today-like

Notes on Casting
Medea's and Jason's ethnicities are not specified, but they should look
different from Creon. Medea and Jason do not have to come from the
same cultural background either. All the characters speak English
without an accent.

The play is inspired by Euripides' *Medea* (431BC).

> A shabby apartment in NYC.
> Today.

FRIEND

What happened?

MEDEA

We're getting divorced. Jason wants to marry someone else.

FRIEND

Who?

MEDEA

Creon's daughter.

FRIEND

Creon?

MEDEA

He owns the big diner on 95th Street and Broadway.

FRIEND

Right. The place you and Jason wait tables.

MEDEA

I got fired. Jason is going to manage the diner after he marries that little princess.

FRIEND

What're you going to do?

MEDEA

What can I do? I wish I were dead.

FRIEND

Let's not be melodramatic.

MEDEA

How else can I escape my own body that Jason has touched with his lips, caressed with his hands? In what part of my body shall I store this misery, where the memory of love will not collide with it to destroy my soul? Jason has no right to go and replicate the act of our love on another woman's body.

FRIEND

Medea, how're your kids?

MEDEA

I don't know. I can't really look at them. They look so much like Jason.

FRIEND

Does Jason give you money for the kids?

MEDEA

I have to find another restaurant job. That's about all I can get as an illegal immigrant. I was a pharmacist in my own country, you know. I come from a long line of women pharmacists. We owned a large drugstore. I gave it all up to come here with Jason. I betrayed my father by selling the store. It was in my name because my mother left it to me when she died. I needed the money to leave with Jason. Now my father has nothing. I can't even go home.

FRIEND

Your father will forgive you.

MEDEA

No, he won't. Once you leave your homeland, forgiveness is not yours. In the new land, tolerance is not yours. Creon didn't like anything about me. The way I dressed, the way I spoke, the way I ate my lunch. He thought I was in the way of other workers and an annoyance to the customers.

FRIEND

And Jason? He's a foreigner too.

MEDEA

Jason is clever. He adapted better. Where I looked dumb, he appeared exotic and promising. I became a burden to Jason's progress. I know a stranger must conform. I accept my place. But Jason was my whole life. With him, I could have made a home anywhere. Without him, I'm homeless.

FRIEND

Medea, you made the choice to leave your country. Ask yourself if you'd have been completely happy back home. You followed Jason for the promise of an adventure. Marriage is difficult in any culture. Don't make an enormous tragedy out of this.

MEDEA

The same rules of sorrow and comfort don't apply to you and me. You have this city, family and FRIENDs. I'm alone. I have no city. No blood of my own to turn to.

Knock on the door.

MEDEA

Who is it?

CREON

Creon.

FRIEND

What's he doing here? Don't let him in.

MEDEA lets him in.

MEDEA

What do you want?

CREON

I heard from some of my employees that you're telling lies in the neighborhood about roaches and mice in my kitchen.

MEDEA

You *know* they're not lies.

CREON

You don't get it, do you? No one will believe you. I was born here.
You are nobody. You don't belong here.

MEDEA

If that's true, why worry?

CREON

I don't want you to be a nuisance to my daughter. You're vicious enough
to go after your ex-husband's younger and wealthier new wife.

MEDEA

You don't know me.

CREON

I've known people like you.

MEDEA

Listen asshole, think about what's going on here. Your new son-in-law is
the father of my two children. Because of your daughter, I now have no
husband and no job. Do you think I want to live in this hell hole at any
cost?

CREON

If you don't like it, go back to...

FRIEND

Oh, come on.

CREON

Anyway, I've called the Homeland Security and told them you and your
children are illegal. You should leave if you don't want to go to jail.

MEDEA

What?!

FRIEND

What about Jason? He's not legal either.

CREON

Jason is marrying my daughter today.

MEDEA

So I have nothing left.

CREON

Leave with your kids. You still have time.

> Creon exits.

FRIEND

What are you thinking about?

MEDEA

My country.

FRIEND

I'll ask my brother if he knows a lawyer who can help you.

MEDEA

Why?

FRIEND

Don't you want to stay here? Raise your children as Americans?

> Lights change.

Voice "CREON"

OK. Let's take a lunch break. We'll do the rest of the play when we come back.

"Creon" and "Jason" enter.

"FRIEND"

Do you understand this?

"MEDEA"

She's insane. No sane mother will kill her own children for revenge against their father.

"CREON"

It's not natural.

"JASON"

It's not natural to be so alone.

"FRIEND"

My uncle lives alone, but he's not insane.

"JASON"

I mean *alone*. Not understood. Not understanding. Food tastes harsh. Clothes don't fit. You forget the sound of your own voice.

"MEDEA"

No one is that alone.

"FRIEND"

Do you want something to eat?

"JASON"

I don't know. Where're you going?

"FRIEND"

The pizzeria next door.

"JASON"

No, I think I'll just stay here and read.

"Creon" and "FRIEND"
exit.

"MEDEA"

What're you reading?

"JASON"

Hamlet. I think it's appropriate for me to be reading it now.

"MEDEA"

Why?

"JASON"

Hamlet is like MEDEA, in a way. An unexpected tragedy alienated him from love and trust and made him a stranger among his loved ones.

"MEDEA"

You don't like pizza?

"JASON"

It's not that.

"MEDEA"

Come with us anyway. You can just get tea or something. So you don't have to be alone.

"JASON"

I want to be alone for a bit.

"MEDEA"

Are you sure?

"JASON"

Yeah. It's practice.

"MEDEA"

What do you mean?

Calling from off stage.

"CREON"

Are you coming?

"JASON"

I'll see you in a little while.

"MEDEA" exits. "JASON"
sits and reads. Pause.

Everyone re-enters.

"CREON"

OK. We're back.

"FRIEND"

Let's do it.

"JASON" and "CREON"
sit nearby and watch.

FRIEND

What are you thinking about?

MEDEA

My country.

FRIEND

I'll ask my brother if he knows a lawyer who can help you.

MEDEA

Why?

FRIEND

Don't you want to stay here? Raise your children as Americans?

MEDEA

They shall not hurt me and remain free of suffering. In bitterness and pain they will lament their marriage. Regret their houses joined. Repent my banishment.

FRIEND

Child support. Think about that.

MEDEA

I want to kill Jason's new wife.

FRIEND

Stop saying crazy things.

MEDEA

And Creon.

FRIEND

Medea, wild with love, left your father's house and flew over the Eastern sea. And now, living in a strange country of upper west side, your bed solitary, your refrigerator empty. Where can you turn for shelter? Another woman is the mistress of your husband's bed. You poor thing.

> Knock on the door.
> FRIEND goes to open it.

FRIEND

It's Jason!

> JASON enters.

JASON

This isn't the first time your temper messed things up.

MEDEA

You're amazing.

JASON

I did this for you and the kids. We came here penniless. I was really lucky to meet my second wife. The heir to Creon's Diner. It's not that I want a white, American wife. It's good for you and your children for me to do this. This marriage will give me security, a green card. The children won't grow up poor and foreign. They'll have half brothers and sisters who are American. Don't you see? We couldn't have made it without this marriage.

MEDEA

I wouldn't have left my country if it wasn't for you.

JASON

That's a lie. There was no future there. I took you away from a barbaric land. You should have been grateful just to be here. But what do you do? You get Creon angry and now the ICE is after you. What were all the hardships for?

MEDEA

Not for the nights alone, with visions of my husband fucking someone else.

JASON

God, if women didn't exist, the human race would be free of misery. If only we could get children in some other way.

MEDEA

Yes. That would be a good thing. Once women are freed from rearing children, we will be completely free. No more mistakes in thinking some other human beings are part of you. No need to love so much, need so much, control so much. No need to kill one's own children.

JASON

Medea, I know you hate me. But I still care about you.

MEDEA

I need money for my journey.

JASON

I don't have any money right now. I have to pay for my own future. I can't pay for yours too.

MEDEA

But I'm poor. Don't you feel responsible for my well-being?

JASON

It's over. Memories tainted. Hopes broken.

MEDEA

Do you remember when we were planning our new life? Talking about silly things like a house with a big yard and six dogs, all black and white. Like a Disney movie. We thought everything was possible in America.

JASON

But we found out. We didn't know anybody here. You were constantly in despair and rage.

MEDEA

We were having a bad time, that's all. We'd have come out of it all right. If only you were more patient.

JASON

I was unhappy.

MEDEA

You've stayed too long. You should go back to your new wife.

JASON

What will happen to you?

MEDEA

What will happen to *you*?

JASON

I don't understand.

MEDEA

I guess not.

JASON

I tried.

MEDEA

Me too.

JASON

Good-bye.

JASON exits.

FRIEND

Medea?

MEDEA

I'm a long way from home.

FRIEND

From Asia Minor?

MEDEA

No, from how I thought my life would turn out when I grew up.

FRIEND

It happens to everyone.

MEDEA

Where are my kids?

FRIEND

What kids?

MEDEA

Didn't I have children with my husband?

FRIEND

What do you remember?

MEDEA

No? Perhaps not. No.

Pause.

MEDEA

Time passed. I didn't think I could do it. I was a child myself. I needed protection. It's too late now, isn't it?

FRIEND

I don't know.

MEDEA

I wanted Jason to be everything. My best friend, lover, parent, child, country. I wanted him to be everything I lost by leaving my country.

FRIEND

That's a big job.

MEDEA

Yes. He got tired.

FRIEND

What will you do tomorrow?

MEDEA

Kill my children.

FRIEND

I think you've already done that.

MEDEA

Shouldn't I hurt Jason?

FRIEND

It's not worth the trouble, is it?

MEDEA

When I was a little girl in Asia Minor, I used to dream of America. In the movies I saw, everyone was so beautiful with perfect skin, different colored hair, wearing tank tops and driving cars with no roof. I thought I would be just like that if only I could get here. But when I finally did, I realized that people were suspicious of me. To assure them that I was trustworthy, I hung a big American flag on my front door. It didn't help much. The flag didn't belong to me, even though I bought it with my lunch money.

FRIEND

What're you going to do?

MEDEA

Practice.

FRIEND

What?

MEDEA

Nothing.

FRIEND

Are you feeling unnaturally alone?

MEDEA

I'm not so alone. I can go down to the bodega on the corner, and the woman at the counter will say hello to me. Hello. She'll smile at me, even.

FRIEND

Oh, come on. You're not that pathetic.

MEDEA

Right. I was just kidding. I'll look for another restaurant job. See a lawyer about my status.

FRIEND

That's good. See. A happy ending.

MEDEA

This is the land of starting over.

End of Play

José Lauriano Di Lenola

THE LOST KINGDOM

It was the late summer of 1996 when I met my first prison, Great
Meadow Correctional Facility. Quickly I realized how alien prison life
is. An old-timer told me that in order to survive it, I'd have to adhere
unwaveringly, oftentimes ruthlessly, to the prison codes: rules and values that
dictate every facet of prison life, from associations, strength and weakness,
manhood and respect, to how disrespect should be handled—preferably at
the sharp end of a knife. I studied and mastered the rules, followed them
even when they made no sense. Fast forward a year, several serious conflicts
and a disciplinary transfer sent me to Attica. It was October 3, 1997, roughly
2 a.m. I stood shackled and handcuffed in front of the prison's massive wall.
A tower and its guard, clutching his AR-15, stood silhouetted against long
arcs of lightning that blazed across the sky. The roar shook my chest.

I couldn't imagine prison being any worse than Great Meadow, but
then, it's Attica, the most infamous prison one can think of. There is not a
prisoner who hasn't heard a bit of Attica lore, and of Attica's three defining
traits: inmate to inmate violence—one stabbing a day and at least one murder
a year; bad treatment of prisoners by guards—the only thing more common
than stabbings is the beating-down of prisoners; and the infamous legacy of
the 1971 uprising, one of the bloodiest in the nation's history. I didn't know
what to expect. No matter, I knew the rules and played with the best of
them. But after walking around the prison those initial weeks, I noticed how
different it was compared to Great Meadow. Yes, it was violent and bloody,
but there was a feel to the place I couldn't quite pin down.

One day another prisoner and I were walking C-yard, where he
introduced me to prison writer, Eric Reid. Reid was slightly taller than me,
5' 9", his complexion a "high yellow," and had the build one only gets after
years of workouts. What struck me was his smile and how out of place it
appeared on a man who had served so much time behind the wall. Eric was
famous throughout the prison system for his scathing critiques of prison
culture, and his work circulated in prisons he had never set foot in. At that
time, writing had become a serious hobby for me and I always sought
advice, so meeting him was a great opportunity. Many convicts considered
Eric a penitentiary philosopher, the social commentator for his generation:

the cons who came to prison on the heels of the Attica uprising, men who my generation had come to look up to and call old-timers, or OTs.

Through the years I knew Eric, he gave me some great advice about writing. He said that being a good writer involved an ability to observe the world around you, to make sense of what you see and how it relates to what the story wants to say. But the most forceful advice came via his essay, "The Upside-Down Kingdom." The essay warns:

> If a prisoner isn't careful, by the time he's released from incarceration, his perceptions may become so distorted, that virtuous concepts will appear distastefully unappealing and truth become indistinguishable from lies... Prison environments are generally governed by...cave-dweller values, deviant codes of silence, and non-progressive criminal philosophies... [and] those with eyes to see must bear the burden of those who are blind. (1–2)

Immediately, I understood the sinister implications in his warning. Avoid the prison codes. They are a fraud and will twist the mind and harden the heart; and it is the duty of those who can see, generally the old-timers, to help the blind, new guys.

"The Upside-Down Kingdom" challenged everything I believed and saw in prison. I reevaluated the prison codes I followed and realized how destructive they truly are. But that didn't miraculously change my behavior. It took quite some time to extricate myself from the bowels of prison madness. Through this process, provoked by Eric's words, I asked myself some serious questions. Where are the old-timers and how did Attica become this way: violent, gang infested, ununified? Especially since what most old-timers talk about is what prison used to be like. It would take thirteen years behind Attica's gray wall for any answers to come. By that time, after all of my experiences, I wasn't surprised by what I learned.

This essay is not an analysis of why the 1971 Attica uprising (or riot, depending on which side of the issue you take) took place; it is about why I believe another like it and the conditions that sparked it will never occur again. Eric Reid's work helped me to see this.

Several observations support my belief. They are about the conditions of prison prior to '71 and after, concerning old-timers, unity, the housing and transfer of prisoners, stiffer disciplinary sanctions, and the prison codes.

Prior to the uprising, in many ways prisons were vastly different than they are today. Correspondence, visits, prison jobs, education—everything was severely limited and regulated. Old-timers would take new cons under their wings, serving as mentors to instruct new cons in how to appropriately navigate prison life, obtain an education, and offer some measure of protection until the "new fish" novelty wore off. Prisoners would serve the bulk of their time in one maximum-security prison; transfers were rare. Men rarely received additional time for stabbings or for assaults on Correction Officers (COs). Nor would a CO be disciplined for murdering a prisoner. Simply put, prisons were prisons in every sense of the word. They were called prisons or penitentiaries, not correctional facilities, but little penitence was inspired.

Though the uprising changed many of Attica's conditions for the better, the changes that ensured that another uprising will never happen again have made it worse in other respects.

Housing and transfers have changed greatly. Over a ten-year period, men can expect to see an average of three max prisons; some men see far more. My first year and a half, I was in two prisons. At Attica, according to former Superintendent Conway, there is a steady rotation of approximately 800 prisoners a year who are shuffled throughout New York State prisons.

Attica's population is roughly split with regard to the time prisoners are serving. Previous to the uprising, Attica was used only to house prisoners serving long sentences: a minimum of seven years. Now, just under half of the population is serving medium sentences. This change has obliterated a solid population base that had enabled prisoners to form bonds of common cause and collective awareness. Medium prisoners want nothing to do with Attica's politics. Most stay an average of eight months and their only concern is to get back to medium prisons where conditions and treatment are better. This continuous shuffling prevents any pro-group collective from forming, essentially eliminating opportunity for unity.

The unity that existed pre-uprising no longer exists. Sure, there is a semblance of unity found in the gangs, religious groups, or in one's city of origin. But without a wider cohesiveness these groups present only a type of order amid chaos. Within the gangs there are different cliques that follow different leaders or rules. Groups of city origin are split between west side vs. north side, or Brooklyn vs. Bronx. Though within each group there is a core population that remains in Attica longer than the average prisoner, they must contend with a seemingly endless rotation of men—severely undermining any efforts to unify.

Most gangs initially formed as a way to protect members from rival gangs, or from oppressive authority. For example, the *Netas* are a gang originally formed in Puerto Rican prisons to combat severe abuse by staff. Eventually, their members entered the American prison system where their purposes strayed from group protection and empowerment to drug abuse and prisoner extortion. No longer about holding prisoners together to protect them from the COs, rivalries between such groups here in Attica have caused a significant portion of the violent prisoner-on-prisoner assaults.

Groups also claim ownership over state property: phones, tables, weights, even window rights. Violate these and a fight will erupt. When a table is removed for two weeks for "repairs," conflict inevitably occurs when one group attempts to seize a table from another.

Phones are regulated by men who pick and choose who can use them and when. If you're not down with his crew, you may have trouble getting on the phone, unless you're respected, or have money, or drugs. Phones are a regular cause of fights; you don't mess with a man's ability to call his loved ones. Each yard has five phones for an average of 230 prisoners per yard. Each call can be only fifteen minutes long during a two-hour recreation period. Not everyone gets a chance to make their call. I have witnessed five knife fights over these phones. In the late 90s there was a period when each week one phone was shut down. Because COs can switch them on or off, some prisoners believed it was purposely done to incite conflicts. Perceived ownership of state property has resulted in hundreds of bloody fights, several involving anywhere from five to twenty-plus combatants—what security considers a mini-riot.

After all these years in Attica, I thought I had seen it all with regards to how unity is undermined by conflicts between prisoners and in the ways in which it is swiftly stamped out by administration. But recently I had a conversation with a CO that proved me wrong. One morning I was woken up by the gallery officer, who asked if I could "help the COs" by going to lunch. According to him, a CO who worked "up-front" was locked out of the facility because of an altercation with a visiting Investigator General from Albany. I don't know if that was true, but it was strongly suggested that I go to lunch as a sign of solidarity for the banished CO.

The significance of this request related back to the '71 uprising. It was once common practice that when the anniversary of the uprising arrived, men would virtually *all* go to chow but abstain from eating and sit in silence to commemorate what they'd sacrificed in '71. (There is a common misconception in society that all prisoners attend every meal served. There are three reasons that a good portion of prisoners do not attend every meal: the long wait one has to endure on steel seats after the meal is done; the poor quality of the food; and their ability to cook their own food, purchased from the commissary, in their cells using small hot pots.)

Since it wasn't the anniversary, security would notice so many men going to chow and take it as a sign of support for the banished CO. The "prisoner" side of me was reminded of what the old-timers told me: never do anything for a CO, ever, regardless of whether he is a respectable person who wears his authority well and treats you like a human being. The side of me that agrees with Eric's words would consider the behavior of the CO I would be supporting, and of the one who asked the favor. In this case, my analysis of the particular situation led me to decide to stay in my cell, thereby appearing to side with the OTs. But only two others remained behind with me.

So why would prisoners go to chow at the behest of a CO? Today's generation of prisoners doesn't even commemorate the uprising with a silent chow hall. Some would go from ignorance. Others, to curry favor. In this case, men went to chow in hopes that when their turn for a cell search came, the officer would look the other way when he found a little contraband—i.e., extra books or cassette tapes—or just not search the cell at all. Some did it for an extra shower, phone call, or food ration. Another reason is fear. If they don't go, the CO would find a way to make the man's time uncomfortable. This is why prisoner unity is a thing of the past. How could a prisoner trust a peer who avoids a show of unity for an extra food ration? In this case, I was in the minority.

I recently heard a CO state that the early 80s through the late 90s were some of the most violent years in Attica. As a result of a lack of unity and gang activity, there was an upsurge of prisoner-on-prisoner assaults. Men were willing to go to the "box," or Special Housing Unit (SHU), because the lengths of the penalties were so inconsequential. For a first-time stabbing the average box time was four months, a blink in time for a man serving fifteen, twenty-five, or thirty years. But all that changed when staff became targets of the assaults. A series of incidents caused this new trend.

In 1997 and in 1999, the Bloods in Attica organized a series of attacks against the COs. In the early 2000s, in another facility, there was a stabbing of a Deputy Superintendent for Security and the wounding of a CO. Couple this with an increase in men throwing urine and feces at staff, and the result has been stiffer disciplinary sanctions, and the creation of more SHUs.

These facilities, often called SHU 2000s, were instrumental in breaking prisoners from chronic disciplinary infractions, especially against staff. Now, instead of an average of four months for a stabbing, one receives at least two years. Doing time in a SHU is like living in a void. The mind is not made to endure long periods of silence, inactivity, and solitude. SHU 2000s mean twenty-three hour lock downs, one hour of recreation, sparse food and property, and mostly, being double-bunked. Prisoners can earn more time in a SHU for anything from hoarding a food ration (four slices of bread) to assaults on cell mates.

But the most powerful reason that another '71 riot will never take place is the codes prisoners adhere to. Eric said it best. These are "cave-dweller values, deviant codes of silence, and non-progressive criminal philosophies."

What Eric means by calling prisons upside-down kingdoms is that what should be respected and honored—responsibility, compassion, etc.— is despised and perceived as weakness. The respected man today is the murderer, the dealer, the gang leader, the cunningly violent. These men can do most anything and the majority of the population will turn a blind eye. Reputation governs all social interactions. Prison culture is based on codes of honor. When one's honor is violated, the appropriate response is violence— sudden, unexpected, and savage enough to discourage others from doing the same. There were fights and stabbings in the past, but fistfights were more common. Afterwards, no matter who won or lost, the men would part ways with mutual respect and no desire for retaliation.

Some men practice what I call selective gangsterism. An inmate will tolerate certain offenses from another because the man is respected or feared, but retaliate against a man who can command neither fear nor respect. Similarly, a man will suffer certain behavior from a CO in silence, but will stab a prisoner if he does the same. The man fears the CO or violent inmate more than he does the nonviolent, respectable prisoner. And most conflicts are petty. With a little communication and empathy they could be avoided, but that would be a sign of weakness, and no one wants to be seen as weak.

These codes are not limited to prisoners. Even among the COs, conflict resolution is perceived as a weakness. When an officer feels he's been offended by a prisoner he'll dispense "gallery justice," inciting other prisoners to beat the man up in order to have him removed from the tier. An inmate will assault the man to curry favor with the CO.

I witnessed some gallery justice in late 1997, just after the first attack on the officers by the Bloods. I was new to Attica and housed in B-Block where prisoners served long-term disciplinary sanctions, sixty days or more. Another prisoner and I were standing at our gates and talking, with our mirrors out. It was shower day and because only one of the two stalls was operating, the CO started the shower run earlier than usual. As we were talking I heard two cells open, then saw a Latin King with a knife run into the cell of another inmate, who I later found out was a Blood. There followed a commotion. The COs responded, separated and then restrained the man. Both prisoners received more confinement time and were moved for security reasons.

Aside from the fact that the man was a Blood, the CO wanted to get rid of him because of an argument they had had weeks earlier. Instead of filing a disciplinary report, or speaking with the inmate about his unacceptable behavior, he employed gallery justice. At first, the CO shut off the water in the cell of a third prisoner, the Blood's neighbor; then he told the neighbor that if he wanted it back on, he had to get rid of the Blood. The Blood was feared for his gang affiliation and propensity for violence, but when the Latin King moved onto the gallery, just a few cells away, the CO exploited their rivalry and was able to rid himself of the Blood. Of course, this also ensured future conflicts between these gangs.

Another disturbing trend is the harassment of sex offenders. Most are beaten, subjected to extortion, pressed into prostitution, or raped. (The man who rapes a sex offender is never viewed as a rapist himself. People call him a booty-bandit.) However, there are respected (that is, feared) sex offenders. If he is willing to stab indiscriminately anyone who threatens him, then he will be respected. In here Machiavelli is right. It is better to be feared than loved.[1]

---

[1] The fact that prisoners learn what crimes other men are convicted of, including sex offences, is another disturbing trend. Some men's cases are widely publicized on local news stations. Most are exposed by staff, with little thought given to verifying their claims.

Such acts encourage an inmate's belief that it is acceptable to victimize others. One might say, who cares, the man is a sex offender. But what happens when inmates carry this type of thinking outside? What happens when he is released? Who will be the next acceptable victim?

But no matter their crimes, the economics of prison employment have left everyone more likely to suffer extortion and abuse. Since I have been incarcerated, prisoners' pay has not been increased, and remains, on average, at twenty cents an hour. Yet the cost of living (from the commissary) has skyrocketed over 200 percent, and the quality of the food has decreased. So extortion, drug dealing, and thievery are now necessarily rampant.

Men who engage in these behaviors unwittingly undermine unity, and enable men in their addictions—which ultimately feeds the evidence that in Attica there is mayhem—that the savages are out of hand, stabbing, cutting, assaulting staff, and that more control is needed, more COs, more money, stricter rules. I agree that something needs to be done, but I believe there is a purpose in allowing such behavior to persist, as long as it's confined to prisoner-on-prisoner violence. The purpose is to generate support for the COs' union, to expand CO budgets and power, to justify an oppressive viselike grip of control over Attica's prisoners. The ultimate effect is to perpetuate society's stereotypes and fears of prisoners, that is, we are inherently evil, beyond redemption, can only be controlled by (expensive) iron fists.

There is a balance, though, a counter to that segment of the violent population in Attica. There is a core group of men who have chosen to stay here by not requesting a transfer to another facility. Either because they are close to Buffalo or Rochester (where their loved ones live), housed in the Honor Block, or just weary of constantly moving from facility to facility. (If, for whatever reason one were to request a transfer, it can be delayed anywhere from six to twenty-four months, or flat-out denied, stating "present placement appropriate.") According to former Superintendent Conway, there are approximately 1,000 men that constitute the "core": men who have been in Attica ten years or more who are doing the right things—staying out of trouble, focused on their rehabilitation, and in many ways serving as peacemakers. They are needed as much as the guards. Most hold key job positions (e.g., clerk or teacher's aid) and are looked at less distrustfully by staff. Many are considered old-timers, myself included, at this point.

So what happened to the old-timers of Eric's generation? They are tired of fighting the good fight. They see all that they gained after the uprising steadily decline back into insanity. I am ashamed to say that into their positions arose OTs from my generation who prey on the naive. The movie *Shawshank Redemption* depicts the convict named Red as the quintessential old-timer, but real OTs like Red are so rare you hardly see them anymore. Now they're opportunists, extorting for protection or drugs, pressuring men to engage in homosexuality, or inciting prisoners against one another. This is the most grievous loss I have witnessed for the prison population.

I finally understand what Eric Reid meant in "The Upside-Down Kingdom." In some ways I contributed to the state of prison today by buying into the prison codes. Now, almost sixteen years into my sentence of 26 and one-half years to life, I can understand why old-timers give up on the next generation. Look at what we have to face: victimization by peers, fear of staff, disregard for rules, no unity, and the perception that society really doesn't care about how prisoners are treated.

When Eric was released I thought at the time that life would bring him something good. Sadly, a couple of years ago I read a news report that he took his parole officer hostage with a knife and refused to let her go, and in the end he was killed. I don't know what happened, what his state of mind was. If everything in the report is true, I wonder, was Attica able to twist even his mind?

As much as I would like to say that I am a perfectly reformed, rehabilitated criminal and that when and if I am paroled I will not be a danger to society, I have not been released yet. I have some years to go and have to survive this place even to make it to the Parole Board. I agree with Eric that these prison codes are thoroughly destructive. As much as it galls me to say it, some codes I have to abide by to live without fear of assault, extortion, or rape. What options do I have?

What will my condition be when I'm released? Like Eric? What will society think of me? What is prison doing to me? To the other prisoners? Not many people think about this, at least not openly.

What society should fear is not another '71 riot. You should fear those incarcerated men who are made bitter and vengeful by prison and believe that these prison codes are an acceptable moral system to take out into society—into the community where you live, where your children live. ≋

Angela Arzú

VILLANELLE FOR THE MIXED

She runs her fingers through her lifeless hair
Drags a brush and instantly smoothes it flat
I touch my curls and sigh, like I don't care.

We go to the store for a shampoo/conditioner pair
I see the label "ethnic" and prepare to attack, but
I touch my curls and sigh, like I don't care.

She doesn't understand why this isn't fair
What the "ethnic" has that the "normal" lacks
She runs her fingers through her lifeless hair

You and I, we both breath the same air
Who has the right to pass judgment like that?
I touch my curls and sigh, like I don't care.

"Black hair and white hair are different, so who cares?"
She says as she picks up the shampoo/conditioner pack
And runs her fingers through her lifeless hair

"What makes me ethnic?" I spat
"Just because my skin is darker and yours is matte?
I touch my curls and sigh, like I don't care
As she runs her fingers through her lifeless hair

Georgia A. Popoff

THE AGNOSTIC LOCATES UGANDA ON THE MAP

November wind rattles and moans, unravels
desperate leaves. At the polls, Joy signs in vote.
Locals are the elections that matter.
School board, councilor-at-large.

Sacred ceremony, she has cast
a ballot for 40 years, since turning 18.
She is Viet Nam protest. Civil Rights insistence.
One of a wave of women seizing the streets.

A volunteer greets Joy with a BIC pen.
She is wrapped in orange and brown batik, cheeks
nearly cobalt under fluorescent lights.

Joy wonders if nightmares chase the woman down
like a wildebeest. Who has she left behind
by a roadside? What witnessing must she erase?
Joy is being presumptuous. She is grateful for the woman
greeting neighbors as they approach the table.

The retired judge arrives, the first black man elected
to the city bench. He is one who knows firsthand
that opposition lays in wait like a predator.

The thick honey of the woman's first language
pools beneath her tongue; on her face, the map
of all those who stepped through the other,
lesser acknowledged *Door of No Return.*

She admonishes the judge as he approaches.
Don't forget East Africa, now!

The woman smiles *Welcome.*

JANIS JOPLIN'S COWBELL

I'm a victim of my own insides

Pearl was every kind of fire

I still smell her fingers
all smoky and urgent

gripping me
the way she clutched at life

doubt
the men who played her

She was the region between
drumstick and silence

I was her flint

Forgotten
on this shelf

I bear her brand
on my flank

Maud Poole

YOUNG GIRL WITH CHUTZPAH

Don't be fooled by knife-sharpened
shadows crossing crazy behind me,

the squirrel dangling upside down
from the branch, or the dried-out

finch perched on my finger pointing—
make-believe playthings of a painter,

who tries to force my smile. Of what
do you think I'm capable, if hungry?

Little Angel, Mary's Lambkins? No.
Change my name to Hard Black Thing,

twist my pigtail into a sailor's knot.
Don't call me devil child, for I'm not

a boy (nor would I be). I don't
resemble him—I'm leaner, colder.

Young Girl in Ochre

I was a blue baby, tattooed with marmalade,
licked clean by a mother cat, then forgotten next
to amputee limbs pickling in embalming fluid.

Why keep what's already dead—ashes on a collar,
a tire-built landfill, the petrified turtle. Our ambiguous
bloodlines, curdled. I sew the letter shut on all four

sides, cover my name, the address, the Dutch
stamp with a hundred tiny stitches—silk
thread, creamy like the paper—then fashion

an envelope folded from lead, crinkle
the edges. The strap slips from my shoulder—
like the bridge in London falling down—

I no longer fit the shape of my dress. A jar of crickets
decorates the dining table; the fox hangs from the tupelo.
Warblers steal my yellow ribbon to build their nest

beneath the porch rafters: five white eggs with brown
specks; I eat one, suck the fertilized yoke out
to taste the unborn bird—it's sweet, like a bull's testicle.

Young Girl with Wasp

Though they've forgotten I'm here
I am here, small, quiet of tongue.
Ten people around the long, harvest

table. I fear being given away. I wish
to be an infant again, or a very old
man. A wasp beats on the window,

tries to reach its nest on the other side
high in the sycamore. It won't give up,
nor will I. Mother, I change my name

to Jugular Vein. I bite fresh ginger,
slivers burning. The wasp splits
its skull, frantic to find its way home.

Does my brain measure up? Nothing
from nothing comes, fated. I bruised
my knee on the blackberry wall.

Blood's on my pink nightgown; I left
my bones for the bears to chew down.
I'm a two-headed goat, a drowned

cow. The wasp is dead! I swallowed
ten pennies and peed one out. I saw
a picture of a hermaphrodite, naked.

William Michael Lobko

MILONGA FOR MAUD POOLE

The chances this gauze is infinite
doesn't affect the fact I unwrap
as fast as I can the yellow & blue
blood dries into, all of the affection
red enjoys with them, camaraderie
fake until I make. A moment ago
the trees in the park were both crossbow
& bolt, now they're javelins nodding,
yes they have been thrown, but here
is good, here is water enough to drink
up & convert back into lavender,
buttercream, all of the colors we love
in nightshirts. Scarlet originates
with the cochineal bugs who nested
deep in the brush of the New World.
Unfortunate the natives volunteering
to stain the vestments of cardinals,
a shade they had to protect like
precious metal. I want to dance with you
in spirals like the idle tornadoes
appearing out of nowhere on homework,
on notes on American history highlit
triply, yawn, only the doodle is free.
I won the subway game when the baby
syllabled over & over the shape
of air in its mouth, a concord grape
straining with sun. It is impossible
to choke. The grey-haired guy was kinda
too old but the girl in the sapphire skirt
sculpted him into her bliss, confirmed
the nape of his neck as though to feel
the absence of the alien chip, he's real,
& she must contend with the fact.

The social network is over. Next big thing
is internet-in-things, the car to converse
with the fridge about carbon footprints,
lipstick to tint itself to the hue you want.
You think nothing is the new black,
what can I do but agree that black
expands in the chest like outer space.

Jesse Nissim

Toward an Activist Poetics:
A Conversation with Minnie Bruce Pratt

Minnie Bruce Pratt is a lesbian writer and white antiracist, anti-imperialist activist, born in 1946 in Selma, Alabama. She took her Ph.D. in English Literature at the University of North Carolina at Chapel Hill. In addition to this academic education, she received her education into the great liberation struggles of the 20th century through grass-roots organizing with women in the army base town of Fayetteville, North Carolina, and through teaching at historically black universities. Her essay, "Identity: Skin Blood Heart," now considered a feminist classic, chronicles some of this organizing and is used in universities nationally and internationally. Her poetry as a lesbian mother, *Crime Against Nature,* was chosen for the Lamont Poetry Selection of the Academy of American Poets and as a *New York Times* Notable Book. Other honors include the American Library Association Stonewall Book Award, the Lambda Literary Award, the Audre Lorde Lesbian Poetry Award of the Publishing Triangle, and the Lillian Hellman-Dashiell Hammett Award from the Fund for Free Expression. Her tenth and most recent book is *Inside the Money Machine,* described by one reviewer as "anti-capitalist poetics in action." She does organizing with the International Action Center and the National Writers Union, teaches at Syracuse University, and can be reached at *www.mbpratt.org.*

Jesse Nissim is the author of three poetry chapbooks: *Alphabet for M* (Dancing Girl Press); *SELF NAMED BODY* (forthcoming from Finishing Line Press); and *Day Cracks Between The Bones of The Foot* (forthcoming from Furniture Press Books). Her book manuscript, *Diagram Her Dream of Flight,* was a finalist for the National Poetry Series and a runner-up for the Cleveland State University Poetry Center First Book Award. Her recent and forthcoming poems can be found in *Barrow Street, Requited, H-NGM-N, La Petite Zine, Shampoo,* and *Women Studies Quarterly.* She currently teaches in The College of Arts and Sciences at Syracuse University, where she is a Humanities Faculty Fellow and coordinator of the first year seminars.

This interview is a compilation of several conversations that took place between 2010 and 2012, many of which occurred over breakfast at Mom's Diner on Westcott Street in Syracuse.

Jesse Nissim: How did poetry first enter your life?

Minne Bruce Pratt: It was really about breaking out of a matrix of oppression. I first started writing poetry seriously when I was in college, after I took a class with the professor who taught us Sound and Sense [*Sound and Sense: An Introduction to Poetry,* by Laurence Perrine, first published in 1956, by Houghton Mifflin Harcourt]. Everybody had to write some poems at the end of the semester, so I wrote some poems, and at the end of class, he said, "Well, you all wrote your poems." And then he said, "This is a real poem," and he read one of the poems that I'd written.

I felt like, oh, approval! But I'll tell you an anecdote that goes back to when I was in the 6th grade. This is to say something about how poetry was viewed in my economic, cultural, social matrix. I was about 11, in the 6th grade in Centerville, Alabama, at Alexander Grammar School. We had a geography lesson in which we learned how cold it got up north, and how it was so cold that the cold would force the stones up out of the soil to the surface of the fields, and farmers had to pick up those stones and take them out of the field, and that's where stone fences came from. And that seemed so amazing to me. I thought of the soil as having grown the rocks.

So, I was walking home from school on the day that we had that lesson, with Randy Chisholm, who was a year older than me, and Em Hornsby, who was a year younger than me. I was excited and I was trying to explain the North to them. Of course you understand the North was the enemy, because everyone white in the South was still replaying the Civil War. I was trying to explain this amazing thing about the North to them and I said, "The dirt grows rocks! It's like the dirt grows rocks!" I was trying to explain the mechanism to them. Randy became enraged with me, and said, "Dirt can't grow rocks. The ground can't grow rocks." He was fighting with me over the metaphor.

JN: You believed in the metaphor.

MBP: I was saying that's how it is. And he said no, it cannot be. He was being a literalist, I was being a poet, right, and we were having this quarrel. Then he punched me in the face! My nose began to bleed and he ran off, appalled at what he had done, rightfully so. And Em—this is again part of the moment and the place—Em just happened to have a pair of white gloves. She's a 5th grader and she happened to have a pair of white gloves tucked away in her pocket. She's the perfect lady to this day. Never goes anywhere without her gloves. So she pulled her gloves out and gave them to me and I sopped up my bleeding nose, not able to understand why I couldn't communicate by bringing these disparate ideas together through poetry. Where I grew up, people believed that the Bible was the literal Word of God; every word was true. Metaphor had no place. My kind of metaphor—literally, the bringing together of disparate realities in a truthful way—had no function in a social structure that was essentially fascist on the state level. So this other moment with my poetry at the university in Alabama, this moment when my instructor says that this is a real poem, and he thinks it's good, has to be held against Randy Chisholm punching me in the nose for using a metaphor.

JN: So this matrix of oppression included your relationship to the history of institutionalized racism and capitalism, among other things. The themes of racism and capitalism seem to come together in your latest book, *Inside the Money Machine.*

MBP: I think it's related to the long shift in my family's economic status. They went from land owners and property owners—indeed, from the claim of ownership of other people in the 17th, 18th and 19th centuries—through the long shift of loss of ownership, and the segue into the working class. After the Civil War, the family still had land but everyone had to work. They either had to farm or they had to have an occupation. Teaching and social work are what the women did. But it took until my generation for someone to say, "I'm a member of the working class." I'm the first one who would make that statement.

I understand that just because I'm teaching at a university—that doesn't mean I'm not part of the working class. And of course my work history—the fact that I've never had job security, never had tenure, only had one-semester or one-year contracts, maybe three-year contracts—that history reinforces my understanding that I'm part of the working class.

All the women in my family had earned their living. Nobody assumed that there was gonna be a man who was gonna take care of you in that way. My grandmother had worked for a living, all my aunts had worked for a living, and my parents were part of the working class. They wouldn't have identified themselves in that way, but they were. And when I got to graduate school—to the English Department at the University of North Carolina at Chapel Hill—I knew I was gonna have to earn my living.

JN: It sounds like you had at least one instructor who encouraged you to become a poet. Did you have any faculty support around your political interests? Were any of your graduate school professors in the English Department involved in Women's Liberation?

MBP: No, no. There were no women faculty. There was no program called Women's Studies, but there was Women's Liberation that put out a little mimeographed newsletter for 2 cents each, and they passed out literature in front of the library and had consciousness raising groups. Some of the people who were involved were in the English department. But there were only a bunch of women grad students, because it was the middle of the Vietnam War and the men were being drafted, and the department had to fill their slots somehow to keep the graduate school going. They let women in. So there were an unusually high percentage of us in the graduate program, some of whom were involved in Women's Liberation. I didn't know them right away. I was married and I had this baby, and I would walk past their literature table in front of the library, but I would cross to the other side of the quad so I wouldn't go near it because it frightened me. And I often tell that story in my classes to explain how you can be frightened of something that then you understand you were frightened about for a good reason, in the sense that if you open yourself to those ideas, then profound change will happen in your life.

JN: I know what you mean, when you feel the pull towards something that you know you identify with, but that would break things open…

MBP: And—you feel the pull, and it's terrifying.

JN: Because who knows what that means?

MBP: Right. And you know something will happen. If you're honest with yourself, that is.

JN: Exactly. And you don't know what your life will look like as a result of that change.

MBP: So, I stayed away, but one of the women who worked at the literature table was in a Shakespeare seminar with me. This was during my second pregnancy when I was pregnant with Ben. That was the fall of '69. I was very pregnant. I was in my last trimester, and I was trying to finish the semester without going into labor. And the atmosphere was just…the male professors would refuse to get on the elevator with me and they'd make jokes about how they were afraid I would go into labor on the elevator. So they just wouldn't get on the elevator when I was on it.

JN: That sounds so demoralizing to have these supposed mentors behave with such disregard and to have them foster an atmosphere of fear toward the female body. Of course, now we would call it sexism, discrimination, harassment, but at the time, what was it like for you?

MBP: I would say it was tremendous loathing, loathing of the female body, an incredible level of sexism that was quite commonplace. For example, I tried to get Married Student Housing, and they wouldn't give it to me because I wasn't a man with a family, I was a woman with a family. In response to this woman-hating, there was Women's Liberation, and the beginning of Women's Studies. One of the women in my Shakespeare seminar was active in Women's Liberation and she did a paper on the women in *Henry V* or one of those history plays. She did this early piece of what we would now call Women's Studies in that seminar. And she was just ridiculed as being crazy, as being silly, as being trivial. They ultimately failed her. They failed her at her comps twice. They wouldn't let her through. There was nothing wrong with her scholarship at all; in fact, she was a forerunner, but they wouldn't let her through the program. I was very, very pregnant at the time. I didn't know her at all. The seminar was at night, and one night I got out and we were parked near each other in the parking lot, and she came over to the car, and I rolled the window down, and she said to me that she just wanted to tell me that she thought it was very brave of me not to drop out, but to keep going and to stay in school while I was this pregnant. She said she knew it was hard and that she wanted me to know that she understood that. And I said thank you and then I cried all the way home. I had a 20-mile commute. I cried all the way home because it was the only time anyone had acknowledged female oppression and solidarity at the same time.

JN: It sounds like she recognized what you were trying to do, and against what forces, and with no support. And then it wasn't invisible anymore because she had verbalized it to you.

MBP: Right. And she had a consciousness because she was involved in Women's Liberation. She could see exactly what was happening. I got to know her and later we shared an office and she gave me a copy of Robin Morgan's book, *Sisterhood is Powerful.* We had lots of conversations, and I began to go to some of the Women's Liberation events. They would have these all-women parties, before there was a big gay/straight split in women's liberation or in anything, so everybody went. All the heterosexual women came, and all the lesbians, and all the bisexuals, and all the everybody came, but there was no discussion or theorizing at that time that some people at the events might be female-born but identify as more complexly gendered or as transgender.

JN: I imagine that at the time, the "all-women" inclusiveness made it easier for you to attend than if it had been a "lesbian" party, since you were identifying as straight.

MBP: Well, in that case I couldn't have gone because I was married. But I went, and there I was with women who were making out in the corner. And also that was where I danced with the first woman I ever danced with. So there was all of that, and over time I was reading more and increasingly understanding feminist theory. I started writing for *The Newsletter,* which eventually turned into *Feminary.* I did reviews for them for a while, and I wrote articles for them, and that was while I was still married. That was the beginning of my being a political writer, the beginning of my work that eventually emerged into poetry and essays.

JN: I know you've told me before how you've used your own life as the core for the theoretical work that you've written, and that you don't separate your scholarship from personal experience. I was wondering if you engage in a similar process when making poetry. How do you open out your poems to engage different voices and subjectivities?

MBP: That's really important because it raises questions about the relationship between the I and the many. For example, what's the relation of the "I" to the "us", or the "I" to the "we"? And who is the "we," you know, theoretically, politically, and poetically, who is the "we"? To write the poems that would become *Inside the Money Machine,* I went back and reread a lot of left-identified writers and so-called "proletarian poetry" that was being written by so many different people, especially in the 30s. I looked specifically at how poets were dealing with their pronouns. When are they using "I," when are they using "us," and when are they saying "you"?

Overall, I saw a distance between the speaker of the poems and the working class. They were exhorting the working class, or they were appealing to the working class, or they were describing the working class, but they were not being *of* and *in* the working class in their poems. One poet for which this was not true was Langston Hughes. Not necessarily early on, but eventually, he began to write poems that merged his life as an African American person in the U.S. with his class consciousness. In these later poems, I felt like these consciousnesses were united, and with his use of the pronoun "we," Hughes was quite concise and precise about the black working class. I think those are his most tremendous poems. I became interested in watching him work through this conscious identification with workers while at the same time claiming the specifics of other aspects of an oppressed identity, and I started to take that very seriously for my own work. I also looked back at Neruda, re-read Nazim Hikmet, and did a lot of other reading. I had read *The Communist Manifesto* very late in my life and so much of its language was poetry, so beautiful. Theoretically, I understood that I was part of the working class because I'd had enough education in Marxist economics to know that. But I started to ask myself if that's where I was with my poetry and what it might mean to write about the things in the *Manifesto* from the inside out. What would it be like to write about the life I'm living, I mean, to really be in it, really notice the things that are covered up by capitalist ideology?

I very definitely related this idea to my thinking about growing up under segregation, and how that was an oppressive ideology that was laid down on top of reality, and that had educated me to filter my experience of reality in a certain kind of way. The result was that, because of white supremacy, I didn't see things. I didn't look, I didn't hear, I didn't pay attention, except in little bursts. I didn't see injustice running rampant in the daily lives of people.

I started thinking about capitalism that way too. That oppressive ideology is laid down on top of our perceptions, and it causes us not to look and hear and see and feel. I thought, can I write poems that will break through that in some way and reveal what we're living, what we're actually in the middle of? In particular, in relation to me, how do I really understand myself to be part of the "us," the working class, and how can I claim that? I think these questions are certainly related to my being of the generation in my family who understands that we're not the people that the powers-that-be kept telling us we were. Even though my parents were living it—the working class life—they weren't claiming it. That's how I began working with the poems that would go into the book, *Inside the Money Machine*.

JN: A poet can strategize and form an idea and she might say, okay, I'm going to write a poem about this idea. And that's a very different process than being engaged with physical perception and current events and consciousness in a kind of holistic way, going about the day and then seeing what arises. My process as a poet usually involves composing in that kind of a perceptual space, and it always involves my not knowing where the poem will take me. I'll start with a method and find my way through that procedure or task into the subject matter. If I'm not having some kind of discovery about language, I lose interest in it and I start to wonder, well, what's the difference between this and writing a thesis or an essay or a prose narrative? What about you? You were saying earlier that you used to work from a more thematic agenda.

MBP: For many years, my process generally was very tightly tied to my political process. And I might produce prose, journalistic articles or creative nonfiction, or even straight theory on those topics that my political activism addressed. But of course I would be wanting to write poetry also, and I would. What that meant was whatever I was working on politically was closely tied to what was happening in my personal life. For instance, *Crime Against Nature* was about what happened to me as a lesbian mother, and it was theoretically about notions of femaleness, motherhood, sexuality, sin, the female body and outlawed sexuality. I was thinking about all of that, because I was living the experience I was writing about. The same is true of *S/HE,* which is creative nonfiction from a point in my life where I was trying to understand the fluidity and flexibility of gender, the complexities of gender in a new way, as someone who's a feminist and an antiracist white person, and as someone who's attracted to transgender, and has been from a very early age. So I'd say my poetry has been very different from the poets who write as poets first, where the poetry is a collection of moments, or moments of thought. My poetry is the expression of a life lived in political struggle. The moments of experience that are touchstones for my poetry are lived as moments in a consciously political life. And I have to say I have never written as a poet first and foremost. I've written as a political person who's a poet.

JN: How do you go about making poems differently than you'd go about writing in other genres? What does your poetry-making process look like day to day?

MBP: Well, I started writing the poems in *Crime against Nature* about the experience of losing custody of my children. And I had enough encouragement from people, like audiences at readings and Nancy Bereano, my editor at Firebrand Books, specifically, to think that maybe if I went toward those poems, there would be people who would want to read them. And that gave me enough confidence, or enough support to go into something that was terribly painful. Then I went back and I looked through my notebooks at that time, and I made notes of different situations, or themes, or images that resonated, and so I had this raw material that I would browse through, which is not unlike my going out now and walking in the world.

JN: It sounds like recently you've been taking walks outside and starting poems while on the walks, and earlier on you were gleaning and gathering more from your own notebooks?

MBP: Yes. And then I'd see what would pull me, what would bring me into the poem. So it isn't a totally rational or intellectual decision, but it's the decision to take a topic or a theme and plummet, you know, drop the words like a plumb into the depths, and see what's there. That has been my mode. And I do think it's tied to narratives also. It's tied to the fact that my cultural grounding is absolutely in communication through narratives, out of my rural southern background. The way one communicates to another person is through a narrative. Especially if you have something very important you want to say to them, you absolutely would communicate that through narrative, which lends itself to these longer expositions.

JN: I think what we're really talking about is the long-term writing process. It's not simply making a poem, but sustaining that practice of plummeting down in the way you describe, and following it through. We have to keep dropping into language to explore things and then move through the material we have generated and shape it, ultimately, in one direction over another. That can be hard for me because I don't always want to decide for sure in which direction to take a poem. I often try a few different directions with the same material to see which interests me more.

MBP: I would always be testing my poems with an audience as well. I would take the poems I was writing to a house party or a little community reading or something, and I'd read and people would talk to me about the poems afterwards. So I was always testing what I was communicating through the poems, which tended to be strongly narrative, though often impressionistic and metaphoric. With *Inside the Money Machine,* not as much, but I definitely tested drafts of the poems with actual people. I'd give the poems to the woman who worked at the laundromat, or the woman who opened the letters at the office, or the woman who cut my hair. I'd want to hear from several people that the poems rendered a certain common reality accurately to their satisfaction before I'd be willing to publish them. And that's happened a lot with these poems. It's a very important part of my process.

JN: That "testing" reminds me of Mark Nowak's work. I teach *Coal Mountain Elementary* in my "Documentary Poetics" class, and Nowak talks in interviews about how he brought the book manuscript back to the workers in the mining community of Sago, West Virginia, and since their voices and testimonies comprise a huge segment of the book, he worked with them to create a play from the book, so he could test the accuracy of the work with the people who had lived it before he published it for a wider public.

MBP: Every book is shaped by its context, and the project of the poems for each of my different books was part of my dealing with a context, a moment, that had political significance. And the audiences for each book are people who take that issue, not just seriously, but for whom that issue is their lives. For *Inside the Money Machine*, the process was with people who were workers and people of oppressed identities within capitalism. And not because I said to myself, oh, I'm gonna write about those people, but because I am of that struggle. I love that part of being a poet. I love it, you know. I love putting up the poem about cutting hair on the bulletin board in the writing program area and having one of the staff come to me and say, "Would you print that out and autograph it for me because I wanna give it as a holiday present to my sister who is a beautician." And I love what happens when all of the poems are put together in a book and they become a longer narrative argument, not just about individual people or moments of work, but about the entire system.

JN: I think the multivoiced aspect of the book allows readers to imagine many different experiences. I know from our other conversations that it's very important to you that the work be relatable in a direct way to whoever might pick it up.

MBP: My language and my poetics, my decisions around style and voice were very fundamentally shaped back at the beginning, by my emerging out of a political cultural movement where we talked very rambunctiously about these issues. Like what does it mean to be "accessible," and how do you use a language that is interesting and accessible? I really translate that into the question of how to have a poetry language that's as interesting as people's real language. Because often "accessibility" is talked about as if ordinary working people have a really dumbed down, uninteresting language. But that actually isn't the case. Standard academic language is perhaps the most boring language I've ever encountered. But ordinary people's conversational language is incredibly lively. So I went in that direction, as you can see.

JN: I appreciate the way these poems are rooted in the world in all of those textures of language and machines and bodily movement. Being poets allows us the opportunity to really listen and to hear, you know, the music and the rhythms that create truly stunning patterns from ordinary speech and mundane motion. Something physical in a poem, a machine-like opening and closing over and over, gives readers a sense of time moving, which itself becomes a kind of poetic pattern that holds a poem together and creates structure.

Inside the Money Machine uses language to show the transformation of communication and experience into a measurement. By this I mean, the poems reveal how people's life stories are held captive in actual money, in the dollar bill. And it raises the question of how to decode their lives so we can make contact with these people and know their stories. If the dollar bill is a little book that contains a life's work, then when the bill changes hands, someone's life is no longer known. These kinds of moments pop up throughout the book. They show a possibility of truth within language and also a threat of invisibility or erasure. It's especially the case when the bills get counted and translated into profit. I'm curious about whether those metaphoric choices were conscious or not. Maybe you could just talk a little more about the significance of language. What's at stake with language in the context of the larger objective of the book, which is to expose the capitalist regime and what it does to us, how it reduces us?

MBP: I spent years and years studying to understand the world I was in the middle of. And that meant going back and trying to understand what enslavement of other people meant within the economic system, and going forward and trying to understand industrial capitalism and capitalism within the dominations of colonialism and imperialism. It took me years of study, including studying Marxist economics with Milt Neidenberg, to whom I dedicated the book. For instance, how the dollar bill even came to *be* had a very profound influence on me, because of course we handle dollars every day, and that money becomes "naturalized," just like the sun, or the rain, or the roads. Money is thought of as being completely natural, but, in fact, it's artificially constructed by the capitalist system. The history of the physical form of money influenced the poems, because of what money represents in human labor, what the dollar bill actually holds in its exchange form, that is, it conceals the value of human labor that has been exploited and seized under capitalism.

And so the book is an attempt to say, we need to look at this from another angle, that is, we're inside the money machine, and it's our lives that are in those dollar bills. Could we think about the millions of lives that it took to produce that dollar bill and all the other dollar bills? Our labor is hidden in this flimsy piece of paper. But, of course, our power is so much greater than that piece of paper. The book is not just my story, but all these other stories that we don't know, that we don't think about, unless we liberate ourselves from being held imaginatively captive, and intellectually and politically captive, within an economic system that we're told is natural.

JN: What you're saying about the physical evidence of our labor is really interesting. I certainly see that evidence all over these poems. But, when we look at our own ATM balance, we've lost our own story of the effort that makes that number, that number. So for me, your act of gathering all those narratives is like putting the body back into the work, making the time and impressions and sensations during work, making all of that tactile and real again. All of that experience that gets lost in the measuring, comes back to us through the poems.

MBP: I think that, in a general way, what you're describing was absolutely my intent. When I was writing these poems, I would walk around, and I would try to physically and imaginatively and emotionally be with the person who was working or talking to me. And I let myself try to feel as much as I could of what it would be like to be them and to be in their place eight hours a day or more. I tried to imagine this with my body, and my everything. I very consciously cultivated those moments you mentioned because I also very consciously understood that we are living inside an economic system that is hiding the reality of the work and of working people. The relation of our work in our lives as working people is being hidden in the abstraction that you're talking about. In the Dow Jones figures. In the federal debt figures. In the flattening out of the rhetoric that is applied to just about anything. Like an NFL strike. Like a teachers' strike. The language and the figures are abstracted to carry out the ideology of the system. Not because there's something intrinsically wrong with numbers, but because the numbers and the abstractions are meant to obscure the relation of those numbers to us. I really want myself and the people who are reading the poems to feel the connection of our bodies with each other. There is this other reality that we live in all the time, but we don't necessarily consciously recognize that reality because the language and the figures, and the voices of bosses and corporations, are telling us something else. Like the word "productivity." What does productivity mean? It means bosses and corporations pushing workers harder and harder to get more and more profit. The extra value produced by workers working harder and harder is not returned to us in benefits, health insurance, vacation days, or retirement pensions. Instead, companies are making record profits but cutting benefits, trying to make people work longer and harder for less money. That's what "productivity" means.

JN: It reminds me of the abstraction in the language of war that so many contemporary poets are working with. Juliana Spahr and Solmaz Sharif come to mind as two poets working to challenge the abstractions embedded in the terms used to describe acts of violence in war. And I'm also thinking about the ways in which we're unaware as consumers. In the act of consuming, we separate that from our own act of working, and there's a real danger in overspending as well.

MBP: We are defined as consumers and not as workers. We hear the language of consumerism all the time. And we're told the solution to the current economic crisis is to consume more. But, people don't have jobs to buy anything, so the answer is not "consumption" but how to create a new, just economic system. It actually warrants a real discussion about why there's a crisis.

JN: As we're talking, I'm thinking there could be a companion book to this about credit card debt.

MBP: And what's striking to me about the way you're reading the poems is that you are reading these poems in the way that I meant to communicate—but without having to have read any of the political or economic theory. Now we're in a dialogue about these issues, you know, we're able to talk about these issues with each other. And that was also deliberate on my part. I wanted to infuse the poems with theory that most people haven't had access to because of the history of capitalism and its suppression of information and conversation about socialism and communism in this country. So that's pretty fascinating to me.

JN: Me too. The poems do generate their own discussions that might lead your readers toward further study and further action. For example, in these lines from "Arwhoolie" the speaker of the poem demonstrates how the collective experience can be shared, felt and voiced:

> The clouds move their light weight without thought.
> Yet we are tired. To keep going we call out loud.
> Now I make that sound here on paper, the unworded vowel
> deep, climbing up out of grief into the mouth... ≋

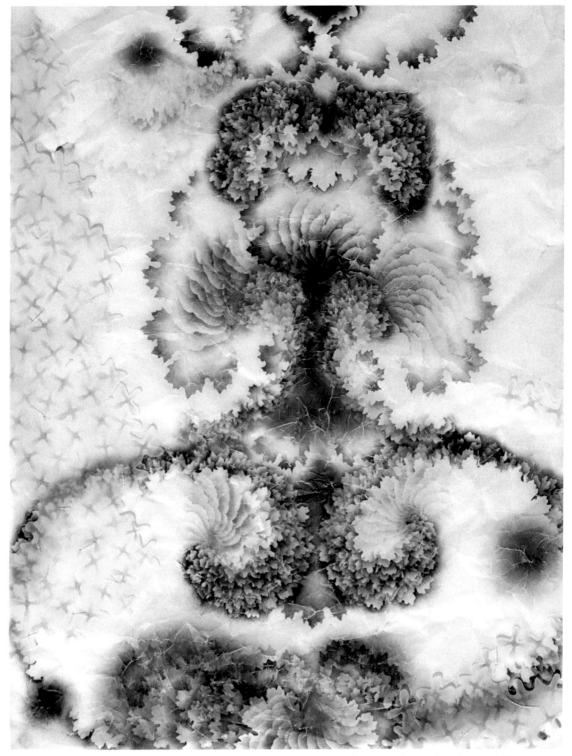

Joy Taylor, *Who's Afraid of Symmetry #1,* powdered graphite on frosted polyester film, 27"x21", 2009

Travis Head, *Sea Spread,* photograph, dimensions variable, 2011

Travis Head, *25 Year Hunt,* photograph, dimensions variable, 2012

GLENN GOLDBERG, *Small Mystery 23,* acrylic, ink and watercolor on canvas, 9"x12", 2011

GLENN GOLDBERG, *Small Mystery 16,* acrylic, ink and watercolor on canvas, 9"x12", 2011

Carmen Lizardo, *Untitled*, tintype, 3.5"x6", 2012

CARMEN LIZARDO, *Untitled,* tintype, 3.5"x6", 2012

STEVEN SIEGEL, *Bridge 2,* Arte Sella, Italy, paper, variable dimensions, 2009

STEVEN SIEGEL, *Carbon String,* Neuberger Museum of Art, Purchase, New York,
shredded rubber tires, 10" diameter x 230', 2001

CRAIG J. BARBER, *Marney with Sunflowers,* wet plate collodion photograph, 8"x10", 2011

CRAIG J. BARBER, *Tom—Vineyard Foreman,* wet plate collodion photograph, 8"x10", 2012

STEVE CARVER, *Four Horsemen,* acrylic and alkyd on board, 30.25"x40.25", 2011

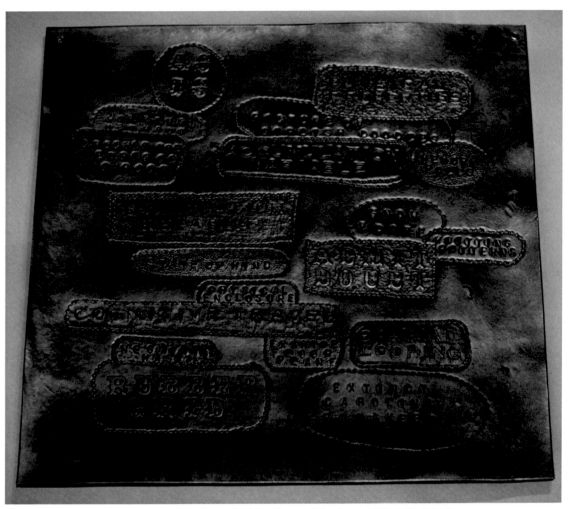

JEN PEPPER, *Admit Doubt,* hand-tooled leather with dyes, 19"x16", 2010

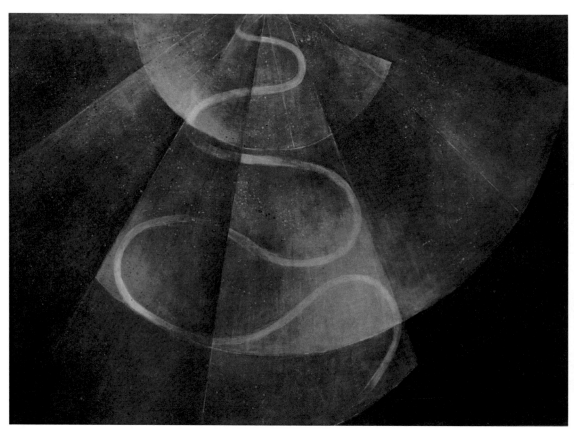

EVA BOVENZI, *From Blue Number Twenty-Two,* acrylic on canvas, 60"x84", 2009

Elisabeth Condon, *Woke Up to Find It Missing,* acrylic on linen, 57"x72", 2011

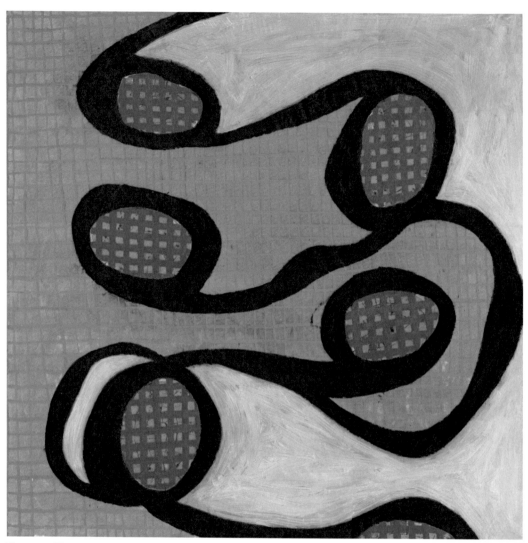

DONISE ENGLISH, *Swoopy,* encaustic on board, 24"x24", 2012

ELIZABETH TERHUNE, *WalkingDreamer, ForestStreamers,* watercolor
and ink on paper, 22"x16.25", 2012

DANDELYON HOLMES-NELSON, *Untitled,* oil on paper, 18"x24", 2012

DANDELYON HOLMES-NELSON, *Untitled,* oil on paper, 18"x24", 2012

ERIK SCHOONEBEEK, *Untitled (C-54),* gouache and acrylic on book cover, 5.4375" x 8.75", 2012 [from the collection of Monica Herman, courtesy Jeff Bailey Gallery]

TAMAR ZINN, *Broadway / Passages 1,* oil on wood panel,
28"x15.5", 2011

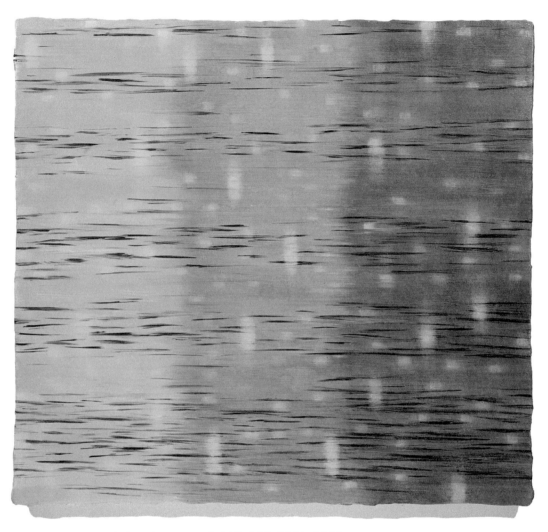

ELLEN KOZAK, *Glade,* oil on panel, 20"x22", 2011–2012

STEPHANIE McMAHON, *Thaw,* oil on panel, 48"x60", 2011

MAUREEN FORMAN, *Refresh,* graphite and charcoal on paper, 20"x30", 2011

DIANE DIROBERTO, *NYC Billboard,* silver gelatin archival print from black and white film, dimensions vary, 2005

Osvaldo Oyola

THOSE ARE THE THINGS THAT BEING IN LOVE'S ABOUT: PRINCE'S "IF I WAS YOUR GIRLFRIEND" AND THE QUEERING OF THE POPULAR LOVE SONG

Probably most famous for the apocalyptic hit, "1999," and 1984's *Purple Rain* album, Prince has had a long and successful career, selling over 80 million records, writing and producing all his music and often even playing all the instruments himself. He's won seven Grammy awards, a Golden Globe, an Academy Award, and in 2004 was inducted into the Rock n' Roll Hall of Fame. He's a flamboyant performer, a demanding bandleader, and a rock guitar virtuoso, and his unflinching and flagrant mix of religiosity and sexuality has often been the focus of both his music and his media-scrutinized personal life. Citing references as varied as James Brown, Santana, P-Funk, Joni Mitchell, and Miles Davis, Prince is considered the founder of the "Minneapolis Sound," a fusion of rock, funk, R&B, and New Wave. In addition to his well-known mainstream success, Prince's deep catalog, said to include over 300 unreleased tracks, demonstrates a wide range of styles and dumbfounding talent that has influenced countless popular musicians.

Leaving aside *Purple Rain,* Prince's 1987 double album *Sign o' the Times* is considered by many hardcore fans and music critics alike to be his best work. Built around the notion that less is more, Prince was initially criticized for sticking to the stock sounds that came with his Fairlight CMI digital sampler and his generous use of the Linn LM-1 drum machine, but the dark, sometimes even muddy, sound of the recording and the minimalist instrumentation on most of the tracks reveal the strength of Prince's songwriting, his creativity, and his willingness to bend and distort expectation with a lyrical and sonic playfulness that challenges the listener to think beyond the obvious gender stereotypes inherent in most popular love songs.

"If I Was Your Girlfriend" is the quintessential example of this playfulness, and I'd argue the best song on an album of standout tracks. Its approach to the "take me back" pop love song complicates the construction of gender roles common to these songs and connects gender confusion to an attitude that makes the song's speaker worthy of being taken back. The second song on the third side of the vinyl (or the second disc in the CD version), "If I Was Your Girlfriend," opens with a sample of orchestral strings warming up, directing the listener away from what turns out to be probably the most stripped down and muddy track of the bunch, and separating it from the over-the-top competitive duet with Sheena Easton, the Top 40 "U Got The Look." A street vendor's voice is capped with a sample of a church organ playing a snippet of Mendelssohn's "Wedding March" (from *A Midsummer Night's Dream*), which introduces the conciliatory tone that Prince will adopt in singing this plea to a former lover, and that is at odds with the idea of "Boy versus girl in the World Series of Love" that "U Got the Look" dwells upon. The conciliatory tone brings the lovers' roles into an ambiguous space that uses the stereotypical positions as guideposts to offer something different from and more intricate than our socialized gender standards that can never quite be escaped.

This gender confusion is characterized by simultaneous masculine and feminine desire in the singular figure of the singer and emphasized sonically through the song's dark sound. "If I Was Your Girlfriend" is muddy as muddy gets: an anemic snare and a muted kick drum, an echoing cascade of electronic handclap with a bit of repeated fuzzed-out synth, and a bass line that seems occasionally erratic, but that keeps the disparate parts in place perfectly. Emerging from the wedding march, the song establishes the admixture of its dark plea and its attempt at reconciliation, suggesting the problems that led to the break-up the song seeks to overcome. Prince's voice comes crying across those sounds, getting ready to do some pleading, since a man should not be ashamed to plead sometimes. These pleas come mostly in the form of questions left unanswered, suggesting the singer's openness to something different from the previous relationship between himself and the beloved. He asks, his voice pitched up a bit in what might be his Camille persona, "If I was your girlfriend would you remember? / And tell me all the things you forgot when I was your man?" The opening lyric immediately creates a distinction between the role of boyfriend and that of "girlfriend" (in terms of a woman's "girlfriends"), but he is complicating the distinction by adding a sexual component to that "girlfriend" relationship through the very desire the song is expressing—reconciliation with a lover. The song's conceit is taking advantage of the tensions inherent in the boyfriend/girlfriend dichotomy and not only the different ways the words are used, but also how "girl/boy" and "friend" are joined to establish something different from generic friendship through the role of gender in its manifestation. His equating of "girlfriend" and "best friend" in the second part of the first verse suggests a level of intimacy absent from typical girlfriend/boyfriend relationships. Prince's play with these tensions asserts a kind of pansexuality that enfolds the surface understanding of the song—which is emblematic of stereotypical male desire to seduce his lady—into broader context.

As the song continues, Prince uses a myriad of vocal overdubs that double certain lines for emphasis. These voices are bizarre in pitch and tone, sometimes a higher harmony, sometimes a very low one, sometimes both, broken into a staccato, low in the mix, slowed down as to be warped, presenting varied depth that is juxtaposed to the simplicity of the instrumentation. Listen to: "If I was your one and only friend, / Would you run to me / If somebody hurt ya, / Even if that somebody / Was me?" in the second verse and listen to the other voices move in around Prince's plea. The weird effect is sonically queer and serves to convey simultaneity of desire that escapes easy categorization. On the surface, the lyrics are directed toward offering a new form of intimacy, but underlying voices, pitched down and delivered in a menacing staccato do not let the listener forget that masculine desire and the sexual interest fuel the song despite its attempts to offer something different.

The differentiation the song offers is not without its problems. The lyrics' characterization of friendship between women is actually rather funny in its superficiality: helping her pick out her clothes, or "go[ing] to a movie and cry[ing] together." But at the same time, he does undermine these assertions. In the lines, "Baby, can I dress ya? / I mean, help you pick out your clothes / Before we go out?" there is tension between that aggressive masculine force and what he is portraying as a gentler, helpful feminine force. The lines that follow, "I ain't sayin' ya helpless, / But sometimes those are the things that being in love's about," mitigate that undercurrent of sexual desire that keeps slipping to the front of the song.

This willingness to play the feminine role also potentially obfuscates the gender of the beloved. Is the song's speaker singing to a man or a woman? The assumption is that it is a woman because it is a man singing, but can we be sure? Not even the fact that he addresses the beloved as "girl" later in the song makes it necessarily clear, given the colloquial language attributable to gay life. The ambiguity of such language is productive in reading this song as queering the normative modes of romantic love to open a space not limited by gendered positions.

The warbling synth of the song's coda rises and falls like a muted orgasmic echo as Prince speaks directly to the song's object. The lyrics ride that tension of the girl/boyfriend relationship: "Is it really necessary for me to go out of the room just because you want to undress?" questions the level of intimacy in different kinds of relationships. Or, "We don't have to make children to make love / and we don't have to make love to have an orgasm," which addresses the ambiguity most directly, refers on one level to the potential consequences of straight sex (pregnancy) and the range of possibilities lovers have to pleasure each other. Simultaneously, the song is also widening those possibilities, explaining that the reproductive function of sex is not what defines it as "love."

Let me take a breath here and say I love how coarse Prince can be, how he mixes profane and divine in a lot of his work. He isn't afraid to be nasty, and he gets progressively nastier in the song (in a good way, as far as I'm concerned) as he further subverts the expected relationship dynamic to put himself in the traditionally submissive role while simultaneously keeping that dark, aggressive—perhaps obsessive—undertone: "You could do it because I'm your friend. I'd do it for you. / Of course I'd get naked in front of you. / (And when I'm naked what should I do?)" The playfulness of it becomes cajoling: "How can I make you see that it's cool? / Can't you just trust me? / If I was your girlfriend you could. / Oh, yeah I think so..." The "Oh, yeah I think so..." is delivered with a cadence that implies he is answering to something the beloved said in response to "If I was your girlfriend you could."

The warbling synth begins its final rise in pitch and he begins to talk/sing faster, further developing the intimacy he desires. After asking what gets his lover off, he adds, "If I was your girlfriend would you tell me? / Would you let me see you naked then? / Would you let me give you a bath? / Would you let me tickle you so hard you'd laugh and laugh? / Would you let me kiss you there? You know, down there where it counts...? / I'll do it so good I swear I'll drink every ounce." Drink every ounce? While this can literally be a reference to cunnilingus, he is playing with those sexual roles and identities again, moving up and down a freaky continuum. "Drinking every ounce" is something a boyfriend would expect a girlfriend to do, and now that he is in the role of "girlfriend" he needs to learn to submit to her desires. Again, the undermining of heteronormativity in the song put so-called "straight sex" into the ambiguous realm where queer sex already exists, where lovers have to adopt, reject and subvert socialized roles to pleasure each other and share sexual intimacies.

At song's end, the orgasmic release narrows down to just the soft, almost heartbeat-like, drum machine as Prince sings, "And then I'll hold you tight and hold you long and together we'll stand in silence / and then we'll try to imagine what it looks like / Yeah, we'll try to imagine what silence looks like..." The idea of visualizing silence may seem on the surface to be a bit of Prince's occasional pseudo-meaningful lyricism, but in light of the farrago of gendered experience explored in the song, considering the meaning of this silence is an important takeaway. Not only does "silence" play on the taboo nature of the song's homosexual overtones, but it also describes a space free of the fixed identities that come along with gender labels. Shared silence is the intimate space where lovers needn't worry about fulfilling the expectations of girlfriends or boyfriends, of men or women or other, but can simply be together.

"Yeah, we'll try to imagine..." The final lyric is left open and unfinished, and with a final fading hand-clap, the song disintegrates into the opening descending tom-tom drums of "Strange Relationship." Given the confusion and competing desires present in the singer's plea, the song's ending suggests that the reconciliation being sought comes ultimately not from the spoken offer to be something different, but from freedom from having to be something specific, to fulfill a particular socially determined role. "If I Was Your Girlfriend," by lyrically queering these roles over a minimalist soundscape, provides an open field which allows the listener to identify more broadly with the song's speaker. Whereas most popular love songs serve to reinforce unrealistically rigid ideas of gender, Prince's questions entertain the possibility of being free to alternately fulfill the specific forms of intimacy the beloved may desire. ≋

David Lloyd

THE MIRACULOUS BODY

I was worrying

about Provincetown,
the lawn to mow, forms to fill,

a reception to attend, and the rip
a jet bound for Iraq can make in a sky distended

with God's angers, opened
like an apocalyptic piñata

to deluge the earth with frogs, gnats,
locusts, viruses—everything

humans deserve—when a hawk screeched
by Limestone Creek, and a cardinal asserted himself,

and the sky remained
unripped, and it struck me

that in a few hours fireflies would perforate the dark,
that bats hadn't abandoned us,

that the grass masks grasshoppers,
that slugs would not neglect

their nocturnal appointments,
that the tousled, deep-red bee balm

by the window where I write
might lure a hummingbird so close

I could reach and enclose within hands
his miraculous body, if he would let me.

Julie Gamberg

Cows, Elephants

Travelers fail to see patterns. Perhaps because
The book refuses to identify them. Each occurrence,
it slyly implies, fabricated for this circumscribed moment,
It's already gone.

Monkeys. Yet monkeys. And small brown
people with profound lines on their upper
cheeks. And hooved creatures. They do seem
to reappear.

And water. Surely these things repeat. The book
enjoys the unique. The *ghost orchid or corpse
flower.* It likes a bit of the macabre too, a bit of
the quietus.

The traveler has questions. Does it all really end in death?
Can it be this luminescent? Are we at the absolute center?
Even when someone cuts in front of us in line?
We've come a long way for this.

The traveler abhors lines. In a line we are spun
back to earth and shoved into orthodoxy.
We want to flash our book and
be moved ahead. We have our aspirations.

To cross all that water, to get to the other side,
to find out what's inside. To be the Pallid Squill
so floriculturists dream of you and pilgrimage
to see where you once grew.

When to Go

The air is rusted metal on the tongue
and every morning the garbage truck clanks
up and down the block. The door to the street opens
onto a line of people waiting to order bacon beignets
and wrap their palm around a mug of coffee.

Now is the time to go.
Not during the dry season.
Not when the wars have ended.
Not when there is enough money in the bank.
Not when the long baton of words leaves you muddled and blurred.

The book asks questions:

1. In the waxy black night,
from the hub of your block,
which constellations are choked from view?
2. In the tender of your belly,
in the nucleus of your skull,
what were you trying to say?

Every morning—
streaming
waxy
crescent moon
the root of it disappearing
wet season, dry season
insurgency, timetable
train schedules, ticket prices
exchange rate, ferry boat
camel ride, tongue-tied,
monastery, sunrise,
lies and guides
this is your world
this is your sea

Neva Pilgrim and Steven Stucky

AHEAD OF THE CURVE—ELECTRONIC MUSIC IN
UPSTATE NEW YORK FROM THE 1960s ONWARD:
A CONVERSATION WITH DAVID BORDEN AND DEXTER MORRILL

John Cage's CREDO, *1937: "I believe that the use of noise to make music will continue and increase until we reach a music produced through the aid of electrical instruments. Whereas in the past, the point of disagreement has been between dissonance and consonance, it will be in the immediate future between noise and so-called musical sounds. The present methods of writing music, principally those which employ harmony and its reference to particular steps in the field of sound, will be inadequate for the composer who will be faced with the entire field of sound."*

Perhaps it was coincidental that our idea for this year's article should focus on two pioneers in electronic music in Upstate New York. Or perhaps it was Cage's spirit that sparked the idea, this being his centenary. Cage was prescient at age 25 to have given the address, excerpted above, predicting the future of music. We in Upstate New York have seen it lived out in the life and work of David Borden and Dexter Morrill, who were influenced early on by Cage's ideas and the development of electronic music.

Neva Pilgrim and Steven Stucky

Dexter Morrill was born in North Adams, Massachusetts, in 1938. As an undergraduate at Colgate he was active as a jazz trumpeter and began arranging and composing. At Stanford he studied with Leonard Ratner and Leland Smith. In 1962 he took up a residency at University City, Missouri, under the sponsorship of the Ford Foundation. In 1964 Morrill continued his graduate studies at Cornell, where he completed his doctoral degree in 1970.

Morrill taught at Colgate from 1969-2001. He achieved early recognition by performances with the Baltimore and Syracuse symphonies and violinist Ruggiero Ricci. Inspired by his 1970 visit to Stanford, and the Computer Music Group at the Powers Computer Laboratory, Morrill decided to build a computer music system at Colgate, which became operational in 1972.

He was a Guest Researcher at IRCAM in 1980, where he worked with two trumpeters from the Ensemble InterContemporain to study musical phrasing. Morrill's scholarly publications include, *The Music of Woody Herman: A Guide to the Recordings* and *The American String Quartet: A Guide to the Recordings.*

Among his best-known compositions are the early *Studies for Trumpet and Computer, Six Dark Questions* (with soprano Neva Pilgrim), and the 1984 *Getz Variations* (with saxophonist Stan Getz). In the 1980s Morrill worked with Wynton Marsalis on a proposed television project, which resulted in an interactive computer/trumpet design for the NEXT computer. In 2008, his seventieth birthday year, Morrill enjoyed a series of "birthday concerts" in Chicago, Dallas, and the San Francisco Bay area.

David Borden, born in 1938 in Boston, is an American composer of minimalist music. In 1969, with the support of Robert Moog, he founded the synthesizer ensemble Mother Mallard's Portable Masterpiece Company in Ithaca, New York. Mother Mallard performed pieces by Robert Ashley, John Cage, Terry Riley, Philip Glass, and Steve Reich. In addition to his work with electronics and the Mother Mallard ensemble, Borden has written music for various chamber and vocal ensembles. He is also an accomplished jazz pianist.

Borden was educated at the Eastman School of Music and Harvard University. At Harvard he studied with Leon Kirchner and Randall Thompson, and at Eastman, with Bernard Rogers and Howard Hanson. He was also a Fulbright student in Berlin, where he studied at the Hochschule für Musik. His *The Continuing Story of Counterpoint,* a twelve-part cycle of pieces for synthesizers, acoustic instruments, and voice, has been called the "*Goldberg Variations* of minimalism." Borden's music is recorded on the Cuneiform, New World Records, Lameduck, and Arbiter labels. He is the retired founder and director of the Digital Music Program (now the Cornell Electroacoustic Music Center) at Cornell University.

Borden and Morrill have a lot in common. Both grew up in Massachusetts and were involved with jazz early on, both having studied with Jimmy Giuffre. David feels that jazz influenced his compositions and taught him to hear every pitch, but not necessarily the chords. Dexter learned to compose with jazz great Bill Russo by arranging for him. As a youngster he toured the mills in New England with his father, who was an inventor who held 25 patents for wool processing machinery. That experience gave him a love of machinery. "It gave me confidence to join the computer music frontier."

Both composers had Ford Foundation grants in the 1960s, and both ended up in Central New York as leaders in their respective fields of electronic and computer music at the dawn of the electronic music age.

Background

NP: In this conversation, can you say how what was happening with electronic music in the '60s and '70s at Cornell and at Colgate fit into what was happening nationally or internationally? And then we can get down to your specifics—David in analog and Dexter in digital.

DB: I only have a limited knowledge of what was going on internationally with the evolution of electronic music, but I do know this: I saw my first electronic studio in Berlin, and as with most European places it was run by engineers who knew all the technical stuff, but the composers didn't. The engineers were there to help the composers, and they told you what the various equipment and modules can do. But then when you wanted to do it, you didn't know how it works. You would go to the person in charge and say, "I want to do this and the other thing."

SS: That's how it was with Stockhausen. He didn't do any of his own stuff.

DM: Exactly. Stockhausen or anybody—Berio, Boulez, any of those people —never touched a piece of equipment. They wouldn't do that.

DB: Was that a revelation to you?

DM: It really was. I went to Europe in 1975 and was shocked that the composers didn't do the technical work themselves. I had been at Stanford and we all shared everything. It's not so much that way now. A contributing part was that the European scene was not university based.

SS: It was mostly the national radios.

DM: Yes, it was radio that got electronic music started there. They had plenty of scientists in Europe, but they were all connected with the radio, and they weren't thinking about things the universities were thinking about.

DB: Well, at the Hochschule in Berlin, where I was studying, they had this guy in the basement away from everyone else. I think his name was Otto. Boris Blacher, who was my teacher, took me down to the basement and said he would like to show me what they were doing because Stockhausen was coming with his group and doing a live performance. And he said, I'm writing an opera, and it needs some electronic sounds. But Boris didn't know anything about how to produce them. The students didn't have a course on electronic music.

DM: He did one piece, didn't he?

DB: It was the man in the basement's piece.

DM: In Europe they had the "great man" [iconic figure] model, and the great man had an institute. The great man in Holland had the institute in Utrecht, which is where I went to work. I was told the building was closing at 5 p.m. because the engineers had certain hours. The students couldn't stay after hours in the building. I thought that was crazy. At Stanford the students had worked all the time around the clock. So students in Europe asked me if they could come to work in my studio in the U.S.

In terms of the larger relationship between the Colgate studio and the international trends, what mattered in my case was the fact that in 1969 Colgate bought a PDP-10 (Boston-built mainframe time-sharing computer) and everyone interested in computers worked on it. They didn't buy an IBM 360.

SS: When you were an undergrad, or when you went back?

DM: I went back to teach there in '69, and they bought the PDP-10 in '69.

DB: What is that? I don't even know.

DM: It was a mainframe computer by a Boston based company that started in the '60s, Digital Electronic Corporation (DEC). They built the first time-sharing machine. Stanford had a huge machine at the artificial intelligence project housed in back of the University. They let the musicians in the door, but I'm not sure they were all that happy about it. But, again, it was the University that made it possible because of the collaborative work going on in these places. For example, Roger Shepherd at Stanford was interested in perception; he wasn't a composer. They had signal processing people there, obviously, and people from different disciplines—psychology, acoustics, moon buggy, whatever—and they'd come together in these places around this big machine. It was the *machine*. There was nothing about Colgate or Central New York that was unique, except that I had a computer music studio there. The interface work was built by Joe Zingheim, who built the Milnet interface for the PDP-10. He was a crazy guy, and it was just a fluke that he got it going. In my case, it was just a miraculous thing.

DB: I worked with Bob Moog[1] in Trumansburg beginning in 1967, in the first really good state-of-the-art analog studio in Upstate. I worked there on my own. I wasn't employed by them. I couldn't even hook up my home stereo, so it took me about six months before I stopped ruining equipment.

DM: Moog was from Central New York, and he built all that equipment from scratch.

DB: Although I had no background in electronic music, I started working with Moog and was redesigning modules in no time. We were redesigning them so no matter how a person hooked them up, they wouldn't blow up.

DB: Jerry Hiller came in 1968 from Illinois and worked with Moog before going to Buffalo to set up the studio there. That was one of the first electronic studios in Upstate New York. He wrote the *Illiac Suite* there, which was surprisingly tonal. He was a chemist. I think Max Matthews, who was a frustrated violinist, was his model.

SS: Then what about Bell Labs and the relationship of their research in all this?

DM: The first conversion took place in 1957 at Bell Labs in New Jersey from analog to computer. They had so much money. Max Matthews spent his life doing this because he wasn't a very good violinist. Jean-Claude Risset, a good friend of mine, went to work at Bell Labs in 1964. He had a degree in music and in mathematics, and really knew about signal processing. He and Max became good friends. Risset asked Max if I could come to Bell Labs and work on trumpet sounds. Later, Risset went back to Paris to help set up the lab at IRCAM.

DB: I came very late to the computer. But I knew the computer was the thing when a student said her boyfriend was making music on his computer, so I went with her to his dorm room and there he was on his Atari, making some sounds, and a very primitive read-out, and I thought, uh-oh, this is the future. Shortly after that, the first Mac came out that said "hello," and I said "hello" back, and I'm still saying "hello."

DM: Moog came in 1964 or '65 and gave a demonstration at Cornell, and it was fabulous.

DB: And Joel Chadabe, SUNY-Albany, was working with computer music beginning in the late 1960s.

DM: Moog had a sense of community, making something for musicians—there was a spirit there. He did a lovely thing. Stanford had a big concert and they brought over this theremin player from Russia who was 102 years old, and Bob Moog presented him with one of his modern theremins.[2]

DB: He was making them since he was in high school. Moog figured out how to make theremins because RCA had bought one and didn't want it, so he got the rights to it and then developed and built them himself.

SS: And they are now becoming popular again.

DM: Electronic music did bring people in different fields together when it was new. Computer centers are inherently collaborative. Moog was the first to make an instrument, although Don Buchla might disagree. And Moog was regional, based in Trumansburg. DEC became the powerhouse in academia in the '60s, and later the IBM computer was enormously powerful.

SS: All Cornell students now use digital audio in their music, but when I was in college, I wasn't good at it and therefore didn't pursue it.

Career and Context

SS: I want to go back and ask about stylistic issues in the '60s.

DB: I was actually trying out a lot of things and was confused about what to do and where to go. I remember once at Tanglewood I had a spiky, pointillistic piece titled *Detour*, performed with a little triadic part in the middle. George Rochberg came up after the performance and said "nice try." I was impressed with Bill Albright who was out there and wrote in all sorts of styles, ragtime, piano-a-go-go, and with no apologies. That took a lot of courage. Then, afterwards, I got involved with the dance program at Cornell and got to know the dancers around Merce Cunningham, and they were doing something in a different direction. I heard *In C* (Terry Riley's composition), and I got it because an old friend from Eastman was on the recording. After that, I went out and got Riley's *A Rainbow in Curved Air*, and I thought that's what I want to do. That changed my whole approach. So in 1970 I had learned all the intricacies of the synthesizer, and I wrote a piece for two live musicians with tape called *Easter*, which we premiered at Cornell as part of the dance program. So that's how I changed—going from discovering Ives and all that humor and crazy stuff, getting away from a European style, and that's where I stayed. Shortly after, I became friends with Steve Reich and Philip Glass.

NP: Did your music move from dance and pop into classical?

DB: No, I think it all came from classical music.

NP: So you didn't feel more accepted in the dance world? But dance was important?

DB: Absolutely it was, and I felt accepted there. Then a lady who was from Cornell moved to New York City and was a part of Arts Services for avant-garde artists. They got me concert dates, and I realized after the first concert at WBAI radio in NYC in 1971 that I had an audience. It wasn't a pop audience. I realized they really came to see the equipment on stage, but they did like the music too.

DM: In the 1960s I felt limited by the performers available at Colgate, and the same was true with Cornell. There were terrific performers, but they weren't interested in experimental new music. That's why I wrote for one or two people who were terrific performers and excellent collaborators. That's what got my career going.

SS: Where were you going in the 1970s?

DM: I wanted to be a composer, to write music!

DB: Meeting Moog was the thing that changed my life, which led me to teach others, and to have a performing group. I just kept composing that way. Then digital music came in, and I continued with that, as well as performing.

NP: Did you feel more connected with musicians elsewhere who were doing similar things?

DB: I felt more connected to musicians in other places than to local performers, especially with musicians in New York City.

DM: What kept me alive was traveling, then touring, going to Stanford, Paris, Austria, Scotland, to take your music out and do something with it. The administration at Colgate and people in Hamilton gave me the support I needed in order to accomplish that.

DB: I had a group of musicians who were willing to rehearse two to three hours every night whether we had concerts or not. Then we were really tight by the performance.

SS: When did you actually start teaching at Cornell?

DB: I started Mother Mallard in 1969,[3] but didn't join the Cornell faculty until 1987-88.

SS: Between the mid-1970s and 1987, there was nothing going on at Cornell in electronic music, except that Marice Stith offered a course on it.

DM: Marice Stith[4] was a fine trumpeter and had a wonderful ear, and therefore was tapped to teach recording and electronic music. Bill Austin was an agent of change at Cornell, and helped break barriers and open up the curriculum.

DB: Mother Mallard gave outdoor concerts, often connected with art museums, and the audience of mainly young people was fascinated, mostly by all the machines on the stage.

SS: I knew about all those early electronic pieces and liked them, for example, Subotnick's "Silver Apples," one of the first "hits."

DM: That was a tremendously important piece. He really understood how to use the equipment.

DB: I was more interested in making music than working in a lab. My first work with synthesized music was used in dance programs. Choreographers loved it. I was influenced by John Cage and worked with Cage and Merce Cunningham. Then, I wrote that work for a Moog sequencer and two live musicians for the Cornell dance program.

Machine As Instrument

DM: In the 1970s very few people knew about computers, or they thought they were dangerous because they would take over and put people out of work. And they did.

DB: But by making the machines, we put many more people to work.

DM: That's right, we did. Now we've had this enormous transformation.

DM: One question I thought of on the way here was: Did the equipment make for better music?

NP: No, but it helped open up the sound world and unlocked a stylistic logjam—it blew everything open.

SS: It changed orchestration forever.

DM: I thought the development of the orchestras originated in the percussion department, and much of that interest came from Debussy, and now Saariaho and other current composers. These big machines (computers), big beasts, really, had a huge palette, but it was hard to control it.

SS: And students now know a lot more about acoustics than they did before these machines.

DB: What computers made possible was that anyone anywhere could make music, so there's lots of stuff out there, but not all of it is good.

SS: And with the internet there are no filters.

DM: I worked with Selmer Instrument Company to help build an interface with trumpet when I was working on a film with Wynton Marsalis. I asked Selmer to give me some help to build the interface. The guy at Selmer said: "This is terrific what you're doing, but we don't know anything about it." The manager said: Go get this guy a couple of trumpets, but what I needed was $25,000. This MIDI lab work could have helped the company build better instruments so they could play in tune on every note, like the third valve slide to get the C-sharp in tune, or play quarter-tones, or improve the mouthpiece itself.

DM: What we needed was a Sting, or a rock star to get these things going so companies would be willing to support this research. If you couldn't get a major artist, the companies weren't interested in supporting the research.

DB: Moog was lucky in that regard. He didn't know how to market. He hired Chris Swanson to help promote the equipment, but he really didn't need him because he had Keith Emerson (of the Emerson, Lake, & Palmer rock group) out there performing on his huge system, and it sold itself.

DM: Tod Machover went to Scotland and put a lot of guys on the stage. They had a PC here, a PC there, and a PC everywhere. But they didn't need those guys on stage—it was hype.

DB: Tod knows drama.

DM: When Neva and I were doing concerts, I realized I needed something on stage. A laptop isn't very interesting or even four PDP-10s.

DB: I realized for Mother Mallard's 40th anniversary that we had to have video. You don't want to just watch four guys playing keyboards.

DM: Marice Stith asked me to write a piece for him in 1974 *(Trumpet Studies)*. Until then I had written tape pieces, and people would come to the studio and were fascinated by the sounds. But in the concert hall, the reception was lukewarm. But with the piece I did for Marice, which opened with the medieval hocket technique between the trumpet and computer, the audience really sat up and listened. It was such a success that I thought I'll never write just a tape piece again. Then I did a piece for pianist Dwight Meltzer. I learned how to use the speakers so the performer seemed to be interacting with the computer.

Max Matthews wrote an article in *Science* magazine that the computer is just another instrument, but it's not. It's just a machine! Computers are a part of everything now, but they have lost that special identity they once had. I did nothing but work on mainframe for years. I put the best years of my life into it. I tried to make my music exploit what the machine could do, i.e. microtonal, that instruments couldn't do so easily. It didn't have to relate to European or American style music. The piece I wrote for Neva, for example, had a microtonal drop—the music sinking very gradually by increments smaller than half-steps—which isn't easy to do!

NP: But now the computer is used more in live performance, interacting with and altering what the instruments do.

SS: Now it's part of everything. You even have somebody back there in the percussion section hitting the MAX button.

DM: I did research on trumpet tones most of my career, and that enabled me to launch into the acoustical knowledge and how to match the tone with the computer. The big problem with electronic music is how to shape a phrase. Real sounds were the point of departure for computer composers to try to create sounds with the same rich texture. What impressed everyone was how much information there is in those real tones!

DB: I used to use filtered pink noise and trigger various low sequencers to vary them in some way so it didn't sound totally mechanical.

DM: Bob Erickson writes beautifully about that in his book on timbre,[5] which was very influential: the need for distortion to make it sound human. Later in his career, Erickson was bitter that the field of electronic music was just not there anymore, not distinctive in and of itself.

DM: Bruce Pennycook, one of my good friends at the University of Texas, Austin, has built a New Media studio, and he's impressed with the orchestration potential.

SS: I've heard some of those computer orchestration programs and they sound pretty good. Of course the Hollywood composers who use them have a whole staff to work out details to make it sound like real instruments, whereas university composers have to do it themselves.

DM: Proteus II is one I used quite a lot and the demo was really good. But they chose the sort of music for it that the machine could do.

DB: I don't try to make everything sound orchestral, but rather work to find sounds and tweak them to sound the way I *want* them to sound, and to fit with whatever piece I'm writing. It's more the same old pitch and rhythm thing because I'm mostly a tonal composer.

DM: When I worked in computer music with Risset and [John] Chowning, I tried to convey the idea of synthesizing natural sounds, because we knew what the great sounds were: piano, trumpet, and others. Those instrument sounds had lots of information in them, so they made a good point of departure if you could retain some of their rich information. The synthesizers weren't interesting to Chowning because I think it was very hard to do algorithmic synthesis with those early machines. That became the central focus, the driving force behind the Stanford group, and for Boulez who bought into that when he built the studio at IRCAM.

DB: I'm glad that I had that experience with Moog. The three or four basic things I learned on my own, while working on equipment at Moog, are still with me.

DM: Early on you had to learn it yourself. I learned the macro algorithmic language and an oscillator, and that's where I left it, because I had a very serious problem to resolve in the '70s, and that was—"Where was I going?" I was a composer, and I had to draw the line at some point and make sure that I was writing music. The piece I wrote for Neva, *Six Dark Questions,* took me 6-8 months to write—a 15-minute piece. Several good composers gave up composing to become computer music experts.

NP: David, were you always performing and composing?

DB: When the Moog era was over, I was about 40. I reevaluated and decided I would keep composing and get as many performances as possible. When the digital technology came in, I formed a whole new way of doing my ensemble, and I just kept going. But I never quit composing.

NP: Interestingly, this brings us full circle—two gifted performers who focused on composing and cutting-edge technology, and who then returned to performing and composing once they mastered the machines. ⊜

NOTES:

(1) Robert Moog (1934–2005), founder of Moog Music, was an American pioneer of electronic music, best known as the inventor of the Moog synthesizer, one of the first widely used electronic musical instruments. Early developmental work on the components of the synthesizer occurred at the Columbia-Princeton Electronic Music Center, now the Computer Music Center. While there, Moog developed the voltage-controlled oscillators, ADSR envelope generators, and other synthesizer modules with composer Herbert Deutsch. One of Moog's earliest musical customers was Wendy Carlos, whom he credits with providing feedback valuable to further development. Through his involvement in electronic music, Moog developed close professional relationships with artists such as Don Buchla, Keith Emerson, John Cage, and others. In a 2000 interview, Moog said, "I'm an engineer. I see myself as a toolmaker and the musicians are my customers. They use my tools."

(2) The theremin is an early electronic musical instrument controlled without discernible physical contact from the player. It is named after its Russian inventor, Professor Léon Theremin, who patented the device in 1928. The controlling section usually consists of two metal antennas which sense the position of the player's hands and control oscillators for frequency with one hand, and amplitude (volume) with the other, so it can be played without being touched. The electric signals from the theremin are amplified and sent to a loudspeaker. The eerie sound of the theremin was used in movie soundtracks such as those of Miklós Rózsa and Bernard Herrmann, in TV dramas, and in rock bands.

(3) Mother Mallard's Portable Masterpiece Company was the world's first live synthesizer band. They traveled, performed concerts, and recorded widely during the 1970s, and (with shifting personnel around David Borden) still exist to this day.

(4) Trumpeter Marice Stith was the long-time director of bands at Cornell, and a skilled recording engineer.

(5) Robert Erickson (1917-1997), Sound Structures in Music (1975).

Karen Martin

RE-ENACTMENTS

1.

While I waited, I remembered another railway station: the sandstone tower, clock, hot gardens with their marigolds, canna lilies, gravel sweep. Next morning, in the woods behind your new little city, I kissed you. Your mouth you made available, but none of your night. Your look took me down dim cold stairs to the tracks, smell of iron filings, a leaving feeling, or gone already. But later, in the evening, a room full of people, when we parted, you looked afraid, said, "When will I see you again?" I said, "Soon. In August." I promised.

2.

I was in the train station, waiting for you on a bench, my overnight bag by my side, and the tunnel to Departures ahead. The big clock told me you were late, and so did my little red watch. Everything was fraught, as it ought to be, but I knew what not to do. And there you were: I could see you through the silent sliding doors, walking towards me. *Will there ever be a woman who isn't my mother?* you were thinking. And: *She always wants to go on expeditions; today will be no exception.* And: *I can hardly see the keys at the bottom of the pool, but they are there, and I will dive for them.* You were worried about saying your lines, but I knew you would improvise brilliantly.

In the nights to come, I will weep. I will tear at the bedclothes with my teeth. Where are my dreams when I need them? With my alarm, I leave them. My bed, an island.

3.

You were late, obliging me to wonder, as always, what you were suggesting. I felt like someone else was wearing my brand new skirt. *What is missing in me?* I thought. I entertained every doubt. "Here you are," you said, with your arms spread. Even this, I doubted. You said, "You travel light." Or did you say that closer to the end, at Grand Central Station, when you carried my bag for me at last on the crowded, confusing, bright-lit, unfamiliar underground?

I allowed myself to be taken on your expedition to the library. In the upstairs stacks there were galleries, with narrow windows, and grey light, and writing nooks I could live in. "I still remember a dream from more than twenty years ago," I said. "I longed to turn on every single light. My house, with all the lights inside, blazing." *He doesn't want me,* you were thinking. *How does one bear this? My wiles have failed me. Catamite.*

I can't remember anything from yesterday. I try, but it's almost always disappointing. What comes: a thin thing, and cold. I refuse to use the heating, so I must wear my coat downstairs.

4.

Fast forward to the sex. What is it that dismantled my resolve? There had been colour in the trees, and the grass was green. And clouds scudded across the sky. And an aeroplane was going southwest.

I wake each day having flown from Johannesburg to New York City. The nights are bright. In my dream, you tell me I had misunderstood your preferences. I think about the jet stream, the autumn sky continually cut by birds in long haul transit. In the cities, buildings are no longer in use, boarded up windows, the steps and porches empty. And it is here, exactly, the abandonment tugs, where once there were embraces.

5.

Oh, how dreary that we thought the young boy waiter may have wanted us. What can I have been hoping to demonstrate? I initiated the arrangement for after his hours were up. We would meet at the cigar bar. And then? You talked through the smoke at me about the man who would not love you as you wanted him to. "To know what everything feels like," I said, "can't do any harm."

It can only be ridiculous to have been writing to you daily for years, and rarely a reply. In my wilful blindness, I turn your slights into my mistaken expectations. But the sudden cruel light of someone else's kindness, yesterday, obliged me to let my stupid heart contract for its hurts.

6.

It's simple: things happen one after the other and all I have to do is tell them.

You were late just a moment short of rude.

I could see us in the windows of the library.

I was clumsy at the cocktail bar, spilt the concoction on the long shining wood, talked to the barman despite all his signals that I should not.

That bouncing child on the seat beside me at the dining table. The careful poetry of the menu. And the rain through the window, May. Our slim-hipped waiter with his thin moustache. The words between the words a foreign language we were all quite naturally fluent in. He suggested the cigar bar, and agreed to find us there later.

Through the smoke, you spoke: How nothing else mattered when he called you. How you would do anything. How he sent you away before breakfast. You said, "Perhaps it's what I deserve." I said, "Perhaps."

Of course not. I said, "Of course not."

We left without reminding ourselves about what we had not been waiting for. It was impossible to share your umbrella, but it wasn't raining hard; in fact the drops floated.

Our last stop, a sad gay bar, was too dark. Three sad men sat at one end of the counter. The barman couldn't pretend to care. I drank the bourbon that would undo me. In the Ladies, strange, I stared at me. I should not have been taken to that place.

In your sitting room you had me watch while you unwrapped the new blue sheets for the couch you had elected to sleep on. I was undressed in your bedroom when you stepped into the doorway wearing something you wanted me to see you in. And I did see a you. Inevitable, deliberate, mistaken, we entwined. Good to feel your hipbones. And your mouth. Bring me your sucking and your sighing. But through the buzzing in my ears I remembered: Dee. I said, "No fucking." And, well, I guess then what's the point? I would have liked more kisses, but no. I said, "Don't go." There is a lot of room for two small people in a big, white bed.

I heard Ahmed in the kitchen in the morning. When he walked past your open door he saw me. I heard him. He said, "Jesus Christ." He saw us and I was glad to be seen so.

When I kissed you on the hilltop, I refused what I could tell as clearly as if you'd recited it. But I was hungover; I hadn't slept; I was giddy with the sorry possibilities. Nothing gave me more pleasure than when you took my light luggage from me and shouldered it on the walk to our train to New York.

At the talk, we sat with Dee between us. I hate the way she slouches in her chair, crotch bulging, as though everyone wants to know. At the end you held onto me, your fingers digging into my arms, your frightened eyes: "When will I see you again?" you said, like a promise.

Dee started limping on the way home. I had to take her briefcase. "I can't stand to see the two of you together," she said, "like a golden brother and sister, some other kind of substance. And I am made of meat." I wondered would I be able to make love to her, and I could.

7.

Someone has been watching me, all these years, drip the wrong medicine in my mouth. With the failing light: anxiety. My waking feeling: distaste for my interior. I pull the covers off me, soaked, and they tear. I tear them some more. The difference now: I know what wants to live. When shadows tremble and the floor beneath my feet, I know the room is moving. What about a house, nowhere, broken, calls me? Due to fierce and early frosts, the mountains will be red and orange with the burnt lightning bushes. Behind, there lies another world. Thousands of motionless ladybirds bejewel the tree trunks. And a pair of wild ducks will leave their evening water in my presence. ▧

Carol K. Howell

Jews Who Come Back

The living die so that the dead may live.
 —Isaac Bashevis Singer

It was her idea to go. I said traveling was dangerous, there were terrorists, bombs, but she scoffed: "Who's going to blow up a nothing little village in Poland?" It never occurred to me that she would. I watched her fussing over tickets and passports, packing for both of us, telling me what I was going to see and taste and love, fooling nobody. I wasn't going along to shlep suitcases: I was the niece, the substitute daughter—when Tzippy shattered, I would be there to pick up the pieces and bring her home.

The last time she'd seen her Polish village, she'd been twelve, an early bloomer who could pass for fifteen, Tzipporah, "little bird," always Tzippy to the family. Her last glance was over her shoulder as the Jews were crammed into covered trucks. She told me what she saw: the neighbors, opening their doors to watch, eyeing the empty houses the Jews were leaving behind.

It turned out Tzippy's prematurely developed bosom saved her at Auschwitz, for instead of being gassed with the other children, she was sent with the women to be starved and worked to death. When liberation came at Dachau two years later, she was so flat and shrunken, so shriveled and toothless, that the American soldiers called her Grandma. Too bad nobody in the family was left to share the joke.

And did she go back to her village, to Lipiny, place of linden trees? Did she go back to gather mementos—a platter, a quilt, clothes that might someday fit again?

"No," she told us. "Right after liberation we heard of a Polish Jew who went home and tried to get his farm back from the neighbors. He was found hanging upside down with his throat cut like a pig, a note pinned to his body that said: *This is what happens to Jews who come back.*"

But sixty years later Tzippy still longed for the Lipiny of her childhood. She longed for the linden trees with their heart-shaped leaves and flowers that smelled of warm honey and didn't start blooming until all the other trees were finished. She and her friend Malinka had climbed each one, addressing them as "Princess of Green Emanations"—a word Tzippy heard from the old men who sat discussing Kabbalah—and crouched in their leafy tops for hours, telling stories of demons and angels, playing Gypsy tunes on wooden flutes Malinka had carved. No one below knew where the music was coming from. It was their own exclusive magic.

So when Tzippy read on her Polskie news links that the village of Lipiny would be celebrating its 500th anniversary in early June, she knew the time had come. Early June was linden season. She had to go back.

The banner stretching across the road seemed bigger than anything in town. Tzippy translated: *WELCOME HOME ALL SONS AND DAUGHTERS OF LIPINY! FIVE HUNDRED YEARS OF HISTORY TOGETHER!* It was even longer in Polish. In the solitary hotel, the owner seemed to have a problem with our reservation, which was soon solved by handing over Tzippy's credit card twice.

"You bribed him, didn't you?" I said when we were in our dingy little room.

She shrugged. "Here you do things their way."

We went out to walk. We'd been tourists in Warsaw—we'd seen the brilliant houses on Castle Square and the shiny glass wings of the Metro; we'd seen the graves of the Home Army soldiers, rows and rows of white crosses, fetchingly twined with moss; we'd seen the cathedral and the red marble tombs. We knew how to appreciate.

But as Tzippy pointed out the arched doorways and the houses with bright painted bottoms—pink, yellow, sky blue—I noted their dull tops, peeling and neglected, as if no one ever expected you to look up. People with big noses and missing teeth smiled at us, wearing dirty jackets and jeans torn not in the fashionable way. Lipiny was not an affluent town. Most of the Jewish section had been built over, but Tzippy remembered where everything used to be and pointed, picturing the Jewish bakery, the shul, the kosher butcher shop. She even pointed out trees, insisting they were the same ones she and Malinka had climbed, all decked in white flowers now like brides—you could smell the warm honey. I thought she was about to ask me for a boot-up into the branches when she suddenly came to a halt, looking straight down instead.

She stood quite still, staring at the stones beneath her feet. At the very odd paving stones. So I did too. I could read some Yiddish, a little Hebrew: *This is the gate of the Lord into which the righteous shall enter. That sounded like a psalm. He shall cover thee with His feathers and under His wings shalt thou trust.* Psalms, names, dates. Tombstones. These were tombstones underfoot. We were walking on them.

"From the cemetery," Tzippy said in a thin moan. "Come, Shaindeleh, we have to see."

She pulled me through narrow streets onto a rutted dirt road that must have once been open country. Small dark houses, broken fencing, chickens and geese, and there—a low stone wall with gaps, reminding me of the toothless smiles in the village. No sign hung on the ancient iron gate, but I didn't need one. This had been the Jewish cemetery.

Tzippy wandered, hand over her mouth.

"What happened?" I said, though that was clear enough. I just wanted to make sure she was breathing.

She raised brimming eyes to me. "They took the stones."

"When?"

"They were here when I left." There was the tiniest bitter bite in that last word, but for Tzippy that was a lot. Usually I had to be bitter for us both.

So, when Lipiny knew the Jews were never coming back—when it heard about the fatal showers, the efficiently packed ovens—when Lipiny knew its Jews would be leaving no more pebbles lined up on the graves of loved ones, they tore out the tombstones and used them to pave the streets.

"Recycling," I said. "Can you argue with that?"

Tzippy didn't hear. She stood swaying over a patch of cracked mud.

"My grandparents," she said as I went to sway beside her. "They were lucky."

I knew what she meant: no truck, no train, no gas. But their stones were out on the street where the sons and daughters of Lipiny daily ground them underfoot, erasing their names.

"Tzippeleh." A voice spoke from the shadows and we whirled. "Little bird."

Tzippy didn't hesitate, though it had been sixty years.

"Malinka!" she cried, and they flew into each other's arms, hugging so hard I feared for their old-lady bones. Malinka's skin was dark and her hair pure white, chopped rough, unlike Tzippy's neat chignon. She looked skinny and tough, dressed in a combination of men's and women's clothing, four layers deep. She had about half of her teeth, including two gold beauties right in front that gleamed even here in the cemetery dusk.

"I've waited here every day for a week," she said, Tzippy rapidly translating for me. "I knew if you came, you would visit your grandparents."

"But Malinka, the stones—" Tzippy's voice broke.

Malinka's face darkened even more. She uttered a sharp word and spat on the ground. "They are pigs. They have always been pigs. They have not changed."

Tzippy embraced her again. "Neither have you, raspberry. I thought you'd be long gone!"

Malinka smiled and her teeth lit up the dusk. "Come and have tea."

We visited Malinka—"little raspberry"—in her unquaint cottage that was part brick, part mud, part sheet metal, and odd bits of lumber. I didn't see how it possibly kept out rain and snow. She served us tea and poppy seed cookies, and showed me a picture of the two of them as girls—Tzippy with blond braids, Malinka with black, arms wrapped around each other.

"Little Bird eats Little Raspberry," Tzippy shook her finger in a game that was evidently as old as God.

"Yes, but Little Raspberry has the last word!" Malinka made an unladylike noise, and they giggled like six-year-olds.

Then Malinka opened a chest, unwrapping a bundle which turned out to be an ancient looking pair of wooden flutes. "Remember this?" She held one out. There was a crude bird etched along the side.

Tzippy gasped something, forgetting to translate, and I realized the flute was her only possession from before the war, the only thing ever restored to her. She turned it in trembling fingers, finally raised it to her lips.

Malinka's gold teeth flashed. "Think you can still play, old woman?"

"You try to keep up!"

I wished for a video camera as the two of them began to play simple melodies falling just short of familiar. Tzippy's face was pink again. They ended with a tune I knew, a *niggun*, something Tzippy had hummed to me when I fussed as a child. The tune had three intricate sections and she'd keep repeating them faster and faster—that was its charm. Tzippy always called it her magic song. To hear it now, played on a flute, two flutes, was like hearing it brand new. They played faster and faster until both of them collapsed, laughing, in need of more tea. When Malinka walked us back to the hotel, it was very dark. We made plans to meet tomorrow. I opened the small window in our room and the linden honey drifted in like a promise that nothing bad could happen here.

"Americanski," I kept saying, rapping my chest till it was sore. "I don't speak Polish, sorry. Lauren, Tzippy Kirschaum's niece, Americanski."

They smiled as if I were slow. Tzippy was engulfed in embrace after embrace as the good churchwomen of Lipiny discovered her identity. Not that they recognized her or the family name: it was as if Jews had never existed in Lipiny. No, it was the idea that thrilled them. A lost lamb who made good, coming back with fond memories of home. Or so they assumed—I could tell by their proud glances around the banquet walls hung with handcrafted quilts and embroidered tablecloths, the long table laden with homemade delicacies, the scrubbed colorful buildings outside glowing in the sun—at least the half you could see without looking up. The older ladies seemed to love hearing about my aunt's life with us: the big American house, the gardens, the shopping malls. But no husband, no children or grandchildren? They pointed out their own.

"Tell them why, Tzippy," I said. "Tell them what was done to you at the camp."

But she shook her head. "They're asking when did I leave."

I watched her. This was the moment. "Tell them about the trucks."

"I went to America in 1946," Tzippy answered, translating automatically for me.

It wasn't a lie. I glared at her.

"Oh, then you will remember Pan Gorzynski!" the ladies exclaimed and tugged her toward the back of the hall where a hugely obese old man in a wheelchair with enormous wheels seemed to be holding court.

Tzippy clutched me. "He was mayor when I was a child. He yelled at us for climbing his trees. Shaindeleh, I can't, I can't—"

I wrapped my arm around her, backtracking through the crowd, making excuses, till we were out the door into the cool air, where we found Malinka waiting—Gypsies, of course, would not have been welcome inside. Malinka grinned, took us each by the arm, and said: "Now we will have a stroll in the sun."

I was beginning to understand why Tzippy loved her so much.

We strolled. I tipped my face to the light. Malinka chattered to Tzippy. But Tzippy had begun to mutter under her breath, sometimes in Yiddish, sometimes in English: *Beloveds and friends in their life, even in death they were not separated…Yehoshua Elhanan, son of Reb Yekhiel Hacohen…Frotka Bila, daughter of Reb Eliyahu HaLevi and her mother's name was Leah. May her soul be bound in the bond of everlasting life. Here lies our honorable father…our beloved mother…a perfect and upright man…a son of good deeds…important, modest, a precious soul… God-fearing, a scholar, a teacher…a modest woman…a woman of valor….*

"Tzippy." I opened my eyes. "What are you doing?"

But I knew. She was reading the tombstones beneath our feet. She was looking for her grandparents.

"See the willow trees?" she said. "That means tears. *By the waters of Babylon, there we wept and there sat down; Hung our harps on the willow trees; Zion yet we remembered thee!* The ones with upraised hands mean they were descended from kohanim, high priests. The crown means he was a scholar. The ones with pitchers and a bowl? The tribe of Levi. Women have a menorah or candlesticks."

Malinka spoke, and I didn't have to know Polish to understand.

"Tzippy," I said, "why don't we go back to Malinka's house for a cup of tea? You can rest a little."

She took another step. Stopped. Sucked in her breath and shrieked. It was a piercing young-girl's shriek that made people stick their heads out their windows. She was facing a corner where the pavement met two walls, two angles coming together. There was a small dark space where a single short stone had been neatly fitted. One look and I figured it out. Small stone, broken candlestick, *Hannah Kirschaum, 1936-1941.* Tzippy'd had a baby sister. She'd never told us.

I wrapped my arms around her, then Malinka wrapped her arms around us both. Gradually, we worked her down to boneless sobbing, and the three of us stumbled back to the cottage. Without Tzippy's translation, Malinka and I resorted to sign language. She held up the canister of tea and shook her head sadly. Not potent enough. Then she opened the ancient chest where she'd stored the flutes. Tzippy had told me that Malinka, like her mother and grandmother before her, made her living selling potions to those who believed in the old magic. The chest was crammed with tins, pouches, and tiny jars, smoky gray so you couldn't see what they contained. Malinka swiftly combed through these till she found a wooden box deeply carved like ivory, unlocked by pressing three hidden spots. When she got it open, she held it up to her nose and smiled.

I glared. This was no time for a Lipton moment. Tzippy was weeping in my arms. Malinka seemed to understand and nodded. She swiftly brewed a drink and held the cup to Tzippy's lips, murmuring tenderly. Tzippy took a swallow, grimaced. After a few more, she drew a shuddering breath and wiped her face. Another minute and she was able to speak. She stared up at the ceiling and whispered: *"Sprawiedliwość."* Then she turned to me, eyes flaring. *"Justice!"*

My head snapped back. Such a word out of my Tzippeleh? And what would justice be? What could possibly constitute justice for the act of erasing your links to a chain, millennia long, down to the smallest child?

Another sip and Tzippy jumped up and began to pace, wringing her fingers, worrying her knuckles. "Hannahleh was five years old. She was always following Malinka and me."

Malinka said something and Tzippy replied: "I know, but it's always *felt* like my fault." She looked at me. "We were in Pan Gorzynski's orchard, up a tree. He didn't see us—he saw her, tagging after us. He rushed out. She fled up another tree. He came roaring after her, grabbed that tree and *shook* it. He was like a bull, that man. You saw how big he is even now, in a wheelchair. We were all terrified of him. He shook that tree and little Hannah fell out. Hit the ground. Broke her neck. He walked away and left her there. Never said a word about it, and neither did we—we were too frightened. Shattered my mother's heart. It has always felt like my fault." She interrupted her pacing to cup my cheek. "You looked just like her when you were little, Shaindeleh. I think she would have grown up to look like you."

So that was why she'd always called me Shaindeleh—*pretty little girl*—though my name was Lauren.

She was striding again, her steps eating up the space in the tiny cottage. Her eyes glittered. She seemed taller.

"Listen!" She faced us, hands clenching air. "I recognized some of those quilts on the wall. I *know* one was my mother's. Some were taken from other Jewish homes. And some of the crockery as well—that big blue soup tureen belonged to my Aunt Rochel—it had the same spiderweb crack along the bottom. The platter with the cabbage roses—the rebbe's wife served sponge cake from it every shabbos. They took those things because they knew we were never coming back!"

I turned to Malinka. "Was this supposed to calm her *down?*" I pointed to the empty cup and mimed sleep. She just shrugged, grinning.

"Tzippy, why don't you sit?" I said.

"I will never sit again!" Tzippy strode to the ramshackle door, threw it open, and howled: *"Sprawiedliwość!"*

The wooden flutes were still lying on the table. I grabbed the one with the bird. "Here, channel that energy into this." It was an instinctive move, the way you'd give a teething baby something safe to chew on.

She seized the pipe as if I'd offered a choice weapon, held it to her mouth, and blasted out a note. And all three of us froze as the other flute, the one etched with raspberries, lifted from the table and rose into the air. Tzippy looked at me, looked at Malinka, then raised her pipe and blew again. The hovering flute came closer. When she stopped, it stopped. Malinka jumped to her feet in glee. The two of them seized each other's arms, jumping up and down. They were twelve years old again, shrieking. I finally got Tzippy to look at me and speak in English.

"Gypsy magic!" she said. "Did you think it was *all* just stories?"

"Tzippy." My voice was hoarse. "Why does it work on just the flute?"

She looked at me proudly. "Because it is *mine.* And now I will restore everything else that is mine!"

Malinka said something rapid and they shrieked again. Then Tzippy turned back to me, and I could swear she'd grown another inch. Maybe her bones were just straighter. "We will restore *everything* to its rightful owners. Malinka can help because she made the flutes."

"What are you talking, Tzippy? This sounds a little meshugeh."

She gave me a fierce grin. "You go get our passports. Then I'll show you meshugeh."

Malinka snatched the other flute out of the air, linked arms with Tzippy, and, with me trailing, very much the baby sister, we marched back to the village square where people were just leaving the hall. Here in this open space lined with linden trees, the covered trucks had waited, rumbling. Here twelve-year-old Tzippy had looked over her shoulder and seen the villagers cast appraising glances at the homes their Jewish neighbors had just emptied.

No doubt the trucks were scarcely out of sight before the citizens of Lipiny were fighting over Jewish furniture, linens, china, featherbeds. And no doubt, to judge from what Tzippy had noticed today, the booty had been handed down, cherished as heirlooms, and no one had noticed any bloodstains. After all, businesses, farms, the houses themselves had been appropriated—why fret over a few domestic items? No need to worry—the message was clear: *This is what happens to Jews who come back.*

"Everyone listen!" cried Tzippy in a voice that seemed disturbingly rich and resonant. She didn't wait to see if they complied. She and Malinka raised their flutes and began to play the *niggun.* I ran to get our bags and passports.

When I came out, people were frozen in place, standing on the steps, the sidewalk, the street, looking out windows and doors, all staring up. Everyone in Lipiny was finally looking up. Even Pan Gorzynski had been wheeled out to watch. I looked, too, and gasped. Tombstones were dancing in the air. You could smell the fresh mud. There were screams as people backed into the square and more tombstones clunked against the others above our heads. You could hear the grating, gravelly, squelching sound they made as they wiggled loose from the street, then the mud below, finally tearing clear and rising into the air, keeping jaunty time with the flutes' melody. Pebbles and bits of dirt rained onto the upturned faces, making people cough and gag.

"This is not happening," I explained, though nobody spoke English or cared to listen.

Malinka and Tzippy wielded their flutes skillfully, piping the stones in line, keeping them high above our heads, making room for more. The residents of Lipiny, including its two policemen, seemed utterly paralyzed. Tombstones dancing overhead! Fresh ugly gouges in the street! Tzippy's playing grew soft as she piped in the last stone, the smallest, the one with the broken candlestick. But this stone separated itself from the flock. It danced over to the steps of the town hall where the bloated mayor, Pan Gorzynski, sat in his mammoth wheeled chair. The little stone whirled about his head and Pan Gorzynski cried out in fear. Several men made a grab for the stone but it always danced back out of reach. Finally, it hovered before his face where everyone could read the chiseled words. I heard Hannah's name. The men were squinting, asking questions. Then the stone darted forward and struck Pan Gorzynski on the side of his head. He cried out, touched the wound, saw blood on his fingers. They all saw the blood on his hands. Tzippy smiled as she played. The stone danced back to join the others.

Playing strong again, Tzippy and Malinka piped the entire mass of tombstones over to the Jewish cemetery, the crowd following, and played the stones firmly back into place. I wondered if the policemen—or perhaps the village priest—would have anything to say about that.

But Little Bird and Little Raspberry were not done. They returned to the square, piping faster, and the crowd followed, gasping, as certain quilts and tablecloths detached themselves from their place of honor on the banquet room wall, joined by certain tureens and platters, beat upon by ladles, dancing merrily into the open air above our heads. The gasps turned to shrieks of dismay as windows and doors of certain houses popped open to let out sets of silver cutlery, china dishes, enameled trays, embroidered linens, featherbeds, pitchers, antique clocks, teapots. From underneath beds, from inside hope chests, strong boxes, safes, and secret caches buried in the garden sprang silver menorahs, candlesticks, and goblets engraved with Hebrew names and dates. All these things burst forth to join the dance in the public square. But Tzippy and Malinka played faster and faster, and some of the women squealed as gold rings, earrings, and necklaces—melted and reformed, unidentifiable to the uninformed eye—answered the pipers' call, sliding off fingers, unclasping—none too gently, it seemed—from earlobes and necks, and bobbed like bits of pure light, flashing in the sun, among the household goods that were all that remained of an annihilated people and a vanished world.

Finally, it seemed, the pipes were satisfied. The pipers took a step back. The objects followed. They took another. The objects, likewise. The two portly village policemen finally stirred as if they thought there might possibly be some action or gesture they were called upon to perform. Tzippy piped a few notes in their direction and instantly the silver knives lined up, forming a rigorous first line of defense. So the constables did what their grandfathers had done in 1943. They averted their eyes.

Then the music grew merrier and the dance swifter and I had to run to keep up, dragging our wheeled suitcases, our coats clenched under my arms and our purses slung around my neck, hoping I hadn't forgotten anything, because I knew this time there would be no coming back. I stumbled after Tzippy and Malinka as they capered and strutted down the gutted road, laughing and piping, looking younger by the minute, younger than me, followed not by rats or a crowd of children but by a bobbling, tumbling procession of old dishes and linens. As we left the village, one sharp blasting note tore down the banner: *WELCOME HOME ALL SONS AND DAUGHTERS OF LIPINY! FIVE HUNDRED YEARS OF HISTORY TOGETHER!* Malinka spat and said a naughty word that I didn't need to have translated, and we started down the long dusty road. I didn't have to ask where. Tzippy had already told me: to return the stolen things to their rightful owners, as she had returned the tombstones. We were heading west. Unlike the first time, unlike any other Jew or Gypsy, Tzippy and Malinka would enter Auschwitz dancing. ≋

Teresa Sutton

A Pillar of Salt

He's found the entrance to the underworld
in the plaque and tangles of his brain.
The distant past drags him down to the ninth circle

as he recalls a deed he never did in painful detail.
He thinks of his brother and drinks a little
less water. Car brakes screech inside his head

while the brother he should have minded bleeds
again in the street. He forgets the word for dead
and takes less food at dinner. To atone,

he leaves a wreath at Christmas and a palm
cross at Easter. He clips away the tuft of grass
that always tries to cover Rex's name. His treachery,

to run with the guys down to the boat docks,
to forbid his baby brother to tag along,
brings December and snow that's too heavy

to be shoveled away. Chunks of time
disappear, ten or thirty years at a clip,
yesterday's trip to the grocery store,

his granddaughter's graduation. He stacks
another six cans of soup in the cupboard and asks
who is that girl in the picture. Rex's

accident replays in clear detail. And he says
he wishes he had just turned around.

Leila Ortiz

AT LECHMERE

Customers wander the aisles bathed in neon light.
I check myself out in the security camera.
Yesterday I had a fake customer.

The manager called me into the back office
and said I scored well in geniality. I wonder
who this person was. Maybe it was the woman

Who only bought a remote control.
Or the man browsing lamps the whole day
without buying anything.

There's a better mall across the highway.
The theatre stays open till midnight,
the food court smells like pastries.

When I first started, a woman with a baby
waited in line to ask for an application. I directed
her to the manager, but she disappeared.

Once I came to work in a blizzard.
I checked myself out in the security camera.
Outside the sliding doors, everything was white.

Christopher J. Michel

OFFICE PORTRAITS: TED

Ted runs accounts. He's always at his desk,
which hemorrhages reports, but he always
knows your budget's specs. Some say Ted
speaks only on the phone, others, only
in his office. Every day Ted's in ahead
of Dana, and he's there when Dana's left,
except for Fridays, when he's nowhere
to be found, though no one says he's out,
and he'll insist he's here. *You must
keep missing me,* he'll say, some coy grin
on his face. But Ted knows the location
of every penny in the company. He would be CFO,
but he fucked it up. At Brown LTD. Larceny,
they say. It took them thirteen years to figure out
the how and what he skimmed, and he got
off by naming names. Now he's here, underpaid.
But if you know him, and he likes you he will
find your project funding even after Colleen turns
it down. He's put me in the black, but man:
Ted hates small talk. Do *not* ask about his wife,
or weekends, or the pictures on his desk. He won't
go drinking Thursday after work
                    no matter how you ask. I've heard
he flies first class to his hippie girlfriend's cabin
in the sticks. She fries fish he catches in a creek.
I'll bet he does it with the money they found gone.
I'll bet the girl-next-door and two brats on his desk
are just for show, to keep us off his back. The guy
even eats his lunch alone, deskbound, I've seen it:
whole wheat wrapped in butcher paper, and if he
forgets his door is cracked, he pulls a bottle from
the drawer and pours a shot of single malt.

Paul Linczak

SAILING SOLO

In the fifth grade there was Lassi O'Rourke, a pale, freckled, black-haired girl with whom I exchanged fervent notes folded into paper nachos. She wrote about the torment she suffered under the terrible reign of the Thompson twins, who were pig-tailed and merciless. I declared my love. She accepted my request to be my girlfriend—in writing—but during a momentous snowy recess, screamed when I tried to kiss her. The notes came to a stop; I moved on.

In middle school I courted Tricia Haverford, a cheerleader and flautist, with sandy freckles and a slight retrusion of the front teeth. She liked high-top sneakers, black culture, lima beans, and, for a while, yours truly; but we never progressed beyond what my parents would have called heavy petting. It turned out the specter of pregnancy held her libido in chains, forcing on her a recurring nightmare about a mucky gremlin emerging from between her legs. She sobbed; I caressed her hair and told her it was okay.

I sailed into high school mad for a glimpse of real nipples, buffeted on all sides by gym locker-room stories of glorious conquests—Davey went to town; Michael got to third base. I alone seemed to be stuck at home, and I couldn't understand why. If my friends were to be believed, girls embraced Eros as much as we did, and they weren't particular about their partners. Why couldn't I find one willing to join me for a little splendor in the grass?

By my junior year my strategy was to chase after the most promiscuous girl in our class: Natasha Birkovic. Sallow, waif-like, her eyes piercing from a bandito mask of dark makeup, and with nicotine on her breath, Natasha was widely thought to be destined for adult films. The stories about her made quarterbacks giggle—they meld in my mind into a collage of ganja, rings and studs in painful places, searching female tongues, broken wind, a stalwart shih tzu. After several kind gestures at school (I helped her with Spanish homework during study hall, let her copy my quiz answers in health class, and so on), we finally met in someone's crowded basement amid red plastic cups, thumping bass and drums, and teenagers breathing free. She had brought her own vodka, the bottle tucked into her handbag. We talked about our teachers, the others at the party, and then nothing at all before finally coming to rest in a towel-filled laundry basket and locking lips. She smelled like pears and alcohol, and I worried the one beer I had nursed all night wasn't enough. When I timidly ventured south of her border—finding what fire I could in my belly—she slapped my hand away and whispered with sultry half-sleep, "Do you think I'm going to have sex with you?" Her poor-little-thing intonation stopped me cold. "What's that supposed to mean?" I asked. She laughed and tried to kiss me again, but I stopped her. "What's so funny?" I demanded. "Why *wouldn't* you want to have sex with me?" She looked at me as if she just realized who I was. "It's not you," she insisted. "It's just I don't…I don't know…I'm not really doing that anymore." "Sex?" I said. "Yeah, I guess," she shrugged. "I'm worried about my number. I don't want to be that girl. Can't we just kiss for a while and go back to being strangers from study hall? No one will know the difference…." I looked at the dryer across from us in that small laundry room and wanted to crawl in. The kissing that came after was joyless and brief.

If it is half as painful for you to read this as it is for me to write it, then you have some idea of what I suffered. I became paranoid that my sleepy northern village was some kind of erotic capital, bedrooms and basements everywhere filled with intertwined adolescents putting the ancient bathhouses of Europe to shame, and I wasn't invited. And, yes, I suffered because I loved girls, loved everything about them—loved the way they held their handbags when they walked, loved the way they cleared their hair from their faces, loved their high voices and low voices, loved their slender crossed legs when they sat, loved the shape of their bodies, loved and loved and loved…. I marveled at the positively feline nubility of cheerleaders, the stern prettiness of flight attendants, the tamed, sophisticated movements of assistant professors. Where, finally, was the one who would see some irresistible beauty in me?

She was in Krakow, it turned out. (Here I want to linger a bit; indulge me.) I went there for the summer between my sophomore and junior years of college to take literature courses at the Jagiellonian University, meaning that after two full years of urban coeducation (having succumbed to Columbia), I was still untouched by the fairer sex. I arrived feeling like an exile rejected by his homeland, my shorts stained by the orange juice I had spilled during a spot of turbulence. (I also felt strangely at home, walking in the garden that provided my genetic stew.)

In one of my classes I met a young American woman named Anna. She was tall, slim, blond, and beautiful, but what caught my eye was the novel

I saw among her belongings—one of those abstruse works of Polish literature that lights up the scholarly eye. I caught up with her after class one day as we returned to our hostel among a virus of Fiats parked at the curbs, and hoping to appeal to her as a fellow American, I offered, "Everyone here drives these really tiny cars."

"I noticed," she laughed. "I think gas is expensive here."

"Either that," I said, "or the Poles are in fact a race of little people."

Her laughter was firm but ended in a mumble. She offered her hand and we introduced ourselves. It turned out she had just graduated from Princeton with a comparative lit degree, and we fell into a conversation about books. The way she spoke—calm and knowing—suggested elegance, but her hunched shoulders and inward-facing feet (scuffed sneakers and sockless, bruised ankles) betrayed her awkwardness. We talked about our interest in Poland, which lectures we wanted to attend, our appraisal of the pierogies. Just before we reached the hostel a burst of hail fell from the sky; we ducked under a balcony, laughing with disbelief as ice pebbles stung our legs. Then, as quickly as it had come, the hail stopped, and we laughed at the randomness of it as we entered our hostel. In front of her room she said she wanted to shower and nap, and I asked, with determined nonchalance, "What are your plans tonight?"

"I wanted to see a movie in the city, just like a real Polish person," she said. "Do you wanna come?"

Dear gods on Olympus! I didn't even ask which movie we would see.

When I knocked on her door a few hours later, Anna opened it with a smile that blew me aloft.

"Your roommate's not here?" I asked.

"Don't have one," she said as she joined me. "There are other girls in the suite, but my room is all mine."

This was excellent news. I pictured us spending the night *in flagrante delicto* as I told her about my lousy roommate (a bald young Pole obsessed with skulls and knives, about whom the less said the better).

We took a tram to the city center. At the theater we waited in a ticket line, where I saw a German girl I had met in class but whose name had evaporated from my mind. The three of us talked about our homework, and when the conversation lulled I commented on the Polish graffiti gracing the theater ("I love Janka" and "Jerzy + Basia Forever!"). "It's too bad they have graffiti like this here," I said. The German girl looked at the wall. "You don't have graffiti where you are from?" she asked. "We don't have love in America," I answered, and she stared at me, baffled. Anna suppressed laughter as we bought tickets.

We lost the German girl and sat toward the back of the theater. The film was about an eccentric Polish poet who was rejected by publishers and women and finally stuffed his head into an oven. It was depressing and beautiful, and we watched it without a whisper, both of us, it seemed, being adamant about silence during good films.

When the movie was done, we filed out into a violet darkness and found the German girl again, waiting for the tram. Her eyes bugged and she grabbed my arms. "I finally understood your humor!" she said. "Zey don't teach humor in our English classes. I had to write down ze words. But you are quite funny!"

I thanked her. Anna invited her for a drink, but she needed to meet with a study group back at the hostel, so we left her and wandered past a gate of the ancient brick wall protecting the city center. The streets there were forbidden to cars; people meandered through a park, the lawns bordered by green plastic curlicues and lit eerily by tall lampposts.

As we passed the shops and galleries on the bumpy brick Szewska, she took my hand in hers. No looks, no smiles; just her rough, bejeweled fingers interlaced with mine. I was elated. Not even the sight of a McDonald's could force the happy air out.

"You think this is the Little America section of the city now?" Anna said.

"It could be," I said. "Every city has its own Little Something nowadays. Little Italy, Little Tokyo. I bet somewhere in Krakow there's a Little Krakow."

Her laughter seemed genuine. At an outdoor café we found a table facing the public square. A skinny waitress lit a tea candle between us and after a few minutes we had our beer; like natives, we wished each other a hundred years before savoring the first sip.

"May you live a hundred years," I mused. "Why not forever?"

"They're not a very ambitious people, the Poles," Anna said.

"All evidence to the contrary," I said, and motioned generally to the square. Before us was the enormous Sukiennice, a Cloth Hall of yellow arches and windowed layers, gold spires along the roof. Behind that towered the old town hall, a wide structure of pink and white brick that rose to a black clock on all its faces and was capped with a steeple that glowed dimly from inside. Guarding the Cloth Hall was a monument to Adam

Mickiewicz, who faced the square's tallest attraction, the Mariacki Church towers. "The legend of the church towers is all about ambition, isn't it?"

"The one about the two brothers trying to out-build each other?" She observed the towers, which looked like gingerbread creations in dramatic light from below. The taller one had a gothic spire at the top; the shorter, an iron cupola. "Okay, professor. So I was wrong."

"Ambition can be good, I think. You're ambitious. You're going for a Ph.D., right?"

She looked surprised, then nodded. "Harvard," she said. "How did you know?"

"You seem the type." I smiled at her. "And, ahem, *Haaavard*?"

She swirled her beer. "It's nothing. My grandfather gets me into these places. He's in publishing. For a while he took me to these fancy parties in New York just so I could meet the right people from Ivy League schools."

"You would rather he hadn't?"

She nodded pensively. "I did well in school, don't get me wrong. But now I'll always have to wonder if I could have made it in at all without his help. And I felt so smarmy at those parties too. Everyone wanted to hear me say something smart. Well, being smart is more than just knowing facts or memorizing stats."

"Oh?" I said.

"It's putting two and two together and knowing how to handle it when they don't always equal four."

"Ah," I said. "Be prepared: the Gospel according to the Boy Scouts."

"Maybe," she answered. "There is something pragmatic there. It's just weird—how we want to be the best, break down barriers, assert ourselves as individuals, the kind of 'I can survive on my own' mentality that the Boy Scouts preach, but then those Boy Scouts grow up and join the football team, the fraternities, get married, find a company job somewhere…."

"They joined the Boy Scouts to begin with," I said. "So what's wrong with that?"

"I don't know," she said, shaking her head. "Maybe nothing. Maybe everything."

She looked at the poet's statue. A couple lugging backpacks paused not far from our table and hugged. Anna looked at the ground then, a breeze playing with her hair, and I suddenly imagined waking up with her in connubial sunlight, seagulls yelping into a tropical wind: white sheets, blue eyes, and the puppyish panting before breakfast.

"You don't want to go to grad school, do you?"

"I do," she said. "That's the thing. I still have this little-kid desire to just spend all my time reading."

"There's nothing wrong with that."

She smiled. "Says the English major."

She sipped her beer. A horse and carriage with sleepy tourists left a spatter of manure on the pavement. A craggy-faced woman wandered by with a satchel of flowers, proffering roses and quoting her price ("Three *zloty*, ladies and gentlemen!" she called feebly. "Only three *zloty!*"). The air cooled, and from the belfry of the tallest church tower a trumpeter toned the hour, a commemoration of the medieval call that saved the city from invasion, and the bugler who died in the act. I leaned to catch a glimpse of the man and his trumpet, thinking that this minute would likely be the most romantic of my life, but I couldn't find him. The whole square seemed to stop and watch the tower, listening to the plaintive horn, and Anna gazed too, a beaded necklace crossing her collar as she leaned. Then the song cut off in mid strain, and everyone came back to themselves.

"That's so cool," she said.

A squirrel-haired guitarist set up close by and began screeching something in garbled English. We turned and listened. Passersby dropped coins in his case.

"It's funny," she said, "but when I was in Budapest it seemed a lot of the people there were listening to old American music, stuff we laugh at now."

"You were in Budapest?"

She nodded and ran a finger around the mouth of her glass. "I went there last week with my husband, but then he got called to London for work. Some corporate emergency."

"Oh," I said, my tender heart imploding.

"He works for a shipping company," Anna admitted. "It's not very interesting."

The simple ring on her finger glared at me, but she wore several rings, and beaded bracelets, and with all that jewelry I hadn't noticed the wedding band, hadn't even thought to check, and how old do you have to be, anyway, before you start routinely checking fingers? I cursed the gods and clenched a fist against tears.

"How long have you been married?" I asked.

"About four years. I was a freshman. Or is it *freshperson* now?" She looked at her empty glass. "He should be here any day now. London was too expensive, and I figured while I was waiting and in Europe I might as well come here."

My heart wouldn't slow, and despite the cooler air my face burned. I see myself sitting there, quietly devastated, and wish even now that I'd had the strength to erupt, to force whatever angry words boiled down below up past the fear in my throat. But it's no use; what happened next is written in stone: I called our waitress and we paid.

The liveliness had gone out of the square as we made our way back the way we had come—the bread and cheese stands were packed away and the only loiterers in front of the McDonald's were friends of the employees. So there would be no Chekhovian affair, no secret trysts. I wondered (and still do): What had she meant when she held my hand? What was I to her—a rook? A pawn? I didn't want to ruin her marriage (here my scruples enter, hands on hips and twee little legs crossed for the cameras) just as much as I didn't want to be her pliable Pip. We didn't even know each other's last names.

We joined a small group waiting for the last tram of the night. When it arrived we crowded at the door, and I made sure Anna went in front of me. As she climbed into the car I backed away, then hurried down the street. I saw her inside the lighted car, pressed to a window looking for me, and then I turned a corner and the tram rang its bell and left. That was the last time I saw her.

Wandering the dark and abandoned streets, surrounded by moonlit windshields, I gave in to tears. I'm not proud of it; there is no relief in that ocular wine. Nevertheless, truth be told, I did more than cry. I collapsed into the entryway of a china shop and wept, lonely, unloved, my youthful hope spilling into my hands. I hated women; I hated myself. I understood nothing.

When my face dried, I wandered again, eventually finding myself in a pub with Polish beer in hand, determined to drink myself senseless. Eyes on my mug, nape of my neck burning with anger and shame, I let the room and its *tak-tak-dobrze-dobrze* waft over me, wishing I had a newspaper to read. A song came through the stereo that everyone seemed to know; they bashed their mugs with hooligan shouts; the older men shook their heads and smiled. I had finished my second *piwo* when a girl tapped my shoulder and asked something in Polish. After telling her I didn't understand, she said, "American? I like American! When I was little girl, for two years I eat only pancakes, nothing else, just to be like American. Then I passed out in school, you know, from no vitamins. So I quitted the pancakes. But I still like American!" I told her that sounded about right. Like many Poles, she had the blond-and-blue DNA of the Swedes who had conquered her forebears, with a stark, concentrated look to her eyes and a thin, aquiline nose. Behind cumulous red lips I could see thin spaces between her teeth that I found exotic and lovely. She was heavier than Anna and not as pretty, but I was not about to turn away a girl who liked Americans enough to eat nothing but our pancakes.

After another three glasses, my memory of the rest of that night is hazy. I'm certain I asked my newfound inamorata her name and how she came to know English so well; possibly I even propped open her personal basement door and watched her fumble for the light. I remember laughing, both in the pub and later on the street when my belch frightened an alley cat. I remember a dark stairway, a painting of the earnest virgin with hands pressed in prayer. I remember anointing the girl's commode and then wiping it down with a hand towel. And then, suddenly, I was without pants on a soft surface and panicking that I couldn't feel anything; *it doesn't feel like anything!* My mind conjured other instances of head spin: the time in grade school when an older boy punched my jaw; the moment before the removal of my wisdom teeth, when the anesthetic made the ceiling swirl. I think, at one point, I knocked something off her dresser. I may have expressed out loud the difficulty of the task before us.

Thus was I introduced to the pleasures of the flesh by an anonymous Polish barfly, and if she knew she was my first—bless her—she didn't let on. Naturally, I was disappointed, and not just because I felt nauseous and unplugged through the whole thing, but because it was petulant and sad. Because I could still feel tears swelling my head. Because it wasn't Anna. Because it meant nothing to me. (Yes, I had expectations—not candles or dewy meadows or a wedding night's white peignoir, but at least a glimpse of some deep and abiding beauty, a taste of the elixir of life. Oh, well. In the end, I figured children expect magic; adults just take their clothes off.)

After returning to New York I went immediately to the campus clinic to get tested for disease; the results left me free to fire at will. The monkey of virginity was finally off my back, but there was no golden glow, no sudden profusion of birds—just a searing honesty that emerged from under all of the pomp and circumstance that at night, behind closed doors, people stripped and played with their bodies. This was true of everyone. My professors did exactly what I'd done in Krakow; so did the bankers and executives in their townhouses; so did the mayor; so did my parents. It was a messy act, full of wetness and sounds and smells, and, contrary to the example of my own history and the teachings issued from churches and temples and mosques, everyone was involved. Everyone wanted it! I began to see the hidden desires of every barista or librarian, the experience etched in the face of the mailman, the food cart vendor, the cab driver, and felt enlivened to find myself but one subject in the vast, bustling kingdom of desire.

Still, it grieves me to report that, despite my new sexual citizenship, the wise old man who lives in my head had to watch sixteen months of security camera footage of me reading, writing, eating hoagies, jerking off, watching movies, doing push-ups, and reading some more before the camera finally captured another midnight rendezvous. This was with an anthropology major named Dina, a perky sorority girl who was fond of headbands and spoke dreamily of founding a kibbutz in Kansas. She was far from Jewish, hailing as she did from the rich ports of Puerto Rico, but the socialist mainframe ran a line to her brain, and she wanted to be an expert on justice in different cultures. Our relationship lasted five weeks, during which we had raucous sex and argued about the assumptions of anthropologists, why they studied the Korubo of Peru or the Siberian Yukaghirs, but not the Catholics of Staten Island. I missed her when she was gone.

And then, after four mostly monastic years, Alma Mater pushed my little dinghy out into the ocean. At first, it seemed there were a lot of us, enjoying the wind in our hair, shouting to each other across the waves, but gradually more people headed for ports, some traded for bigger boats, others gave up on the water altogether, and I found myself bobbing listlessly on the open sea with nary another sailor in sight. Three years went by.

Finally, at a publishing party, I met Molly, who was introduced to me by her agent as a bright new star in the American literary firmament. She had written a collection of stories about eccentrics who had encounters with angels in the guise of talking salamanders, winged hobos, and the like, which had received a surprising amount of attention for a work of what publishers refer to by the detestable phrase "up-market fiction." I attributed her success to her age—she was twenty-three, though enough twentysomethings had published books by then—and the stunning and remarkably misleading author photo that greeted readers at the turn of the last page. I never shared my opinion of her book, and she never asked. (Today the curious might find a copy in the bargain bin.)

We began innocently enough: a placid dinner in the West Village; a stroll along the Hudson; an independent film; a rock concert. I liked her quietness and intelligence. She was at home in jeans and sneakers, had pert breasts and a handsome face that was framed by full golden-brown hair that fell to a straight cut at her shoulders, like that curtain of soft strops that awaits you at the end of an automatic car wash. We talked about books, politics, families. I spent a number of weekends at her apartment in Brooklyn, which was picture perfect—jade plants in terra cotta by the window, an oven mitt hung from a peg by the stove. We drank green tea and read the newspaper.

I must admit her domesticity was comforting, and it felt good to have a companion, someone with whom to hold hands at the museum or the occasional party. We bought groceries together, spent Friday nights lying on a futon with a movie on TV. It was wonderful not to feel so alone anymore.

But there was one place we were never comfortable: in bed. Molly took nine dates to get there, and then controlled how we did things, mostly, I realized, to alleviate her fear. The first time she was shirtless with me she repelled my attempts to unhook her bra until I sulked in gentle annoyance and she relented, leaving her hands prudishly over her breasts. When my lips neared her nipples she squirmed. I asked her what was wrong; she said she didn't like her breasts, they were too small. My assurances failed to convince her. The rest of her body was similarly *verboten*. I foraged, she blocked. I held her in place, she shut down completely. Our soundtrack featured no spankings, gagging, screaming, or dirty talk. She simply lay on her back and waited for the deed to be done.

I feared the worst. Was she not really attracted to me? Was she only clinging to me to keep from drowning in her own solitude? Had she been abused as a child? Had she been fed a youth full of fire and brimstone? Was she a germaphobe?

Our discussions went nowhere. She said she was not a plaything, and people simply didn't do "such things" where she came from. I surrendered, though I was certain at least some naughty people lived in Nashua. I told myself that sex isn't so important; after all, there were couples who waited until marriage, and most priests waited their whole lives, and anyway, look at everything else we had—we laughed at the same movies, voted for the same candidates, devoured the same foods.... But it was no use. The thrill was gone, baby, and no argument was going to bring it back.

Our last chapter was written in tears and insults; there were quickly collected belongings and a door slammed in my face. We had lasted almost exactly ten months—the longest relationship of my life—and so, when a story of hers appeared in a glossy magazine a year later, I was pleased to see a character who fit my description die an ignoble death in the jaws of a Yeti. At least I had made an impression.

Well, that's it—the whole history up to the present. No scholars will snuffle over it in years to come. Whatever lessons there are to be learned are better left for others to say. And now, like many stories, like life, I'm right back where I started: sailing solo.

After all, who needs commitment when you can have this much fun? ≋

Adriana Grant

SARGENT AVE, BY THE NUMBERS

A six-minute walk to the library, five to the park. The neighborhood pool doesn't come recommended. Spanish is spoken at the nearest bodega. The in-house butcher makes fine linguiça. A gallon of Pearl Street milk: four thirty-nine. Scratch tickets lie ripped into rough squares: their numbers secret. Lucky, even if they've yet to win. Take a left at the front-yard catamaran. Can't miss it.

Rob Enslin

Raymond Carver said that the secret of good writing wasn't talent—there's plenty of that around, he added—but a person's ability to put his signature on everything he does.

"A writer who has some special way of looking at things and who gives artistic expression to that way of looking: that writer may be around for a time," he said.

Surely this ethos was alive and well in the early Eighties, when Carver taught in the creative writing program in The College of Arts and Sciences at Syracuse University. Since then, his commitment to capturing the world "according to one's specifications" has become an inspiration to poets and authors everywhere.

Raymond Carver

SU Archives and Records Management

It's no secret that SU's creative writing program is one of the nation's best. Nary a year goes by in which some faculty member doesn't bring home a major award or honor, such as a Guggenheim, MacArthur "Genius" Grant, or National Book Award nomination. Further validation comes from *Poets & Writers* magazine, which ranks SU's program the fifth best in the country. Michael Goode, chair of SU's English department, says the distinction confirms what everybody in the field already knows—"our M.F.A. program is among the best out there."

Ben Marcus, associate professor of Columbia's creative writing program, offers similar praise for SU. "They have it all: brilliant faculty who teach their hearts out, excellent programming, and the best students I have ever encountered."

Ever since Margaret Habrect G'65 was the first student to enroll in the program 50 years ago, Creative Writing has been launching the careers of authors, poets, scholars, and teachers. Every year, hundreds of applicants from around the world—approximately 500 fiction writers and 150 poets—vie for a mere dozen openings. Part of the allure is the faculty, which is front-loaded with talent. Mary Karr, George Saunders G'88, Dana Spiotta, and Bruce Smith are just some of the professors one might bump into in the Hall of Languages or Tolley Humanities Building. Former faculty members include Tobias Wolff, Mary Gaitskill, Douglas Unger, Tess Gallagher, and Junot Díaz (who, at the time of this writing, is a MacArthur Grant recipient and a National Book Award finalist), as well as the dearly departed crew of Carver, Philip Booth, Donald Justice, Hayden Carruth, W.D. Snodgrass, and Delmore Schwartz.

If proof of a successful creative writing program is turning out one notable writer per decade (a metric often used with the Writer's Workshop at The University of Iowa), SU is well ahead of the pack. A snapshot of former students and alumni might include: M.T. Anderson G'98; Stephen Dunn G'70; Phil LaMarche G'03; Jay McInerney G'86; Claire Messud (who attended in 1989-90); Iain Pollock G'07; Tom Perrotta G'88; and Cheryl Strayed G'02, who is enjoying national celebrity with her memoir *Wild: From Lost to Found on the Pacific Crest Trail* (Knopf, 2012).

Director Christopher Kennedy G'88 attributes the program's success to its star faculty, many of whom have been hired before hitting it big. "I mean, we get Raymond Carver *before* he becomes Raymond Carver, Toby Wolff *before* he's Toby Wolff, George before he's George Saunders. And Dana Spiotta—she's everywhere you look," he says during a recent office meeting. "Syracuse hires people who want to teach, and who are good at managing their time between teaching and writing."

For a program that got a late start compared to, say, Iowa's or Stanford's, SU's prides itself on selectivity and personalized attention. Creative writing is composed of 36 students in two divisions (fiction and poetry), who are taught by eight full-time faculty members. Each professor is not only a consummate writer, but also a dedicated teacher, closely involved with the inner workings of the program and with the intellectual lives of his or her students. That each student receives a full scholarship, in addition to an annual stipend, gives the program added value.

"We don't want our students to worry about money while they're here," says Kennedy. "We want them to hone their craft and nothing else. It keeps the process pure."

Karr agrees. "We get writers who are slightly older and understand the wisdom of not needing to work four part-time jobs or to go into thousands of dollars of debt. ... It's important that we invest in our students."

He Was Huck Finn, That's Who He Was

SU's creative writing program unofficially began in 1891 at the Delta Upsilon house, where Stephen Crane penned fiction in his upstairs bedroom. He wasn't much of a student, completing only one course in a single year at two different colleges, but his desire to report on what couldn't be taught in the classroom (e.g., prostitution) made him a gritty author. Crane's coming-out party was the 1895 novella *The Red Badge of Courage*, which did wonders for his career and the area's reputation. Years later, other notable writers, including Lillian Hellman, Toni Morrison, and David Foster Wallace, would find their way to the Salt City.

What's not to like about Syracuse? The combination of long winters, cheap housing, and close proximity to New York City (the publishing capital of the world) is all a writer needs. Arts and Sciences alumni Shirley Jackson '40, John A. Williams '50, and Joyce Carol Oates '60, H'00 thought so. They were already best-selling authors by the time the creative writing program roared out of the gate in 1963. Other undergraduates who went on to shape the program (or to be influenced by it) were William Safire '51, H'78; Alice Sebold '84; Koren Zailckas '02; and Steve Sheinkin '90, another 2012 National Book Award finalist.

Many writers chalk up SU's allure to a certain mystique or romanticism. For example, one would be hard-pressed to talk about the University without mentioning Delmore Schwartz, who famously mentored Lou Reed '64. "I will always love Syracuse for giving me the opportunity to study with him," the gravel-voiced rocker told a packed room in Manhattan, several years ago. "Delmore inspired me to write, and, to this day, I draw inspiration from his stories, poems, and essays. His titles, alone, were a writer's dream."

Despite the fact Schwartz was nearing death, he was a formidable presence on campus, and instilled in Reed an abiding interest in poetry.

Christopher Kennedy admits these yarns are ratings gold. "There are several legacies associated with us," he says between sips of coffee. "You have the Schwartz-Reed connection, which is popular among musicians and poets. You also have Stephen Crane, who, despite being a lousy student, wrote an American masterpiece. And then there were Raymond Carver and Toby Wolff, who were such literary giants....These things are important to 18- and 19-year-olds who are thinking about where to study writing."

As SU's program gained traction, so did its students. Novelists Mary Gordon G'73 and Jay McInerney succeeded by dint of hard work and helped usher the program into a kind of golden age. At the center of it all were Carver and Wolff, soon to become the best fiction writers of their generation.

Much has been written about the pair, individually and collectively, and their impact on modern literature. Born and raised in the Pacific Northwest, Carver achieved critical success in 1976 with the short-story collection, *Will You Please Be Quiet, Please?* (McGraw-Hill). Other volumes followed, many of which drew on his experiences as the child of a small-town sawmill operator. Carver quickly amassed a large following, as well as his share of imitators, before dying of lung cancer at the age of 50.

"Anybody who knew Ray knew what a serious artist he was," says Karr. "He had enormous enthusiasm for other people's work. I remember Ray reading my poems and stories when I was in my twenties, and being very encouraging."

Calling from the West Coast, where she and Rodney Crowell are promoting their country album, *KIN,* Karr recounts story after story about her mentor. Like the time Carver tried to stop drinking. "Ray had lost everything—his wife, his home, his car—and was living out of a trailer," she says. "When he skipped out on paying his bankruptcy fees, his lawyer took him to small claims court and tried to have his dog taken away. ... He was Huck Finn, that's who he was."

Karr also recalls a piece Wolff published in *Esquire,* shortly after Carver's death in 1988. "The piece Toby wrote spoke of a kind of tribal connection he had with Ray," she says. "Here were two sincere writers who didn't care about making millions of dollars or getting their faces plastered on billboards. They were simply devoted to the art of writing. It's almost religious, if you think about it."

This fall, Karr is helping organize a special event in New York City to mark the 50th anniversary of SU's creative writing program and to raise support for the "Raymond Carver Reading Series," which annually brings 12 to 14 writers to campus for readings and discussions. Past readers have included Dave Eggers, William Gass, Lorrie Moore, Alice Fulton, Mary Gaitskill, and various SU faculty members.

"It's a way of honoring Ray's legacy," says Karr, who will be one such reader in November. George Saunders echoes these sentiments, citing the "egalitarian impulse" that Carver instilled in his students. "Ray came from a working-class background, and fought his way up, so I think there's some of that in our spirit—the idea that writing is for everyone, regardless of their background," says the award-winning writer, during a recent interview in his office.

Mary Karr

Perhaps no one benefited more from Carver's insight than McInerney, who shot to fame as a student with *Bright Lights, Big City* (Vintage, 1984). The renowned novelist and wine columnist has credited both Carver and Wolff for teaching him "a hell of a lot about writing, about the basic craft… that has to be mastered before you can do original work."

When McInerney arrived on campus in 1981, the jet-setting student had already been married and worked for *The New Yorker* and for TIME-LIFE Books in Japan. It didn't take long for him to publish his first short story in *The Paris Review* or to polish off the initial draft of *Bright Lights, Big City*, notable for its use of second-person narrative and explicit drug references. By the time he graduated, McInerney was a bona fide star, with a second novel under his belt and a film adaptation on the way.

McInerney credits Carver and Wolff for "helping him to find his way." "Their styles were completely different," he tells me during a recent airline layover. "Carver treated his work like a living thing, and was not bound to it. He'd nurse it along. …Toby was more methodical, and viewed writing like a watch, which could be taken apart and reconstructed. He was also very objective with his teaching."

The Eighties were good to SU. Carver's and Wolff's creative gears were working overtime, and the program was flush with talent.

But with success came the public's need to label and categorize. Carver and Wolff, for example, found themselves lumped into the "dirty realism" camp, a term coined by Bill Buford of *Granta* magazine to describe fiction that captured the "belly-side of contemporary life…with a disturbing detachment." Carver also had the dubious honor of being tagged a "blue-collar minimalist." "Ray had been sort of an underground secret among literary types, until he published 'What We Talk About When We Talk About Love,' which made him a literary sensation," McInerney says of the 1981 short-story collection. "That was when the minimalist label got hung around his neck."

Most writers fail to accept such designations, despite their apparent associations and affinities, and Carver and Wolff were no different. "The purpose of an M.F.A. program is to allow each writer to develop his or her own voice, rather than to impose an aesthetic," says Deborah Treisman, fiction editor of *The New Yorker.* "Otherwise, it would be a failure of the program. What Syracuse professors and alumni have in common is an abundance of literary talent."

Wolff concurs: "I don't even know what 'minimalist' means, frankly. I guess it was more of a journalistic term than anything—a term of convenience, much like the 'blue-collar' label. Sure, some of Ray's characters worked in lumber mills or lived in housing developments behind the highway, but those stories took place in a world that Ray knew. They were stories of social observation, without being preachy."

Interestingly, Carver studied with John Gardner, a novelist and classical scholar who probably did more to nurture his style than anyone else. "Just as Gardner helped Ray find his voice, Ray and Toby helped me find mine," says McInerney. "The direction I ended up going in, as a writer, was not typical, but I could not have done it without them. I was from Manhattan, so I wasn't going to write about trailer parks and the working class."

Gallagher, an accomplished poet who briefly directed the creative writing program, was grief-stricken after her husband's death. "Ray died in August. When I went back to campus that fall, it wasn't the same," says Gallagher, who later collaborated with filmmaker Robert Altman on two Carver-inspired projects: the drama, *Short Cuts,* and the documentary, *Luck, Trust, and Ketchup: Robert Altman in Carver Country.* "So I decided to leave Syracuse—which was hard because I had quite a good life there and loved my vocation as a teacher—to concentrate on my book, 'Moon Crossing Bridge,' which I dedicated to Ray."

Recently, Gallagher worked on *Beginners* (Library of America, 2009), featuring the collection *What We Talk About When We Talk About Love* in its original, uncut form. The book has, among other things, prompted a fresh

SU Archives and Records Management

Tobias Wolff

consideration of Carver's style. "Writers can now see what kind of writer he really was," she says. "A great lesson has been taught here about the overzealousness of his editor."

Like Carver, Wolff was a product of the Pacific Northwest and a consummate storyteller. Yet as a writer and teacher, the latter's style was vastly different.

A member of the U.S. Army's Special Forces in Vietnam, Wolff has channeled many of his wartime experiences into sharply etched stories and longer works, including his novel *The Barracks Thief* (Ecco, 1984) and his memoir *In Pharaoh's Army: Memories of the Lost War* (Vintage, 1995). Wolff's collection of short stories includes *In the Garden of the North American Martyrs* (Ecco, 1981). Another memoir, *This Boy's Life* (The Atlantic Monthly Press, 1989), was made into a film with Leonardo DiCaprio and Robert De Niro.

George Saunders was one of many writers fortunate enough to study under Wolff. "He was as good a teaching mentor as he was a writing mentor," says Saunders. "Plus, it was a pretty big time in the life of the program. Ray Carver was here, as was [poet] Hayden Carruth, and Jay McInerney had just published 'Bright Lights, Big City,' and was the most famous writer in America."

Tom Perrotta was a classmate of Saunders' who also learned from Wolff. If Carver was the reason Perrotta came to SU, Wolff was the reason he stayed. The author of *Little Children* (St. Martin's Press, 2004) and *Election* (Berkley Trade, 1998), Perrotta describes Wolff as a "careful and sympathetic reader," and credits him for developing his sense of identity and literary aesthetic.

George Saunders

"I recall Toby reading an excerpt from 'This Boy's Life,'" says Perrotta. "The book was still in progress at the time, and the excerpt he was reading was amazing—funny and mortifying and deeply moving. It was one of those great moments when you realize you are in the presence of something special."

All in the Family

Cheryl Strayed remembers it like yesterday—new student orientation for the creative writing program. "Brooks Haxton stood up and told us that we were all there to be writers," she says. "Nobody had ever said that to me before. I knew it was a tremendous gift then, and I know it even more now."

Despite enormous changes in the field (e.g., the proliferation of e-publishing, low-residency programs, and online courses), SU has remained loyal to fostering creativity and strong writing skills. Strayed is the latest example of alumna-done-good. She is currently the proud owner of two *New York Times* bestsellers, including *Wild*, which was the inaugural selection for Oprah's Book Club 2.0 and has been optioned for film by Reese Witherspoon's production company.

Cheryl Strayed

"What hasn't changed is the fact that becoming a good fiction writer requires years of dedication, learning, and growth," says Deborah Treisman, whose magazine has published pieces by George Saunders, Mary Karr, Dana Spiotta, and other SU writers. "The best thing a writing class can do is save the writer some time—both by requiring him or her to produce a lot of work in a short amount of time and by forcing him or her to experiment and actively develop his or her voice."

But not everyone can be like Strayed, and faculty members are quick to point out that they're not in the literary agency business. "We're here to make you the best writer you can be," says Kennedy. "All that other stuff about finding an agent or getting a book published is important, but it's not our ultimate goal."

Strayed is proof that this philosophy works. At SU, she began writing her first novel, *Torch* (Mariner Books, 2007), which was not completed until after graduation. Torch went on to become a finalist for the Great Lakes Book Award and was selected by *The Oregonian* as one of the Top-10 books of the year by writers from the Pacific Northwest—proving patience is a virtue.

"I went to SU so I could have a concentrated period of time to focus on my writing," she explains in an e-mail. "Writing 'Torch' was tremendously important to me, as a person and a writer. It taught me how to write a book. Everything that followed, professionally, can be traced back to its success."

Strayed rattles off names of other SU faculty members, including that of former English professor Mary Gaitskill ("one of my all-time literary heroes"), who helped point the way forward. Strayed also says the atmosphere they engendered was not just collegial; it was familial. "Their generosity gave me strength. It was also a transformative experience—just that small thing of being treated with seriousness and respect. It has stayed with me."

During the course of researching this story, the word "family" has come up a lot in conversation. Karr stresses it in a forthcoming SU documentary that her son is producing. "The secret of our program is not just the students, but the openness of and connection among the faculty," she says, with a hint of emotion. "I see my students go into SU, and come out with this exceptional shift in knowledge."

Spiotta, author of the award-winning novel *Stone Arabia* (Scribner, 2011), knows what Karr is talking about. She and other female writers at SU, for example, have made strong contributions toward issues of gender, literary credibility, and critical acceptance in the industry. Among the female professors to whom SU may lay claim are Safiya Henderson-Holmes, Malena

Mörling, Farnoosh Moshiri-Rossi, Heather McHugh, Amy Hempel, Diane Williams, Christine Schutt, Heidi Julavits, Lynne Tillman, Mary Caponegro, and program associate director Sarah Harwell G'05.

"We have wonderful women in our program who are ambitious and brilliant," says Spiotta, known for her sometimes difficult and complex female characters. "In 10 years, the literary world will probably be quite different, when it comes to how women writers are perceived. I like to think that our students will be the vanguard of a movement of fierce writers who happen to be women."

Meanwhile, the "egalitarian impulse" that Saunders referenced earlier continues to permeate campus. Poets hanging with novelists, who, in turn, are mixing it up with memoirists—it's all good, he says. "The idea that writing is for everyone, and is important to everyone, and that anyone talented can do it, regardless of background—there's something to be said from wherever you find yourself."

Poets Brooks Haxton G'81 and Michael Burkard exemplify the dramatic range of the program's faculty. Haxton exhibits all the outstanding traits of a Southern gentleman, as well as a flair for classical languages. Students and alumni repeatedly cite him as one of their most favorite professors. "I wouldn't be the writer I am today without the tutelage of Brooks Haxton," says Iain Pollock, winner of the Cave Canem Poetry Prize. "I'm particularly thankful for being exposed to the plain-spoken school of poetry, which helped to assuage some of my florid and long-winded predilections (which you may be noticing right now)."

Strayed is equally appreciative of Burkard. "I will always be indebted to him for all the wisdom he shared with me about writing and for his kindness and support," she says. "Michael made me feel like there was something *real* happening at SU."

Haxton and Burkard quickly deflect such praise onto their colleagues. "From the formal invention and virtuosity of Donald Justice and W.D. Snodgrass to the passionate empathy and urgency of Hayden Carruth and the experimental freedom of Michael Burkard, Syracuse has always had various aesthetic approaches," says Haxton. "As a student, I had the great luck of studying with Hayden, who was a dazzlingly intelligent, learned, and imaginative writer. He was also probably the best teacher I ever had. And Ray Carver—many people don't know that he was a first-rate poet. His practice as a teacher, like his writing, was highly intuitive."

With his shock of gray hair and perennial five o'clock shadow, Burkard is probably about as close as one gets to the starving-artist stereotype. But appearances can be misleading; the oft-disheveled Burkard is not only an accomplished poet, but also a sought-after teacher of community writing.

We usually talk art or music—Burkard is an amateur singer/songwriter—but this time the onus is on creative writing. "I'll never forget the time [Mexican photographer] Flor Garduñu came to campus to discuss her exhibition 'Witnesses of Time,'" he tells me outside the Hall of Languages, a cigarette perched on his lower lip. "She gave a stupendous talk

©Syracuse in Focus

Michael Burkard

about how common, everyday acts take on an added dimension through their ritual associations. I took my students to her talk and the exhibition. Boy, she was a *real* poet-photographer."

Other guest writers work their way into the conversation, but none of them elicits a stronger response from Burkard as SU's Bruce Smith and Arthur Flowers. "I would say Arthur Flowers' reading-performances—his invocations and musicality, the tonality with his work—well, I could see them again and again and again," he says. "Bruce Smith is the same way. His latest book, 'Devotions,' is like a big jazz solo. It's very rhythmic and musical. I just love it."

A self-described "unorthodox minority voice," Flowers says he was hired in the mid-Nineties to give the program some color. (No pun intended.) Since then, he has arguably done more than anyone on faculty to expand the modalities of storytelling. His presentations often include singing and drum-

SU Photo and Imaging Center

Arthur Flowers with undergrads

ming, and have taken him all over the world, from bohemian dives in Greenwich Village to the Lotus Stage in Bali (Indonesia) to the Hotel Diggi Palace in Rajasthan (India).

Flowers is particularly excited about transmedia publishing—a passion instilled in him by his students. "We are constantly influenced by the young guns we bring into the program," Flowers says on the phone from Syracuse, weeks before the New York City event on November 15. "During my first class at SU, I had one student [Jeff Parker G'99] who introduced me to the concept of hypertext fiction. Since then, I've been trying to build a digital persona that's as lasting as my print one."

The professor regards himself as a latter-day "griot," drawing on elements of both Western written and African oral traditions. "I feel like a storyteller who gathers the tribes around the fire and then establishes a sense of community," says Flowers, author of the acclaimed graphic novel *I See the Promised Land: A Life of Martin Luther King, Jr.* (Tara Books, 2010). "My goal is to take everyone a little bit higher and to leave them feeling stronger than when they arrive."

Smith—whose latest book, *Devotions* (University of Chicago Press, 2011), has been nominated for several national awards—has a similar effect on his followers. "Bruce helped unlock the sonic intensity of poetry for me," says Pollock. "Almost immediately upon arriving at SU, I learned from him how to pay more attention to vowel and consonant sounds of individual words and at the line level."

Smith returns the compliment. "Because I can't actually study with Dana Spiotta, George Saunders, and Arthur Flowers, I read them and learn what I can from them and annoy them in the hallways and bug them at dinners," he says rather self-deprecatingly. "They are so fiercely smart and worldly and otherworldly that I get reflected glory in their presence. I try to keep up. I want to ride in the backseat of their convertibles."

Half-joking aside, Smith has his own superlatives at the ready: Burkard ("one of the great associative imaginations in poetry"), Haxton ("one of our great lucubrators who writes poems of heart-scalding beauty"), and Kennedy ("a writer with extravagant power whose poems are like dreams, barely perceptible yet hauntingly real"). You get the picture.

As the creative writing program prepares to usher in the next 50 years, it's a given that some things will change—such as how technology is utilized in the classroom—and others will not. "Thank the Muses we have no common aesthetic or teaching style," Smith says. "Or maybe there is one: care and scrupulous attention and commitment to developing writers."

"If you look at the history of folks who've taught in the program, it's amazing how different they are. None of them shares a common style," says Phil Memmer, executive director of the Arts Branch of the YMCA of Greater Syracuse, which includes the Downtown Writer's Center.

"This strikes me as healthy for the future of the program and for the students who pass through it."

Perhaps Carver was on to something when he said that the writer gets the final word, insofar as the word is ever final. His death may have cut short a career, but it certainly didn't diminish his legacy—and the impact he has had on the possibilities of creative writing.

As long as there are writers, there will be programs, such as the one here on the Hill, to harness creativity. It's a responsibility nobody takes lightly.

"That's all we have, finally, the words," Carver prophetically said before his death, "and they had better be the right ones."

A Sampling of Creative Writing Faculty over the Years

Philip Booth
Michael Burkard
Hortense Calisher
Hayden Carruth
Raymond Carver
Sally Daniels
Junot Díaz
Donald Dike
George P. Elliott
Arthur Flowers
Mary Gaitskill
Tess Gallagher
Brooks Haxton G'81
Donald Justice
Mary Karr
Christopher Kennedy G'88
Delmore Schwartz
Bruce Smith
W.D. Snodgrass
Dana Spiotta
George Saunders G'88
Douglas Unger
Tobias Wolff

Select Alumni

M.T. Anderson G'98

Joel Brouwer G'93

Dan Chaon G'90

Rebecca Curtis G'01

Lee Durkee (attended 1986–88)

Stephen Dunn G'70

Mary Gordon G'73

Paul Griner G'89

Sarah Harwell G'05

Lily King G'95

Phil LaMarche G'03

Adam Levin G'04

Larry Levis G'70

Jay McInerney G'86

Jane Mead G'86

Claire Messud (attended 1989–90)

Robert Olmstead '77, G'83

Robert O'Connor G'85

Mike Padilla G'99

Lucia Perillo G'86

Tom Perrotta G'88

Iain Pollock G'07

Courtney Queeney G'05

Cheryl Strayed G'02

Tryfon Tolides G'04

Paul Watkins (attended 1986–88)

Nina Pick

THE GIFT

I lived in a house on the boulevard,
saw the edges of lawns lined with stones

and pruned. I spent my childhood in stucco

in Utica its pimply walls we had a hamster, a string of turtles,
three cats. My grandmother lived there too and she cooked and she tied

my shoes. You were a kid in Detroit, where you played
soccer and trumpet your mother loved you

she was eating you whole. We moved from those places and
then we both came here and we met. I sat in the front row

stoned at the band concert, looked up at your fingers pressing
the keys and your spray of freckles

and the gold mouth of the trumpet like a cave I wanted
to live in or maybe be. Welcome, it said

the floor woozing beneath me. Welcome, it said
splaying its knees.

I had never seen anything as beautiful as longing and right
then it was handed to me on its glass string

and I took it and slipped it over my head and knew it
was the apple, the bridal gown, the princely gift,

that poisons, strangles, burns one to ash.

Pat Daneman

To Anne Sexton

When I was sixteen, I wanted to be you,
and I wanted you to be my mother. I thought
girls needed gin, not cocoa, to grow up with courage.
I envied your long legs, your cigarettes, your black,
unyielding hair. My heart clutched at your slyness
with acrostics, your unapologetic appetites
brought down on you by madness, brilliance, luck—
all interchangeable once you'd put on makeup
and had a weeping cold glass in your hand.
You slapped the men who needed slapping
and lay down with the men you needed
on lumpy mattresses or towels damp with ocean water.
When Sylvia Plath died, babies asleep, furniture
crammed against the door, and up and down the stairs
melted snow in the prints of policemen's boots,
you said that death was mine and I understood
that it was not a sin for women to aspire
to each other's bitterness, borrow rage
as if it were a tube of lipstick or a comb.

Thomas P. Rigoli

EXPERIENCING SILICON VALLEY

"There are certain periods in history when discoveries and events...create a window when civilization has the opportunity to leap forward. One of these was...the Renaissance...a time of invention, entrepreneurial accomplishments and exploration—very similar to what has occurred in Silicon Valley."

"The Making of Silicon Valley"
©*1995 The Santa Clara County Historical Association*

My romance with electronics took root when I was growing up in Jamestown, New York, in the 1950s. A fascination with radio led me to build my first crystal set using my mattress bedspring as an antenna. It seemed like magic to manipulate a "cat's whisker" atop a small grayish-white clump of germanium and then hear music and radio dramas streaming out of the ether. Many nights I would fall asleep wearing earphones. I never guessed that my early interest in electronics would ultimately lead me to work with America's most innovative high-tech companies and some of the legendary personalities who established them.

After earning my B.S.E.E. from Syracuse University in 1964, I accepted a position with GTE Sylvania, a military/aerospace contractor. I initially wrote operations manuals for about a year and then moved on to become a field engineer working on Top Secret projects. For about

Location: 844 E Charleston Road, Palo Alto, California, about 5 miles from Stanford University

five years, I worked on Minuteman ICBM electronics at both Vandenberg AFB, California, and Grand Forks, North Dakota, and then in 1969, I accepted a brief assignment to oversee the installation of perimeter security systems in Vietnam.

I was subsequently asked to return to the war zone to direct the deployment of large, dart-shaped seismic detectors along the Ho Chi Minh trail. When I learned that deployment meant dropping electronic darts from a low-flying helicopter, I sensed it was time to alter my career path. In a major career shift, I became the first San Francisco editor for *EDN*, a monthly publication for electronic designers. Thus began my odyssey in a northern California region that was to become famously known as "Silicon Valley."

"Found on no map, yet famous around the world...

...Silicon Valley is that great nursery of new companies and technologies that are revolutionizing our lives," wrote the late Gene Bylinsky, the former science and technology editor for *Fortune* magazine. "Silicon Valley is the 20th Century's counterpart to the Fertile Crescent, the cradle of modern civilization in the Near East where wheat and farm animals were domesticated and (the) first writing evolved. In Silicon Valley, this densest concentration of innovative companies in the world, the new kind of writing is done on silicon, in intricate microminiaturized patterns that plot man's path to the future."

"Silicon Valley: High Tech Window to the Future"
© *1985 Intercontinental Publishing Corporation Ltd.*

My High-Tech Odyssey

As *EDN* magazine editor, I had rare opportunities to interview entrepreneurs before they became Silicon Valley legends. I recall interviewing a professorial Bob Noyce a few weeks after he left Fairchild Semiconductor to start Intel. I also interviewed a flamboyant Jerry Sanders shortly after he left Fairchild to start Advanced Micro Devices. And then there was cigar-smoking Charlie Sporck and cerebral Don Valentine, the top execs at National Semiconductor. Don later founded Sequoia Capital, which became the gold standard for venture capital companies. Sequoia was an early investor in many successful high-tech companies, including Apple Computer and Cisco Systems.

I also met the taciturn John Bardeen, who won the Nobel Prize in Physics twice, first in 1956 for co-inventing the transistor at Bell Labs, and then in 1972 for his work on superconductivity. I caught up with Dr. Bardeen in 1970 after he presented his latest esoteric findings on superconductivity at Stanford University.

I was completing my second year with *EDN* when a market research firm hired me to edit its monthly analysis of technology developments for the financial community. I worked one year there, once scooping *Business Week* by publishing the first comprehensive article about digital watches. (Considered high-tech marvels at the time, they originally sold for about $200. The magic of ICs and the forces of global competition quickly drove down prices to less than $25.)

Inspired by the entrepreneurial spirit of Silicon Valley, I set out to "do my own thing" in 1972: first as an independent technology writer and then as a principal in a high-tech marketing and communications agency. Over more than 25 years (and through three different partnerships), I held virtually every management position in the agency as we served cutting-edge companies.

It was exhilarating to be on the front lines as we helped promising startups launch their very first products. We worked closely with Dr. David K. Lam, the founder of Lam Research, who launched his innovative plasma etch system in 1981. Born in China, he became the first Asian American to take a company public on the NASDAQ exchange in 1984. (I am currently a business advisor to Dr. Lam who now oversees Multibeam Corporation, an early stage developer of Complementary E-beam Lithography systems.)

In 1994, I was recruited by Cirrus Logic, one of my agency's clients, to become its VP of corporate communications, and this gave me the opportunity to work closely with the late Mike Hackworth, co-founder and CEO, over a seven-year period as the semiconductor company's revenue rocketed from about $400 million to more than $1 billion annually. Mike's vision was to build all the critical chips around a microprocessor—i.e., chips to handle graphics, communications, hard disk control, power management, etc. Through an aggressive program of acquisitions, his company came closer to realizing this dream than any other semiconductor company. However, Cirrus Logic eventually spun off its acquisitions, which triggered a new wave of startups. When the company relocated its headquarters to Austin, Texas, I chose to stay in Silicon Valley.

Who Named Silicon Valley?

Don C. Hoefler (1923–1986) coined the term in a 1971 series of articles that was published in *Electronic News*, the only major weekly covering the emerging semiconductor industry. Don was the West Coast reporter for *EN* at the same time I was West Coast editor for the monthly *EDN* magazine. I regularly bumped into him at press conferences. In his brief San Francisco obituary, they credited him with naming "Silicon Valley," noting that he later quipped when asked about it, "How was I to know that the term would be adopted industry wide and become generic worldwide?"

The Silicon Valley Phenomenon

Like the Renaissance and the Fertile Crescent, Silicon Valley emerged from a confluence of favorable factors. The Renaissance, during the fourteenth to seventeenth centuries was fueled by pent-up desire to emerge from the Dark Ages and the generosity of wealthy patrons of the arts, most notably the Medici family. The Fertile Crescent flourished some 9,000 years BCE, thanks to the natural irrigation from the Tigris and Euphrates rivers. Key factors creating Silicon Valley included a temperate northern California climate and enviable geography, plus great universities and a community of high-tech venture capitalists.

Comparing the emergence of Silicon Valley to other historical periods gives us clues about its future impact. The Renaissance, for example, started in Italy around 1350 and subsequently spread throughout the rest of Europe until about 1620. The Silicon Valley phenomenon has also spread, albeit more rapidly, from its roots in northern California to other metropolitan centers hoping to emulate its economic success. From "Silicon Prairie" in Dallas-Fort Worth to "Silicon Alley" in Manhattan to "Silicon Glen" in Scotland, the marvel of Silicon Valley continues to migrate around the globe, inspiring many. Perhaps the most remarkable emulators of Silicon Valley culture are now taking shape in China and India.

Moore's Law

Transistor density on integrated circuits doubles about every two years[*]

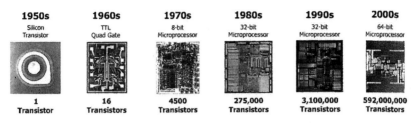

1950s	1960s	1970s	1980s	1990s	2000s
Silicon Transistor	TTL Quad Gate	8-bit Microprocessor	32-bit Microprocessor	32-bit Microprocessor	64-bit Microprocessor
1 Transistor	16 Transistors	4500 Transistors	275,000 Transistors	3,100,000 Transistors	592,000,000 Transistors

Silicon "chips" have grown in capability from a single transistor in the 1950s to billions of transistors today. These extraordinary engines powered the computing and communications revolution of the information age.

[*]Source: "Moore's Law: Raising the Bar" (Intel Corporation 2005)
Photos courtesy of Fairchild Semiconductor and Intel Corporation (images are not to scale)

Microprocessor Magic

Silicon Valley culture seemed to reach a critical mass for explosive growth in 1970, about a year before Intel introduced its 4004 microcomputer, or "microprocessor" as it was later called. The emergence of the microprocessor chip was followed by a tidal wave of innovations throughout the adolescent semiconductor industry.

The advent of the microprocessor propelled us into the Information Age. To appreciate how fast and how far we have progressed, we need only look back about a half century when computers were huge machines operated by vacuum tubes. They filled entire rooms and were costly, making them accessible only to labs operated by the government, universities, and major corporations.

Complex semiconductor devices, which emerged in the 1970s, set the stage for computers as well as a host of other electronic products to be made much smaller and more affordable. The most complex integrated circuit back then was an 8-bit microprocessor that integrated nearly 5,000 transistors on a single chip. Today, IC transistor density is now in the billions. Moreover, semiconductor manufacturing has gone 3D both at the transistor and packaging levels to seek higher densities. Moore's Law, which asserts that transistor density of ICs will double about every two years, is still on track.

When further silicon integration finally reaches its atomic limit, we will no doubt see new materials and processes emerge to store and manipulate binary 1s and 0s so that even more data can be packed into ever smaller form factors.

Throughout the 1970s and 1980s, semiconductor startups blossomed in the Valley, a good number of them tracing their roots to Fairchild Semiconductor. Its progenitor was the Shockley Transistor Corporation founded by William Shockley, one of the co-inventors of the transistor.

Shockley was brilliant but not easy to work with. It's now the stuff of colorful Silicon Valley folklore how Bob Noyce, Gordon Moore, and six other young technologists bolted from Shockley's company and banded together to form Fairchild Semiconductor under the auspices of Fairchild Camera & Instrument. Helping to put the deal together was a young M.B.A., Arthur Rock, also a Syracuse University graduate, who later became a lead investor in Intel and a premiere venture capitalist.

"The Traitorous Eight," as Shockley called them, went on to make Fairchild Semiconductor a leading manufacturer, as well as the incubator for numerous entrepreneurial talents who eventually spun out to start their own semiconductor companies. Most notable among these were Intel and Advanced Micro Devices, which became fierce competitors in the microprocessor market.

Following the proliferation of semiconductor device manufacturers in Silicon Valley, a new class of early stage ventures emerged to build the sophisticated equipment to manufacture and test the chips—the "pipes and plumbing" of the industry, as some have called it. Such equipment included lithography systems, plasma etchers, diffusion furnaces, automated testers, and packaging systems. The strong demand for such equipment led to the formation of the Semiconductor Equipment & Materials (SEMI) trade association, which has since grown in stature and today stages SEMICON tradeshows around the globe.

Megabyte Milestones

A good candidate for the 20th century equivalent to the Gutenberg press in terms of the impact it has had on communications is the IC, which gave rise to microprocessors, RAMs, ROMs, flash memory, and a host of application-specific systems on a chip. A close second would be the hard disk drive (HDD) that has enabled access to an extraordinarily large and increasing amount of affordable mass storage.

Interestingly, both ICs and HDDs—not unlike the Gutenberg press—rely on a printing process to bring information from the one to the many. While both optical and E-Beam Lithography systems facilitate the printing of patterns on silicon wafers to create ICs, HDDs deploy heads that float above spinning disks to imprint magnetic data on the disks.

Without the IC and HDD technology advances that took place in the last quarter of the 20th century, there would be no affordable computers, no highly functional mobile handsets...and no Internet. ICs are needed to control HDDs, which in turn are needed to store the vast amounts of information to make computers and all their derivatives, as well as the Internet, work.

While Moore's Law was conceived for ICs to forecast the doubling of transistor density every two years, it has also been applied to disk storage density. If you begin tracking storage density in terms of Megabytes, starting with IBM's Winchester HDDs that came to market in the 1970s, you would find that HDD storage density has easily doubled (and perhaps more than doubled) every two years.

To appreciate even more the steep ramp of innovation in HDD technology, flash back half a century when IBM introduced the world's very first HDD system, dubbed RAMAC for its designated function, "random access method of accounting and control." Weighing one ton and designed with vacuum tubes, RAMAC controlled fifty 24-inch diameter hard disks to provide access to 5 Megabytes.

The RAMAC was leased for $3,200/month; its cost per Megabyte was about $10,000. Now fast forward to the present when you can purchase for about $100 an internal HDD (that can be installed in a desktop computer), which provides access to 2 Terabytes, which equals 2,000 Gigabytes or 2,000,000 Megabytes, bringing its cost per Megabyte to a mere $0.00005!

Although magnetic recording has been around for half a century, non-volatile semiconductor memory, or "Flash" memory as we now commonly call it, came on the scene about 30 years ago. There has been some speculation that the Flash memory, now so ubiquitous in mobile handsets and numerous other electronic products, will eventually replace HDDs.

Given the much lower cost per Megabyte of HDD and its history of easily keeping pace with Moore's Law, it appears that HDD and Flash will co-exist and complement each other for the foreseeable future. Flash will be best to store data in small form factors and in high performance applications, while HDDs will continue to reign supreme where there are vast amounts of non-volatile storage required at the lowest price point, such as in supporting cloud computing.

Cloud computing continues to grow in popularity as leading Internet companies, particularly Google, provide Internet users with access to more and more Petabytes of storage and applications "in the cloud"—or more specifically from the vast number of servers it has installed around the globe.

Mobile Platform Impact

The widespread use of cell phones that began in the 1990s set in motion a series of rapid technology advances that have transformed the basic cell phone into a powerful touch-screen handset that can now perform virtually any task that used to require a powerful desktop computer. Today's smartphones can operate as an Internet browser, an e-mail port, camera, photo album, music library, GPS, FM radio, and much more.

As a mobile platform for electronics, the automobile has been no stranger to using advanced ICs. By some estimates, a typical automobile today deploys some 50 microprocessors in various modules, each dedicated to controlling a specific function, such as power distribution, airbag deployment, cruise control, climate control, transmission control, and so on. Many smartphone applications are migrating to automobile dashboards, and this increased use of ICs has improved safety, reliability, comfort, and convenience.

New Faces of Silicon Valley

Internet companies such as Google, Facebook, and Twitter represent the new faces of Silicon Valley. Nobody has yet come up with an equivalent to Moore's Law to forecast the growth of time spent online or the rate at which the number of unique web pages is growing, but it looks like these statistics will continue to rise for the foreseeable future.

Facebook now has nearly 1 billion monthly active users, 14 percent of the world's population. Twitter has about 500 million registered users. The rate at which Google continues to grow its infrastructure is truly mindboggling: it quickly, easily handles some 100 billion search queries per month. The number of unique web pages identified by Google has reached 30 trillion, up from 1 trillion in 2008.

Among the numerous content categories available on the Internet, Google's YouTube videos are one of the most popular, with more than 4 billion hours being watched each month. In an earlier report, YouTube reported traffic of over 800 million unique users/month and over 70 hours of video uploaded each minute. Whether for productive or entertainment reasons, more and more people are spending a lot of time online.

YouTube today is localized in over 40 countries and across some 60 languages. Although YouTube has attracted many users because of its viral videos, it will likely attract even more when it adds more original and professionally produced channels. With most new flat-panel TVs coming to market equipped with an interface to the Internet, YouTube is likely to popularize a new class of Internet TV channels.

The demographics of advanced technology adopters have changed dramatically over the years. Thanks to the emergence of the easily accessible Internet and the profusion of affordable computers and mobile handsets, a growing number of "power users" can be found in virtually every population segment, from young children to senior citizens. All have become enraptured by the high-tech products that open up new doors to communications, education, and entertainment.

Coming Full Circle

Technology in any of its forms is simply a tool, not unlike the wheel or fire. However, the easily accessible technology tools of the 21st century can bestow unprecedented power on a single person or small group to involve vast populations in record time. Moreover, the exponential use of social networks is making the world's inhabitants better informed, regardless of borders, race, gender, sexual preference, age, or religion. This increased knowledge sets the stage for positive societal and political change.

We've come so far, so fast, and yet I know that we have only begun to scratch the surface of advanced technology. As I write these final paragraphs on my computer, I am pleasantly distracted by a news headline that has popped up on my screen that reads, "NASA Shows First Color Photo of Mars." Space, the final frontier, will no doubt beckon new generations of engineers and scientists to quicken the stride of technological developments.

I would like to believe that many youngsters around the globe are fascinated with some aspect of technology, as I was so many years ago. My hope is that their individual voyages of self-discovery will take them to exciting new places like Silicon Valley, which I was so lucky to experience. ≋

"There is of course no single answer, no simple formula by which Silicon Valley can be emulated. Rather, this story shows what is possible if the right conjunction of events takes place to release and align human freedom and aspirations. It is a biography of an area, which, as a good biography should, inspire others and other regions to believe in themselves and be the best they can be."

Robert N. Noyce (1927-1990)
Co-inventor of the Integrated Circuit

"Silicon Valley: High Tech Window to the Future"
©1985 Intercontinental Publishing Corporation Ltd.

Betty Lise Anderson

HAVE YOU MET YOUR ENGINEER?

We are all familiar with lots of professions. We know our lawyer and our doctor by name. While we may not personally know a scientist, we all know what scientists do. They unravel how the world works and figure out the laws of nature. Their discoveries are often reported in the news, frequently accompanied by speculation about how some day, this knowledge could be used to (insert incredible miracle here). And then there are the engineers. Who are they? Although you are surrounded by and embedded in a marvelously complex technological system, you probably don't know the folks who built it.

Engineers are the ones who take scientific discoveries and apply them to real-life situations for practical purposes. A chemist (that is, a scientist) might work out what it is about a sugar molecule that makes it taste sweet. A chemical engineer uses that knowledge to design a molecule that tastes sweet, but can't be digested, so it has no calories. Purpose: to attempt to reduce the obesity problem. A physicist (scientist) deciphers how electricity and magnetism work, and writes out the solution in the form of equations. Electrical engineers use the equations to design an MRI machine that utilizes a magnetic field to image your spleen. Purpose: to find out if you're sick.

Everything engineers do is to benefit society. Some ways are obvious; some are not. You've heard of Bill Gates and Steve Jobs. But do you know the person who designed your cell phone? (OK, it was a bunch of people.)

A cell phone is a great example of invisible engineering. Sure, you know it has an antenna inside somewhere. It has a display. (There are engineers whose entire careers are devoted to color liquid crystal displays.) It has either a keypad (mechanical engineering) or a touch screen. The touch screen uses capacitive sensors that were designed by somebody you never heard of. The glass on the front is called Gorilla Glass, which is amazingly tough. A materials science engineer came up with that. There is a tiny speaker in your phone, and a tiny microphone. Somebody applied electricity and magnetism cleverly to make those, even though the concept for each has been around a long time. And the battery! There are engineers who spend their entire careers eking out a few more electrons from a battery. Oh, and don't forget the camera. In addition to the integrated circuit that actually detects and records the image, there is a series of lenses and filters designed by an optical engineer to provide a clear image under variable lighting conditions in an incredibly small space.

But that cell phone doesn't just have to work while sitting on a desk in your house; it has to work while you're outside with it when it's really hot or really cold. It has to stay together while you're running, jumping, or even driving over a bumpy road. It has to be able to withstand shock in case you drop it. It has to do all these things, yet be lightweight, compact, easy to use, and not cost too much. Some cell phones can tell where you are and whether you're moving or stationary. And, if you're waving or tipping the phone, the accelerometers inside it can tell how fast and in what direction.

The cell phone has to be able to find and communicate with cell towers. Engineers designed those cell towers too. If you look at an antenna tower, you might see some long, skinny vertical rectangles. Those are the antennas that send and receive signals from your cell phone. The smaller the antenna's aperture, the broader the beam. Since the antenna is skinny horizontally, the emitted (and received) beam is actually wide in that direction, to spread the beam over a wide area. The antenna is taller than it is wide, so the vertical spread of the beam is narrow, perfect for covering the surface of the earth (instead of an expanse of sky). Those round dish antennas on some of the towers have a large aperture that is as wide as it is tall. Their beams are more directional, for relaying microwave signals from one tower to the next.

And it's not just the phone, the antenna on the tower, and the antenna in the phone that are amazing. The cell tower has to be able to tell which phone call is for you and which is for the lady next to you. That data is all encoded, and someone had to figure out what the code should be so that the most users could share a tower at the same time, yet not have crosstalk with that other phone. And when it comes to phones, it's not just the ones you can see. Every gas pump has a "phone" now, so it can communicate with a computer somewhere to verify your credit card. Who is responsible for all this technology? Engineers!

Look around you. Everything you see that isn't a plant or an animal was engineered by somebody. And a lot of it is made of plastic. Back in Colonial America, if you needed an object of an unusual shape, you carved it out of wood, forged it out of metal, or made it out of ceramic. Then, in 1907, somebody invented a plastic called Bakelite, and suddenly people could make rugged, nonconductive items in all sorts of shapes and sizes. Telephones, dishes, toys, jewelry…the list is long. Plastic was not only incredibly convenient, it was cheap. Since then engineers have created all kinds of amazing plastic, from soft, pliable, and heat-resistant silicone to PVC for pipes to Styrofoam to nylon to a zillion other types in a wide array of colors and patterns.

Other kinds of engineering are less tangible. Civil engineers designed the entrance and exit ramps you take to work every day. They also determined what the speed limit should be on any stretch of road, and how to time the traffic lights. They designed the airport so that enough planes could land to accommodate all the travelers, and so that those travelers could move easily through the airport at any given time. The gates have to be spaced only as far apart as necessary so people can easily reach them. This feature is hard to design, since airplanes are pretty big; you can only put them so close together.

And what about the energy needed to fuel those planes…and our other vehicles? We get most of our energy from burning coal or gasoline. Those fuels are not only plentiful (so far), but they also contain a boatload of energy. Consider a tasty food that you enjoy, such as beef. Beef contains about two and one-half kilowatt hours (kWh) of energy per kilogram (kg). How about the highest calorie food you can think of? Let's say a stick of butter. If you eat the whole stick, that's 800 calories. That works out to around five kWh of energy per kg, about twice as energy-rific as beef. Gasoline, however, contains a whopping 12 kWh of energy per kg, or more than twice as much as butter! If we want to replace gasoline or coal with something greener, whatever it is has to produce a *lot* of energy. Even if a coal-fired furnace or gasoline engine is only 40 percent efficient (and that would be a very *good* engine), it's still effective to burn gasoline or coal, as long as you don't mind the impact on the environment. (For more information on that topic, contact an environmental engineer.)

On the other hand, if you put up windmills, the fuel is free, although it isn't available everywhere and not at all times. New York State, for instance, is not particularly windy, except on Lake Ontario and Lake Erie. The engineering dilemma is that it's more expensive and technically more challenging to put windmills out on a lake, plus you lose some energy sending the electricity to land. Let's say we're restricted, then, to putting our windmills on land.

The average wind speed in New York is between 5 and 6 mph (up in the air where the windmills operate). The National Renewable Energy Laboratory estimates that if you covered all available land in New York (excluding state parks, cities, waterways, etc.), one might generate about 75 GigaWatt hours/year. That is about one thousandth of the energy consumed by New York in 2010: 460,000 GWh.

Can we make windmills more efficient? What if we added more vanes, perhaps four instead of three? It turns out that, perhaps counter-intuitively, the added weight of the extra blade, not to mention the costs of manufacturing and transporting it, makes a poor trade. More doesn't turn out to be better. Significant engineering analysis went into finding that conclusion. Intuition can be wrong. In fact, some engineers are proposing to go down to two blades. What if we put solar cells under the windmills and get a two-for-one deal on space? Oops, solar cells aren't very efficient. The most effective are only about 40 percent efficient, and they are very expensive.

Research like this, on windmill efficiency, is what engineering is all about. Engineers study ways to trade off efficiency versus cost. For example, we can't afford to cover New York with fancy multi-heterojunction cells, but if we use cheap ones, we can afford more of them. Unfortunately, we only get about a quarter of the energy produced by the expensive ones. And, since we need some grazing land, we can't put them everywhere.

Back in the 70s, electrical engineer J. J. Suran talked to my engineering ethics class at Syracuse University. He had been an SU student himself and was the inventor of the GE implantable pacemaker. He told us about the first of those pacemakers installed in a person. It extended that person's life by many months, perhaps a couple of years. When the patient did eventually die, the family sued Mr. Suran, as well as GE, arguing that they had made compromises on the quality of the materials to keep costs down. If, however, GE had used the super-deluxe-platinum version of every component, the pacemaker would have been so expensive it wouldn't have been able to save anybody's life because no one could afford it. (Interestingly, Mr. Suran said that, two years later, at the person's gravesite, one could still detect the pacemaker's heartbeat.) That's what engineering is all about: finding the most effective solutions to the world's challenges.

And what about our food supply? If wealth is measured by access to food, we are obscenely rich in this country. Your friend Bob might have a chicken salad for lunch, then chicken again for dinner. Bob wouldn't give it a second thought. If Bob only likes white meat, he might be responsible for a chicken or two per day. Yet, two hundred years ago, a family might expect one chicken to feed the entire family for a day. Bob doesn't even have to cook his chicken. He can buy chicken dinners already made, cheap enough so he can buy one every day if he wants. If there is a drought, food might get a little more expensive for us Americans, but it is still available and affordable. And it is technology and engineering that make that possible.

Next time you go to the grocery store, pick any aisle and take the time to look at every product there. You'll see food items you didn't even know existed. Some are engineered foods in the sense that plants were crossbred to develop the tastiest tomato. (Hah! Researchers were really looking to develop the tomato that survives shipping the best.) Other foods are engineered in the sense that they don't occur in nature. Rice Krispies, for instance, or diet soda. Still others are engineered to be more nutritious (orange juice with added calcium) or more shelf-stable (the Twinkie is the classic example) or tastier. Some snacks, like pretzels, taste better if the salt is on the outside rather than in the dough. Remember Jello 1-2-3? That was food engineering!

But engineering at the store goes beyond food itself. Take bar codes, for example. Simply printing stripes on products and waving a laser beam over them has enabled much faster and more accurate checkout. It's so common we don't even think about it any more, but there was a time when the checkout clerk read a price tag and punched the numbers into the cash register. And bar codes are used to track your packages so you can go online (another engineering marvel) and find out whether those orange socks you ordered went out on the truck for delivery today.

Most people are never aware of all this engineering. Here's another example: Your computer keyboard keys are laid out in a peculiar way, the so-called "QWERTY" keyboard. Why? In the 1800s, some folks did a lot of keyboard testing to find out which letters people use the most—in English, anyway—and which the least. The keys with the least-used letters are pressed by your weakest fingers, the pinky and ring fingers. Letters are also distributed left and right so that you rarely have to type a word all with one hand, which would be slow. This is an example of ergonomics, a branch of industrial engineering. A more modern example is the computer mouse. When I first saw one, I thought some loser had come up with it.

I found it hard to get used to, and I was sure it was a fad. Now I can't imagine life without the mouse, or the trackball, or even more awesome, the touch screen. Or even a screen that reads gestures! Amazing!

Industrial engineers also figure out how to design a manufacturing process to be more efficient, less costly, and faster. Remember the materials engineering that went into developing plastic? There's also engineering in how to mold it, press it, extrude it, dye it, paint it, and assemble plastic parts. Take a trip to the department store, or the hardware store, and pick any item at random. Who designed it? How did they decide what materials to make it out of? How did they decide whether it should snap together or screw together? Why is the handle (or feature of your choice) shaped this way, pointed in that direction? Why is the battery compartment located here and not there? Why does this thing use button batteries and that thing use AAs? There are engineering reasons behind all these questions.

For example, why is my thermostat so darned complicated to program? Answer: because if you had a separate button for every feature, and a keyboard to enter the temperature, the thermostat would be as big as a microwave. The smaller the device has to be, the more involved the menus necessarily must be to keep the key count down.

Speaking of programming, I heard a computer engineer once talking to a group of high school kids, explaining that a cell phone has 10 or 20 million lines of code, and that's just for the operating system; it doesn't include the apps. Why so many? As Steve Jobs said, "Easy is hard." To make it easy for a person to use a phone or iPad, you have to figure out what a person's intuition is going to tell him to do, and then make that possible. You also must try to guess all the crazy things the user might actually try to do, then prevent him from crashing the device, while at the same time sending him meaningful error messages. The devices that function best in this situation are the best-engineered.

Incidentally, a smart phone having 10 million lines of code is not really that surprising, since it's really a computer that can make phone calls. In fact, the next generation of tech-enabled cars has 100 million lines of code per vehicle. (On the other hand, a Boeing 787 only has 6 million lines of code. Maybe it's to keep the weight down!)

In the early days of computers, the devices used to seize up all the time when users made mistakes. Engineers have gotten a lot better at predicting human error. I remember that, every time I had to buy a new printer, I was filled with dread. The reason? I'd have to locate and install some driver software, usually from a floppy disk, and get the computer to "see" the printer and communicate with it. It always seemed to take a whole day to get it working. Now when you plug in a new peripheral device, the computer says in effect, "Oh, I see you got a new camera. Let me go online and find the appropriate driver and install it for you…there you go. Have fun." That is real software engineering.

When you think of an engineer, what do you imagine? A white guy with a white shirt, narrow tie and calculator, working alone at a desk doing calculations or in the lab with an oscilloscope? That's the stereotype, and it probably comes from the 50s. Or maybe you imagine the cartoon Dilbert—oh, wait, Dilbert *is* a white guy with a white shirt and narrow tie, who works alone in a cubicle. In reality, engineers generally work in teams. Think of the engineers who built the Mars rover, Curiosity. There was a team for the landing system (which is a totally insane design, featuring a rocket-supported sky raft with a crane). Another team figured out where to land, another worked on the antenna, another on the drilling tool, and so on. Maybe you saw a video of the exhilarated engineers in the control room the day of the landing. That's the kind of joy every engineer experiences at the end of a successful project. "Woo-hoo!" is a well-known engineering term.

So remember, while you may see your dentist and your veterinarian and your accountant a few times a year, engineers are everywhere, even if you never actually see one. Hundreds of thousands of them are working for you behind the scenes, making your world a better place. And they're having a blast doing it. ≋

Adriana Grant

Lyric

Half the trouble's in the asking. How she said what she said was very much who she was. Be absolute all over the parquet. A closed-room mystery, solved by a genius-level amateur. Sometimes, one says too much. And suddenly, there's a bird.

Mary-Margaret Stevens

No Damn Good

Just before the train yard the tracks all run into each other and at the mouth of the northeast corridor they come in sixteen across. The ties sink in the gravel, the rails snake over them biting the toes of our sneakers and when we trip we rattle from the aerosol cans zipped against our chests.

Against the corrugated skin of a freight car, Amber lays down the skeleton design and Tori comes in with the color while I keep watch for the yard guards who still call themselves bulls. At my turn I hold the can close and tight for the details and my fingers go colder than February from the aerosol. Amber signs with her own name, proud as hell. Tori's tag is SPY in pink bubblegum letters. At the last minute I scrawl out BASTARD, just to put it in writing. We hear the bulls coming long before we see their big black SUV with the lights put out, sheets of ice popping under the wheels. The gravel crunches slow and deliberate like someone unwrapping candy in the movies. We try to run but the loose stones push our legs out to slow exaggerated strides and we have to settle for rolling under the next row of freight. Underneath, we scratch the ground for snow and push it into our mouths, stones and all, to hide the steam of our breath. They don't notice the fresh paint among the long bright panels of color, which could and have stretched across the whole Northeast.

We wait a long time and crawl out of the dark, stiff and cold as the dead. None of us feel like walking after that and when we find a string of cars panting and sighing into motion we pull ourselves on and wait. The train starts picking up speed two miles out of the yard and we get anxious looking for a good place to jump. The trees close in faster and faster. The snow rises in the dark places along the tracks. Tori rolls off first but I wait for a snow bank, mouth "Geronimo" back at Amber and bale out. When I hit, the fall blows out my breath and punches in my right ribs. There's no snow bank, just a dusted-over pile of pulled-up cement ties with the screws still in. At first I just feel sick and I don't even try to get up. It's hot and I feel like I'm going to puke. I cough for so long and with so much pain I swear I taste marrow. Feeling inside my coat for blood, my hand comes out wet but fluorescent. The spray paint cans broke against my body and I'm tagged blue and orange right through my clothes.

It's a long stumble through the strip of pines to the road. We take refuge in a CENTRO bus shelter and pool our change. The extra goes to Amber who runs across the street against the signal of a frozen street light to the CVS. She comes back with one 16 oz. Pepsi for all three of us, which she rations and administers by the capful. I can't swallow so I just wet my mouth, rinse out the bile and spit it onto the grey snow.

After the bus it's only the snow banks that keep me on my feet. I fall into each side alternately and hug the cold to my sore side for a moment before moving on. On the porch I can't even try to be quiet, not that it matters anymore. It's just after midnight now and my mother's already home. She's taking off her uniform in the kitchen, one piece at a time like always. Her service medals are already pooling in the bottom of a cereal bowl, the brass badge is on the side of her placemat where knives would lay. The holster's hung over the back of a chair, patent leather shoes in parade gloss lined up underneath. Her sergeant's stripes make wings on her shoulders.

"Is this how you're coming home now? Whenever you feel like, after doing God knows what? Don't lean on that wall! You've already made a mess of the floor. Do you want to ruin everything of mine?"

I try to straighten up, pulling my arms in a tight hug around my cracked ribs. I want her to see that I'm hurt. I want her to see that I'm sorry.

"If I'd known you'd turn out just like him I would have never...," she doesn't finish and she doesn't have to. She faces me like I have an answer but I don't. Over her shoulder I can see myself in the hall mirror and in the frame of our last family portrait, when I was still small. For the first time I see myself as plain as she can. Out too late too early, filthy, bloody and stained. I'm no damn good and I never was. She turns the kitchen light out on me when she leaves. ≋

Alison Meyers

WALKING OUT

*When the random patterns on the acoustic ceiling tiles stopped looking as if someone
had covered the tiles with every possible word or phrase (in several languages) that
began with the letter "I" (including every pop song title imaginable), then I knew
I had finally returned to reality, though prior to that day there were several occasions
on which I wanted to point out to Robert how clever whoever had created that
ceiling palimpsest was.*
                            –Reginald Shepherd, "Speech after Long Silence," 2008

Small breasts & slender waist in a striped
jersey dress, hers is the pear shape magazines say
leads to a long life. When she walks off

the passenger bus, her legs are sturdy, likewise
her hips: this woman could wander country miles,
haversack strapped to her back.

You, on the other hand, with your bad habits
of reading sad poems & letting your mind wander,
will never trek the Appalachian Trail or take

a Tibetan walking tour. You'll wait for traffic lights
to change, scribble "epiphany" in notebooks, insist
it's the personal & only the personal that matters.

A woman boards a passenger bus a country mile from
Kandahar. Her legs are sturdy, likewise her hope for
a long life, though just as easily, American troops will

waste this bus with magazine fire, *a tragic loss of life.*
You might strap slender hope to your breast, insist the
world divides into feet & inches. You could wait here, count

the I I I I I s on the ceiling, palimpsest of dying & living.
Or, on the other hand, walk out of this wayward American
century into loosestrife, dandelion, wild pear.

It could be that simple, couldn't it.

Dream Cycle

I. When Is It Over

You dream of him though it's the other you want to remember,
ashes blown into earth, you can call up his body, Noxema, how
he moved in you.

Beetled brow of the moon, your night gown in flight, his loaded
gun, crush of gravel, a key, ignition, Run me down! his shout
a purpling bruise. Regret like the sweat you smell behind
the rolled up car window.

II. You Dream of Paninis

You jostle in line waiting for paninis, your sister scowls, he sees and says,
    Caught you.
For penance the three of you tumble into bed. A corner of your eye
    locates motion:
his wife's backpack, a blue gypsy skirt swirling out the door.
    He's American, this is
Milan, this morning filled with yellow light a sensation before Watergate
    and your long
drunken marriage. A stranger appears, wonders, *What were you thinking?*
    He is crew-
cut and stern as your father. Your sister shrugs, meaning,
    Opportunity knocked. Her
breasts gleam from saunters among sunburned German tourists.
    Your wallet contains
$100, not enough for a ticket home, a fact that might concern you,
    should you suppose
there is some place to return to and someone to forgive your indiscretion.

Christopher J. Michel

GOOD FRIDAY

Out of the blue air into the cherry-wood barbershop
where a plump, bob-cut woman bibs me and wets my head.
You're Catholic too, she doesn't ask. *I don't attend*
much either anymore. Still, it colors us. Gesticulates
with scissors: *And of course you are aware what will*
befall us all at 3 o'clock today. Leans in, conspiratorially:
Jesus dies. *And we must wait till Sunday for light again.*
My glasses off, she's all tinge and blur. I try not to move.
Every year this very day, you understand, it rains at three
no matter what. Isn't that a wonder? Well, I notice
you're a poet from your hair: sloppy. But I'm making you
respectable. Someday you will put me in a poem! As a prophet.
Or not! We must wait till three, and see if I'm not right.
I glance out at the bolt-blue blur of sky. *What a lovely chat*
we've had! But I am done. Stepping back, she hovers
a hand-mirror. *And here is the back of your head.*

EDITORS

KYLE BASS is a New York Foundation for the Arts Fellow in both fiction and playwriting and was a finalist for the Princess Grace Playwriting award. His work has been produced by several regional theatres, and has appeared in many publications. He teaches at Syracuse University and at Goddard College, and is Resident Dramaturg at Syracuse Stage.

AMY CHENG, professor of art at S.U.N.Y. New Paltz, is a painter, printmaker, and multimedia artist who has installed a number of large public arts commissions in cities such as New York, Chicago, and Seattle, and whose paintings have been exhibited in major galleries throughout the country. Originally from Taiwan, she grew up in Brazil, Oklahoma, and Texas, and was educated at the University of Texas at Austin and at Hunter College in New York City.

MEGAN DAVIDSON, former editor-in-chief of Lee Shore Agency and Sterling House Publishers, has edited hundreds of books, including two Pulitzer Prize-nominated novels. She is the author of three historical romances and coauthor of two nonfiction books on writing. She currently does freelance consulting and is on the faculty of the Downtown Writer's Center in Syracuse.

CORNELIUS EADY, Rochester-born poet and playwright, is the author of several books of poems, among them *Victims of the Latest Dance Craze,* winner of the 1985 Lamont Poetry Prize, and *The Gathering of My Name,* nominated for the 1992 Pulitzer Prize. He is cofounder of Cave Canem, a summer workshop retreat for African American poets. He currently holds the Miller Family Endowed Chair in Literature and Writing, and is a professor of English at the University of Missouri-Columbia. In 2013, he will release two poetry/music chapbooks: *Book of Hooks, Vol. 1 & 2*, and *Asking for the Moon: Swamp Rose Recordings 1990-2012.*

DORAN LARSON is professor of English and creative writing at Hamilton College. He has published widely on the topics of American literature and prison writing, and has taught creative writing at a maximum security state prison since 2006. He has written two novels, *The Big Deal* and *Marginalia,* and is the editor of two forthcoming volumes, *The Beautiful Prison* and *Fourth City: Essays from the Prison in America.*

KARL MARLANTES is the author of *Matterhorn, A Novel of the Vietnam War,* a *New York Times* Top 10 Bestseller published in 2010. A graduate of Yale University and a former Rhodes Scholar at Oxford, he is a highly decorated veteran who served as a Marine company commander in Vietnam. His most recent book is a collection of essays entitled *What It Is Like To Go To War.*

KENNETH McCLANE is the W.E.B. Du Bois Professor Emeritus of Literature at Cornell University. He is the author of eight poetry collections and two volumes of personal essays, *Walls: Essays 1985-1990* and *Color: Essays on Race, Family and History,* which was awarded the 2009 Gold Medal for the best book of essays by *ForeWord Reviews* magazine.

E.C. Osondu, originally from Nigeria, is the author of *Voice of America,* published in 2012 by HarperCollins (U.S.A.) and Granta Books (U.K.). He was a finalist for the Commonwealth Prize and a winner of the Caine Prize for African Writing—also known as the African Booker Prize—and a 2011 Pushcart Prize. His work has appeared in many journals, and has been translated into several languages. He is currently assistant professor of English at Providence College in Rhode Island. His novel *This House is Not for Sale* is forthcoming from HarperCollins in 2013.

Neva Pilgrim teaches at Colgate University and is founder/artistic director of Society for New Music, now in its 40th year. She also hosts and produces *Fresh Ink,* a classical music program on *National Public Radio.* She is a well-known soprano, having performed in orchestral and operatic settings throughout the world, and has recorded extensively with several music labels.

Nancy Keefe Rhodes is a writer, editor, and curator whose work covers film, video, still photography, and the visual arts. She is a member of Syracuse's Public Arts Commission, teaches film theory and criticism at Syracuse University, and is founding editor of The Moving Image section of *Stone Canoe.*

Steven Stucky is a Pulitzer Prize-winning composer and the Given Foundation Professor of Composition at Cornell University. He served as 2011-2012 Composer of the Year in residence with the Pittsburgh Symphony Orchestra. His newest symphony, commissioned by the Los Angeles Philharmonic and Gustavo Dudamel, was first performed in October of 2012, and received a rave review from the *Los Angeles Times.* The symphony was also performed by the New York Philharmonic in November of 2012.

Anthony Swofford is a former U.S. Marine whose award-winning book, *Jarhead,* about his experiences in the Gulf War, formed the basis of the 2005 movie of the same name, directed by Sam Mendes. His newest memoir, *Hotels, Hospitals and Jails,* was released in 2012. He is a Michener-Copernicus Fellowship recipient, and his fiction and nonfiction work has appeared in many publications. He lives and works in New York.

Brian Turner, author of two volumes of poetry, *Here, Bullet* and *Phantom Noise,* is the director of the low-residency M.F.A. program at Sierra Nevada College. His awards include a National Endowment for the Arts Literature Fellowship in Poetry, the U.S.–Japan Friendship Commission grant, and the Poets' Prize, and his work has been featured on *National Public Radio,* the *BBC,* and *Newshour* with Jim Lehrer. He is a combat veteran of the Iraq War.

CONTRIBUTORS

BETTY LISE ANDERSON, a Syracuse alumna, is professor and associate chair in the Department of Electrical and Computer Engineering at The Ohio State University.

ANGELA ARZÚ is a tenth-grade student at Poughkeepsie Day School and a recent attendee at the Young Writer's Summer Institute at Skidmore College in Saratoga Springs, New York.

TRICIA ASKLAR is a widely published poet who teaches writing at Nazareth College in Rochester, New York.

CRAIG J. BARBER'S current photography deals with people who have a close working relationship with the land. He creates environmental portraits of farmers, hunters, and gatherers. A resident of Woodstock, New York, he was a 2011 artist-in-residence at the Constance Saltonstall Foundation for the Arts.

DAVID BORDEN is an American composer of minimalist music, an accomplished jazz pianist, and the retired founder/director of the Digital Music Program (now the Electro-acoustic Music Center) at Cornell University.

EVA BOVENZI is a painter from Rochester, New York, who now lives and works in San Francisco, California.

STEVE CARVER, a painter and former graphic designer, currently resides in Ithaca, New York. His paintings, while very different in content from his previous work, often utilize the visual language of the designer.

LILY CHIU grew up in Oneida, New York, and now lives in San Francisco. She misses morning glories and snow days. Her poetry has been published in *Enizagam* and is forthcoming in *Gargoyle Magazine.*

RICK CHRISTMAN served in the U.S. Army from September 1966 to November 1969. He has published one book, *Falling in Love at the End of the World,* and his work also appeared in such journals as *Indiana Review* and *Connecticut Review.*

ELISABETH CONDON (*www.elisabethcondon.com*) is a Pollock-Krasner Foundation Grant recipient and associate professor of painting and drawing at the University of South Florida, Tampa. A former resident of the Cooperstown area, she now lives and works in Brooklyn, New York, and Tampa, Florida.

EDWARD CUELLO, a graduate of Columbia University, is a Syracuse, New York, resident and a financial advisor for AXA. This is his first published poem.

PAT DANEMAN publishes widely in print and online journals. She has B.A. and M.A. degrees in English and creative writing from Binghamton University, and currently serves as poetry coeditor of *Kansas City Voices* magazine.

Suzanne Rae Deshchidn (Des-CHING) has an M.F.A. in poetry from the Solstice Creative Writing Program. She is a freelance editor *(www.srediting.com)* and adjunct professor of English at Passaic County Community College. Of Chicana and native (Isleta Pueblo) heritage, her works are deeply spiritual and rooted in nature.

José Lauriano Di Lenola, an inmate at Attica Correctional Facility, is a mentor to at-risk teens in prison diversion programs. His writing has appeared in *This Side of My Struggle, Stone Canoe (#5), Prison News Express,* and is forthcoming in *Fourth City,* a collection of essays by incarcerated Americans. He received an Honorable Mention in the 2011 PEN American Center prison writing contest.

Diane DiRoberto is a published writer and photographer who formerly freelanced in New York City for a diverse client list, and now resides in Rochester, New York. She is the recipient of a 1997 ADDY Award for a print advertising campaign and the 2000 Hackney Literary Award for poetry.

Paul Elisha served as a press spokesperson for five New York governors and executive director of New York State Common Cause before joining Albany's WAMC, Northeast Public Radio, as a commentator and host for poetry and classical music programs. A decorated Special Forces WW II combat veteran, he received a New York State Council of the Arts award for a series of poems honoring the heroic actions of New York's 27th Infantry Division in WW II. His first book of poems, *SWASH,* was published in 2009.

Amze Emmons, originally from Breakabeen, New York, is a Philadelphia-based, multidisciplinary artist and associate professor of art at The College of New Jersey. Emmons is also a cofounder and contributor of the popular art blog, *Printeresting.org.*

Donise English is chair of the Department of Art and Art History at Marist College. Her abstract, encaustic paintings are represented by the Carrie Haddad Gallery in Hudson, New York.

Rob Enslin is a writer, musician, artist, and communications manager in The College of Arts and Sciences at Syracuse University. His book projects include the Ned Corman memoir, *Now's the Time: A Story of Music, Education, and Advocacy.* He is board president of the YMCA Arts Branch and also serves on the boards of the Society for New Music and Syracuse University Brass Ensemble.

Dewaine Farria is a United Nations Field Security Officer who has been based at U.N. headquarters around the world. A former U.S. Marine, he is a graduate of Excelsior College and the University of Oklahoma, and his writing appears frequently on the World Policy Institute's web site, *www.worldpolicy.org/blog.*

Maureen Forman lives in Bloomington, Indiana, and teaches drawing and art history at Indiana University, Herron School of Art + Design, and Ivy Tech. Originally from Beacon, New York, she was educated at Maryland Institute College of Art and Indiana University.

Julie Gamberg is a Los Angeles-based poet who writes about geography, localism, longing, representation, landscape, and language as told from a mythic trickster guidebook. Her previous book, *The Museum of Natural History,* won the 2005 Blue Lynx Prize for Poetry.

Sam Gifford is a U.S. Army veteran with degrees from Utica College and Syracuse University's Maxwell School of Citizenship and Public Affairs. At various times in his career, he has been a newspaper reporter, a corporate vice-president, and a faculty member at SUNY Buffalo.

Glenn Goldberg is a New York painter who has shown extensively in the United States and Europe. His work is in numerous museum collections, including M.O.C.A. in Los Angeles, The National Gallery of Art in Washington D.C., and The Metropolitan Museum of Art in New York. He teaches at Queens College, CUNY, The Cooper Union, and Parsons The New School for Design, as well as at The Chautauqua Institution School of Art in the summer.

Adriana Grant *(www.adrianagrant.net)* studied literature and creative writing at Skidmore College in Saratoga Springs, and attended New York State Summer Writer's Institute. Her poetry has been published by numerous magazines, including *DIAGRAM, Peaches & Bats,* and *LIT* magazine.

Travis Head lives in Blacksburg, Virginia, where he is an assistant professor of drawing at Virginia Tech. Head's work is included in the Drawing Center's Viewing Program and his drawings and artist's books have been exhibited nationally in numerous solo and group exhibitions. He has also worked as an adjunct professor and artist's assistant in New Paltz, New York.

Dandelyon Holmes-Nelson holds a B.S. degree in Visual Arts Education from SUNY New Paltz. She works as an art educator for the Junior Art Institute and EDAP, an extended day arts program, for the Mill Street Loft in Poughkeepsie. Her teaching experience also includes community-based work for chronically ill children at Vassar Brothers Hospital and programs for at-risk youth.

Carol K. Howell taught writing at Syracuse University from 1986 to 2002. Both her children were born in Liverpool, New York, and consider it home.

Ellen Kozak is a painter and video artist whose work is represented in many museums and private collections. A former research fellow at M.I.T., she has taught in Japan and currently teaches at Pratt Institute. Her video piece, Notations on a River, 2009, was shown in a solo exhibit with her paintings at the Katonah Museum of Art. She is currently working on a new 3-channel video installation in New Baltimore, New York.

J.P. Lawrence is a photojournalist with the U.S. Army. He has produced more than 200 published pieces on Iraq, Kuwait, Qatar, Germany, and Australia. He currently studies creative writing and anthropology at Bard College in Upstate New York.

Richard Levine is the author of *That Country's Soul, A Language Full of Wars and Songs, Snapshots from a Battle,* and *A Tide of a Hundred Mountains.* He was runner-up for the 2010 William Stafford Poetry Award and a finalist for the Ohio State University Press Poetry Award.

Paul Linczak received an M.F.A. from Syracuse University, where he was a Cornelia Carhart Ward Fellow in fiction, and a B.A. from the University of Rochester. "Sailing Solo" is an excerpt from his novel, *Olivia.*

Carmen Lizardo, originally from the Dominican Republic, is a painter and photographer who was educated at Pratt Institute and currently teaches at SUNY New Paltz. Her work has been exhibited nationally and internationally, and she has received many honors and grants here and abroad. Most recently, she has been lecturing in Guatemala City, and collaborating with local artists there on a project exploring the effects of colonialism on indigenous communities.

David Lloyd is a poet, fiction writer, and critic who directs the Creative Writing Program at Le Moyne College in Syracuse, New York. He is the author of seven books, including three poetry collections and a fiction collection. His most recent poetry collection, *Warriors,* has just appeared from Salt Publishing (London).

William Michael Lobko holds an M.F.A. from the University of Oregon and teaches in New York. His poems, reviews, and interviews have appeared most recently in *Hunger Mountain, Boston Review,* and *Slice* magazine. He is currently at work on a novel entitled *The Quick Brown Fox.*

Karen Martin originates from South Africa and is currently a student in Syracuse University's creative writing M.F.A. program. In 2012, she was awarded residencies at the Norman Mailer Writers Colony and Byrdcliffe Arts Colony. "Re-enactments" is part of a longer work.

Maureen McCoy is the author of four novels: *Junebug, Walking After Midnight, Summertime,* and *Divining Blood.* Her short fiction and personal essays have recently been published in *Antioch Review, Mississippi Review, Santa Fe Literary Review,* and *Epoch.* She is a professor in the Cornell University Department of English and the creative writing program.

Mac McGowan is a two-tour infantryman/paratrooper veteran of the Vietnam War. He has traveled throughout Upstate New York on business, and has been a featured poet at the David B. Steinman Festival of the Arts at St. Lawrence College.

Stephanie McMahon is assistant professor of painting at the School of Art & Design at Alfred University. She holds a B.F.A. from Alfred University and an M.F.A. from The University of Texas at Austin. McMahon is a recipient of a New York Foundation for the Arts, Special Opportunity Stipend, and an individual artist grant from the Constance Saltonstall Foundation for the Arts.

Shari Mendelson is the recipient of three New York Foundation for the Arts grants and a Pollock-Krasner Foundation Grant. She has exhibited in numerous galleries and museums in the U.S. and in Australia, and has been featured in *The New York Times, World Art Glass Quarterly, NY Arts Magazine,* and *Art on Paper.* She lives and works in Brooklyn and Schoharie County, New York.

Alison Meyers's work has appeared in various literary journals and is forthcoming in *Blazes All Across the Sky: Writers Respond to the Poetry of Joni Mitchell,* and *Ragazine,* an online journal. She is executive director of the Cave Canem Foundation, Brooklyn, New York. She is a resident of Jersey City, New Jersey, and a graduate of Skidmore College in Saratoga Springs, New York.

CHRISTOPHER J. MICHEL earned an M.F. A. from Syracuse University, and has received a Fulbright Grant to translate poetry from the Republic of Georgia. He lives in Brooklyn's secret Chinatown, and is a stay-at-home dad.

CHIORI MIYAGAWA is a Japan-born U.S. playwright who studied at SUNY Albany. She currently divides her time between New York City and Upstate New York, where she teaches playwriting at Bard College. Her plays have been published and produced off Broadway and in renowned New York City performance houses, as well as regionally.

AMY MONTICELLO was born and raised in Endicott, New York, and currently lives and teaches in Ithaca. She has lived in Ohio and Alabama, but always returns to her home state and its eclectic beauty. She has a new nonfiction chapbook, *Close Quarters,* and her essays have been published in the *Iron Horse Literary Review, Phoebe, Natural Bridge, Redivider,* and *Upstreet.*

DEXTER MORRILL taught at Colgate University from 1969 to 2001. An accomplished jazz trumpeter, arranger and composer, he built the first computer music system at Colgate. His scholarly publications include *The Music of Woody Herman: A Guide to the Recordings* and *The American String Quartet: A Guide to the Recordings.* As a composer, he has worked with such luminaries as Stan Getz and Wynton Marsalis.

PORTIA MUNSON *(www.portiamunson.org)* is a visual artist who works in a range of media. She has taught at Yale School of Art, Vassar College and SUNY Purchase, and her work has been exhibited throughout the world. Her home and studio are in Catskill, New York, where she lives with the artist Jared Handelsman and their two children.

JESSE NISSIM is an award-winning poet who currently serves as Faculty Writing Fellow in The College of Arts and Sciences at Syracuse University. Her book, *Self Named Body,* was published by Finishing Line Press in 2012.

OSVALDO OYOLA, originally from Brooklyn, New York, is a Ph.D. candidate in the Department of English at Binghamton University, where he teaches and writes about intersections of collection, pop culture, and ethnic and gender identity in Transnational American Literature.

LEILA ORTIZ, a Brooklyn native and SUNY Albany alumna, is a social worker in New York City's public schools, and an M.F.A. candidate at the Queens College Creative Writing and Literary Translation program.

JEN PEPPER *(www.jenpepper.com)* lives and works in Upstate New York. Her work is exhibited at Pierogi gallery in Brooklyn, New York, and has been reviewed extensively in regional and national media. She holds an M.F.A. from the University of Connecticut.

BARRY PERLUS, an artist and photographer, is currently associate professor of art and associate dean at Cornell University. In recent projects, he uses panoramic imaging as a departure from conventional pictorial space.

NINA PICK works in Ghent, New York, and resides in Massachusetts. She has degrees from New York University, University of California, Berkeley, and Pacifica Graduate Institute. She has read in the Holloway Series in Poetry, and has published in *Chronogram, TINTA, Written River,* and in a forthcoming anthology from Sibling Rivalry Press.

DAVID S. POINTER was the son of a piano-playing bank robber who died when David was 3 years old. David served in the Marine Corps military police from 1980 to 1984. He currently lives with his two daughters and two cats in Murfreesboro, Tennessee.

MAUD POOLE's poems have appeared in or are forthcoming in *Boston Review, Copper Nickel, Nimrod International Journal,* and *Podium.* She lives in New York City and Upstate New York.

GEORGIA A. POPOFF is managing editor of *The Comstock Review,* coordinator and faculty member of the Syracuse YMCA's Downtown Writer's Center workshops, and poet-in-residence in numerous school districts. She has two poetry collections and has coauthored a book for teachers on poetry in the K–12 classroom.

MINNIE BRUCE PRATT is professor of writing and rhetoric, and women's gender studies at Syracuse University. Her books include *Inside the Money Machine with Nothing to Lose,* and *The Dirt She Ate: Selected and New Poems,* which received a 2003 Lambda Literary Award for Lesbian Poetry, and *Crime Against Nature,* a Lamont Poetry Selection.

THOMAS P. RIGOLI grew up in Jamestown, New York, and attended Syracuse University, where he earned an A.B. in Math and a B.S.E.E. from the L.C. Smith College of Engineering and Computer Science. He has been providing strategic communications counsel to Silicon Valley companies for more than forty years.

ERIK SCHOONEBEEK grew up in the small town of Delhi, New York, in the Catskills. He is a graduate of SUNY New Paltz and Rutgers Mason Gross School of the Arts, and currently lives and works in Highland Park, New Jersey.

HEDI SCHWÖBEL creates site-specific installations that examine one's dwelling, sustainability, and technology. She was educated at the Stuttart State Academy of Art and Design in Germany, and has exhibited throughout her country. She won an Internationale des Arts national grant from Germany, and was an artist-in-residence at Sculpture Space in Utica, New York.

CLAIRE SEIDL received a B.F.A. in painting from Syracuse University and an M.F.A. from Hunter College. She has taught at Hunter and at Hofstra University, and has been exhibiting her paintings and photographs for over thirty years in New York City and in Maine, where she lives and works in the summers.

STEVEN SIEGEL holds degrees from Hampshire College and Pratt Institute, and is represented by Marlborough Gallery in New York. He is internationally recognized for his scale site-specific sculpture, built from enormous quantities of pre- or postconsumer industrial materials. A native of New York City, he currently resides in the Hudson River Valley.

Ryan Smithson is from Upstate New York and enlisted in the army reserve after 9/11. He was deployed to Iraq from 2004 to 2005 and has nonfiction published in various journals. His memoir, *Ghosts of War: The True Story of a 19-Year-Old GI,* was published by HarperCollins in 2009. He currently lives in Schenectady with his wife and son.

Ed Soohoo is a retired electrical engineer who has been writing for ten years about his experiences in Naval intelligence. He served during the Korean War from 1951 to 1954.

Mary-Margaret Stevens was born in Syracuse, New York, and grew up in Madison County. She graduated from SUNY Morrisville with highest honors, and is now in her senior year at Cornell University, where she majors in English with a concentration in creative writing.

Teresa Sutton is a poet and teacher who lives in Poughkeepsie, New York, with her two children. She has three master's degrees: from the Pine Manor Solstice low-residency M.F.A. program, from Western Connecticut State University, and from SUNY New Paltz.

Joy Taylor lives and works in a small house and studio in the country, with woods on one side, and farm fields on the other. Natural imagery and processes inspire her work. The apparent chaos that masks complex structures, repeating forms, and the energy of life around her is a constant presence.

Elizabeth Terhune is a painter and visiting artist at Skidmore College's summer session program. Her work explores the transformative space of personification. For almost a decade, she and her husband have spent part of each summer in a small isolated cabin in the Adirondacks where she would study and paint in the forest.

Tamar Zinn is a visual artist who has spent the past 25 summers in the Hudson Valley town of Plattekill. In her work, Zinn explores rhythm and spatial relationships in the context of geometric abstraction.

Janet Zweig is a Brooklyn artist who was educated at Cornell University and the University of Rochester. She has created large public installations in many cities throughout the U.S. and her work has been exhibited in such places as the Brooklyn Museum, Exit Art, MoMA PS1 Museum, the Walker Art Center, and Cooper Union. Her awards include the Rome Prize Fellowship, National Endowment for the Arts fellowships, and residencies at PS1 Museum and The MacDowell Colony. She teaches at the Rhode Island School of Design and at Brown University.

Coalition of Museum and Art Centers
350 West Fayette Street, Syracuse, NY 13202
315/443-6450, 315/443-6494 fax
http://cmac.syr.edu

Formed in September 2005 by Syracuse University President and Chancellor Nancy Cantor, the Coalition of Museum and Art Centers (CMAC) brings together the programs, services, and projects of several different campus art centers and affiliated non-profit art organizations in the campus community in a collaborative effort to expand the public's awareness, understanding, appreciation, and involvement in the visual and electronic arts. The mission of CMAC is to celebrate and explore the visual and electronic arts through exhibitions, publications, public presentations, education, and scholarship.

THE WAREHOUSE GALLERY
350 W. Fayette Street, Syracuse, NY 13202
315/443-6450 315/443-6494
www.thewarehousegallery.org

LIGHT WORK/COMMUNITY DARKROOMS
Robert B. Menschel Media Center
316 Waverly Avenue, Syracuse, NY 13244
315/443-1300, 315/443-9516 fax
www.lightwork.org

COMMUNITY FOLK ART CENTER
805 E. Genesee Street, Syracuse, NY 13210
315/442-2230
315/442-2972 fax
www.communityfolkartcenter.org

SUART GALLERIES
Shaffer Art Building on the Syracuse University Quad
Syracuse, NY 13210-1230
315/443-4097, 315/443-9225 fax
http://suart.syr.edu

SPECIAL COLLECTIONS RESEARCH CENTER
600 E. S. Bird Library, Syracuse, NY 13244
315/443-2697
315/443-2671 fax
http://scrc.syr.edu

POINT OF CONTACT GALLERY
914 E. Genesee Street, Syracuse, NY 13210
315/443-2169
315/443-5376 fax
www.pointcontact.org

LOUISE AND BERNARD PALITZ GALLERY
Syracuse University Joseph I. Lubin House
11 E. 61st Street, New York, NY 10021
212/826-0320, 212/826-0331 fax
http://lubinhouse.syr.edu/gallery/current.html

SYRACUSE UNIVERSITY
The College of Arts and Sciences

Home of the Humanities

The Central New York Humanities Corridor / Watson Visiting Collaborator Program /
The Jeanette K. Watson Distinguished Visiting Professorship / Syracuse Symposium /
Perpetual Peace Project, including the "Common Ground for Peace" summit, featuring
the Dalai Lama / HC Mini-Seminar series / HC Student and Faculty Fellows Program

Syracuse University
Humanities Center

syracusehumanities.org

The College of Arts and Sciences congratulates the M.F.A. Program in Creative Writing on its 50th anniversary.

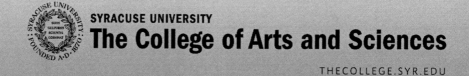

The **L.C. Smith College of Engineer and Computer Science** is proud to support the **Stone Canoe** for its promotion of the arts & the advancement of public understanding of technology and engineering

Whitman
SCHOOL *of* MANAGEMENT
SYRACUSE UNIVERSITY

The Whitman School
continues to support

Stone Canoe

an award-winning example of
Syracuse University's "Scholarship in Action"

SYRACUSE UNIVERSITY
Library

proudly supports
Stone Canoe

The Library is a
center of discovery—
**ENTREPRENEURIAL,
KNOWLEDGE DRIVEN,
& TIMELESS.**

222 Waverly Avenue · Syracuse, NY 13244-2010

COLLEGE OF VISUAL AND

PERFORMING ARTS

SYRACUSE UNIVERSITY

The College of Visual and Performing Arts at Syracuse University is committed to the education of cultural leaders who will engage and inspire audiences through performance, visual art, design, scholarship, and commentary. We provide the tools for self-discovery and risk-taking in an environment that thrives on critical thought and action.

COLLEGE OF VISUAL AND
PERFORMING ARTS
SYRACUSE UNIVERSITY

Delavan Center

509 West Fayette St., Syracuse, NY 13204
315•476•9001

Downtown: Home to
Businesses & Artists

SYRACUSE UNIVERSITY BOOKSTORE

YOUR CAMPUS SOURCE FOR THE FINEST IN READING AND LITERATURE

THE UNIVERSITY
BOOKSTORE
Owned and Operated by Syracuse University

Schine Student Center
303 University Place
Syracuse, NY 13244
(315) 443-9900
www.syr.edu/bkst

congratulations to **stone canoe**
7 YEARS OF THE BEST VISUAL ART AND WRITING.

S STRESS**DESIGN**

THOUGHTFUL BRAND COMMUNICATIONS

STRESS**DESIGN**.COM

The Creative Mind

Le Moyne College is proud of its reputation as a center for creative writing, literature and performance. We hope to see you at the many wonderful events during the spring 2013 semester.
All readings and lectures are free.

LE MOYNE
SPIRIT. INQUIRY. LEADERSHIP. JESUIT.

WWW.LEMOYNE.EDU

Readings

Martha Rhodes and Patrick Lawler
Wednesday, Feb. 20, 5:30 p.m. | Reilley Room, Reilly Hall
Rhodes will read from her poetry collection, *The Beds*.
Lawler will read from his novel, *Rescuers of Skydivers Search Among the Clouds*.

Ron Hansen | Thursday, April 4, 6:30 p.m.
Grewen Auditorium
An acclaimed novelist, Hansen is the Gerard Manley Hopkins, S.J. Professor in the Arts and Humanities at Santa Clara University.

Anne Enright | Friday, April 19, 6:30 p.m.
W. Carroll Coyne Center for the Performing Arts
Booker prize-winning author of *The Gathering*, Enright also won the 1991 Rooney Prize for Irish Literature, the 2001 Encore Awarad and the 2008 Irish Book Award for novel.

David Lloyd | Friday, April 26, 7 p.m.
Downtown Writers Center, YMCA, Montgomery St., Syracuse
Lloyd, director of the creative writing program at Le Moyne, will read from his new poetry collection, *Warriors*.

Concerts
For ticket information, call (315) 445-4200.

The Jazzuits Arts @ Assisi | Sunday, Jan. 27, 3 p.m.
Franciscan Church of the Assumption
812 N. Salina Street, Syracuse
Join the Le Moyne College Jazzuits as they perform in the Franciscan Church of the Assumptions' Concert Series.

40 Fingers | Tuesday, Feb. 5, 7:30 p.m.
Panasci Family Chapel
Join Kathleen Haddock, Amy Heyman, Steve Heyman and Ida Trebicka for an evening featuring the works of Bach, Sousa and Smetana.

The Jazzuits Sing Frank Sinatra | Sunday, Feb. 24, 4 p.m.
James Commons, Campus Center
World-class jazz singer Ronnie Leigh joins the Jazzuits with his renditions of Frank Sinatra's hit recordings.

Vatican II 50th Anniversary Musical Celebration
Saturday, April 27, 1:30 p.m.
Cathedral of the Immaculate Conception
Columbus Circle, Downtown Syracuse
Join the Le Moyne College Singers and Chapel Choir, soprano Janet Brown, baritone David Rudari, and a full orchestra for music inspired by Vatican II. **Free.**

A Night at the Oscars | Tuesday, April 30, 7:30 p.m.
W. Carroll Coyne Center for the Performing Arts

Join the Le Moyne College Chamber Music Orchestra for an evening of film music and a world-premiere soundtrack to the silent short film *Manhatta*.

Jazzuits with Jazz Ensemble and Young Lions of CNY
Friday, May 3, 7:30 p.m.
W. Carroll Coyne Center for the Performing Arts
The Jazzuits will present music from the Great American Songbook and the Jazz Ensemble will perform jazz favorites.

Lectures

McDevitt Lecture: Jesuit Spirituality
and Academic Theology : Karl Rahner and Ignacio Ellacuría
Thursday, Feb. 7, 7 p.m. | Panasci Family Chapel
Presenter: J. Matthew Ashley, Chair, Department of Theology, University of Notre Dame.

McDevitt Lecture: Creation and Cosmology
Thursday, March 14, 7 p.m. | Panasci Family Chapel
Robert John Russell, founding director of the Center for Theology and the Natural Sciences, Graduate Theological Union, will discuss the mutual interaction among scientific cosmology, philosophy and creation theology.

Loyola Lecture
Wednesday, April 3, 7 p.m. | Panasci Family Chapel
John O'Malley, S.J., University Professor at Georgetown University, will address the spirit of change in Vatican II.

McDevitt Lecture: Emergence: Systems, Organisms, Persons
Thursday, April 25, 7 p.m. | Panasci Family Chapel
Nancey Murphy, Fuller Theological Seminary. This lecture will be set against the background of scientific evolution.

Film Talk Series: Film Artists in Conversation
W. Carroll Coyne Center for the Performing Arts
For ticket information, call (315) 445-4523.

Tuesday, Feb. 26, 7:30 p.m.
Thomas Newman: The Art of Film Scoring

Tuesday, April 16, 7:30 p.m.
Siobhan Fallon Hogan: The Art of Acting

Theater
For ticket information, call (315) 445-4200.

Reckless | Thursday, Feb. 14, 15, 16, 21, 22, 23 – 8 p.m.
Marren Studio
W. Carroll Coyne Center for the Performing Arts

Pirates of Penzance
April 4, 5, 11, 12 – 8 p.m. | April 13 – 2 p.m., 8 p.m.
W. Carroll Coyne Center for the Performing Arts

COMMUNITY FOLK
ART CENTER

Community Folk Art Center
805 E. Genesee St., Syracuse, NY 13210
www.CommunityFolkArtCenter.org
phone: (315) 442-2230
email: cfac@syr.edu

Featuring:

Film
Dance
Spoken Word
Photography
Discussion
Food

CARIBBEAN
CINEMATIC
FESTIVAL

Highlighted Presenters: Roger Bonair-Agard | Frances-Anne Soloman | Celiany Rivers | Selena Blake | Sandra Stephens

February 6 - February 10, 2013

QUEEN OF MYSELF
Las Krudas d' Cuba

WHAT MY MOTHER TOLD ME

CUBAN ROOTS
Bronx Stories

CALYPSO R
THE LIONESS OF THE JUN

TABOO...YARDIES

ONE DAY ONE DESTINY

Roger Bonair-Agard:
Friday, February 9th

"The book should be a ball of light in one's hand"
—Ezra Pound

Get the entire *Stone Canoe* series—7 volumes—at 30% off list price, and treat yourself to a sampling of the best art and writing from Upstate New York and beyond.

Order directly at *stonecanoejournal.org* or from our office. Make checks payable to *Stone Canoe,* 700 University Avenue, Syracuse, New York 13244-2530. Individual copies of volume 7 are $20. Classroom use: $10.

NOW: Get e-book versions of our journal online for $7.99.
Read *Stone Canoe* on the web, print it, or download it to your favorite mobile device.

For full details, see *stonecanoejournal.org.*

***Stone Canoe* Number 1**
2007 Edition $14

***Stone Canoe* Number 2**
2008 Edition $14

***Stone Canoe* Number 3**
2009 Edition $14

***Stone Canoe* Number 4**
2010 Edition $14

***Stone Canoe* Number 5**
2011 Edition $14

***Stone Canoe* Number 6**
2012 Edition $14